T0163946

Resurrect Your DEAD MARRIAGE

DIVORCE

DR. REGINALD AND RENEA MORRIS

Published by Clovercroft Publishing, Franklin, Tennessee
Published in association with
Larry Carpenter of Christian Book Services, LLC of Franklin, Tennessee

Edited by Tammy Kling
Cover and Interior Design by Debbie Manning Sheppard

ISBN: 978-1-942557-71-5
Printed in the United States of America

Resurrect Your DEAD MARRIAGE

DR. REGINALD AND RENEA MORRIS

DEDICATION

This book is dedicated to all those who have loved and yearned for and welcomed His appearing.

TO OLIVIA AND AMIRA, *we could not have made in through with the loving support of our daughters. Our hearts are yours forever.*

TO PASTOR FORTE. *My man in the trenches. Peace and love to you.*

TO JOEL AND VICTORIA OSTEEN, *thanks for the seed of hope.*

TO KENNETH, GLORIA, PASTOR(S) GEORGE AND TERRI AND THE KCM FAMILY, *thanks for your prayers.*

TO MOM, *your unwavering support, love and confidence towards us straightened our legs when they were feeble. Blessed are the meek for they shall inherit the earth.*

TO JASON, *thanks for being the man of God you are and your contribution to this work.*

TO PAT, *thanks for lending your ear.*

TO DR. MARK BARCLAY, *thanks for being our man of God and friend.*

CONTENTS

INTRODUCTION

It is vitally important from the beginning to validate with you we are knowledgeable about the subject of resurrecting a dead marriage. Our expertise in this area doesn't come from conducting research with thousands of couples. Instead, like you we are an ordinary married couple who thought we were in a happy marriage until one of us came home and told the other the bomb shell message of "I want a divorce." By the way, did we tell you this didn't just happen once? In fact, it happened not twice but three times over the course of our marriage. Were we just stupid or unwilling to accept that we were not meant to be together? On the contrary, if you want greatness you must be willing to fight for it. Before we ever met each other, the Lord intervened in my life and told me that he would soon be meeting his future wife. And, just as the Lord said, a few days later we met. It was a long distance relationship and sparks of love did not fly immediately. A few months into our relationship, she IRenea) felt she could not spend not another minute on this would-be relationship unless she knew in her heart what we had was real. She bought a ticket and traveled across the country to see what this young man was all about.

She was unaware that all of her prayers to God about finding the right man who would be pleasing to her and God had been answered. That night, when I (Reginald) picked Renea up from the airport, the Lord gave me an open vision as I walked in the baggage claim area. It was a vision of what the future looked like with that skinny young lady waiting for me at baggage claim. When I came out of the vision, I was standing right behind her and uttered these words, "Will you marry me?" and without turning around she said, "Yes."

From that point on, we knew that our life together would be special and in fact, we have had some very special times over our 30 years of marriage. We have had some unexpectedly terrible times that brought us two separations and a contested divorce later. How could such a God-inspired marital match like the one we experienced go so terribly wrong from time to time? We knew our relationship was meant to glorify God, but we had no idea God would use our good times and now more importantly our rough times to bring glory to His name.

During these 30 years, God used us as a marital experiment to show us His love and to unveil to us a redemptive work which has been hidden in the Word for couples in covenant with Him but their marriages are seriously in trouble. With this book you will be exposed to the following 10 things we were mandated by God to share with you:

❦ This book unveils the redemptive work Jesus performs for seriously troubled marriages; God has waited until this time in human history to reveal these hidden truths from His Word.

❦ This book rips off the false lens of a perfect marriage between Adam and Eve in the Garden and reveals the seeds of marital strife which ultimately led to the fall of man and our path to blessing.

❦ Jesus will not only save your marriage but, in the process, will bring reconciliation to spouses who have left and completely transform the relationship between the couple when His work is complete.

❦ This book reveals Satan's master plan and his tactics to destroy marriages with the goal of stealing "the promised blessing" of God.

❦ God desires to start with your troubled marriage to unleash a restoration of love which will fix what ails the Body of Christ and be a catalyst to usher Christ's return.

❦ The book includes a "Special Commentary" from one of the author's partners during a period of infidelity for a behind-the-curtain look at when our spouses are not faithful.

❦ The book is meant to be a candid and open conversation between the author and reader with the bible truths broken down in simple, everyday terms.

❦ Whether you're struggling with abuse or having to overcome your spouse's infidelity, this book shows how you access God's love to find victory for your situation.

❦ This book has been 30 years in the making with the author(s) learning, step by step, from God through 2 separations and a contested divorce about the over 30 truths of Biblical principles and lessons learned along the way.

❦ An entire system in our culture feeds on the carcasses of failing marriages by first encouraging you to make certain decisions while whole industries are set annually to make billions off your heartbreak. With this book, God is exposing these things and setting people free.

REGINALD ᴀɴᴅ RENEA MORRIS

Together, we are about to take a journey that many have not been willing to go. Know you are not alone. We have dedicated our lives to help people get victory and bring restoration to the dead areas of your life. Our ministry will be available each and every day to help in any way we can. Feel free to reach out to us with your questions, prayer requests and testimonies. More importantly, know your Father has already won this victory for you. He has given you His Spirit that lives on the inside of you and is your everyday Helper with the words to think, say and actions to take. Your Lord and Savior Jesus will be overseeing your victory campaign and make sure you have a fresh supply of His strength, grace, love and peace daily as you enter the enemy's camp and take back what was stolen from you.

With the blueprint in hand, fellowship of believers to support and the Spirit of God to guide, let's gets started in resurrecting your marriage.

REGINALD & RENEA MORRIS

SECTION ONE

ADVANCING SEPARATION

Many women started dreaming about their wedding day when they were little girls. They imagined a wedding in a beautiful church or at a luxurious hotel. They pondered who would be their maid of honor long before they met the man of their dreams.

Few boys and men ever gave marriage much thought. They figured they would get married eventually, but few give it much thought until they meet the woman who made their life worth living.

Whether you thought of marriage from childhood or it only occupied your thoughts once you were ready to take the step, divorce was highly unlikely something you thought about. None of us go into a marriage thinking it will end in divorce.

The question is, "Why not?"

The fact is, there is no prototype for a good and lasting marriage. We do not come equipped with everything we need to know about making a marriage work or how to deal with all the issues that arise during the course of the relationship.

It doesn't matter how much premarital counseling we have completed or how long we have known each other before we tie the knot. Dating is not marriage, and pre-martial counseling is not sufficient preparation for living as husband and wife. Thinking your marriage will be successful without understanding what success requires just because you have observed many as you grew up and became an adult is like watching cooking classes and reading recipes to become a good cook. Just like cooking classes do not immediately transform us into gourmet cooks, observing other people's marriage does not prepare us to succeed at our own.

In fact, thinking we can learn from other's marriages might be a huge mistake, especially if we learn from watching movies and television shows about couples. Today's society has given us stereotypical images of what to do when certain circumstances come up in marriage: the man sleeps on the couch after an argument or the woman packs her clothes and leaves after she discovers her husband has been unfaithful. These images and cultural pressures strongly contribute to the way each of us conduct ourselves and the reactions we have to life's daily issues within our marriage.

We claim we do not expect each other to be perfect, yet we get hurt when our spouse responds in a normal human way. We seem surprised we are, in fact, two broken people trying to make a whole life together and remain oblivious to the hurts, disappointments, misgivings, preconceived notions, faults, and idiosyncrasies that walked down the aisle, shared the honeymoon, and moved right in with us. These were all kindling for a fire waiting to happen. The only thing needed was a spark.

The good news is divorce is not inevitable. The decisions we make when we face marital discord is what determines whether the marriage continues or advances to separation.

In the following chapters, I will examine our assumptions, our thinking errors, and the actions we take to both strengthen and undermine our marriage. Most importantly, I will show you that when we respect our marriage as a sacred covenant, we will know harmony even through the most trying times.

CHAPTER 1

STUPID IN LOVE

Spiritual immaturity
is the root cause of all marital problems.

For 30 years, I have enjoyed the love, companionship, and friendship of one woman. Being with her has brought me great joy as well as the worst misery of my life. After spending such a long time with one person, there is no one on the planet I have loved or been hurt by more than her.

At this point, according to contemporary culture's standards, I am supposed to say, "Well, that's marriage."

After 30 years together, which included three separations and one near divorce, I learned that I did not always have a marriage that functioned according to God's design. Had I done so, the phrase, "Well, that's marriage," would never have left my lips.

Marriage is great when everything is going well. Your spouse is your best friend. That person can be your personal fan club, willing to cheer you on when you win and pick you up when you don't. Here's how the Bible describes it: "Find a good spouse, you find a good life and even more the favor of God!" (Proverbs 18:22 MSG).

When you became acquainted with your spouse, you started to believe he or she could be The One. When the two of you exchanged vows, you thought your time together would last forever.

As time wore on, problems set in. If you are reading this book, chances are the problems have become so severe that you do not see any way to rescue your marriage.

What happened?
How did the two of you end up where you are today?

Whenever my wife and I ran into marital issues, I would ask myself those same questions. After the third separation, which nearly cost us our marriage, I realized I wasn't asking the right questions. Even though we tried marital counseling, we were not taking the right course of action to resurrect our relationship.

If you have spent any time in marital counseling, you know the session usually starts with something like, "Tell me what has been going on in your marriage." Our marriage counseling was no different.

Generally, my wife would speak first and tell the counselor all the issues she believed were causing our marriage to fail. Then she would outline all of the things I was doing wrong. Eventually, I would get an opportunity to speak, and I would basically do the same thing, except instead of telling the counselor what I perceived were my faults, I would disclose the laundry list of my wife's shortcomings. Problems with sex, finances, communication, trust, kids, in-laws, church, careers/employment, and infidelity would be aired in front of the counselor as our collective lists unfolded. Once everything was out in the open the counselor would ask, "How do you think your marriage got to this state?"

Personally, I was always dumbfounded by this question. Inside I was thinking, "We just told you!"

The counselors never saw it that way. To the counselor, what my wife and I shared were symptoms, not the root cause of our problems. When the counselor asked this question, he or she considered the sessions could begin.

At this point, you may expect me to share the wisdom I learned from our marriage counseling sessions. I am not going to tell you anything I have learned from counselors, therapists, ministers, or even from books on marriage. Rather I am going to share with you insights I received directly from God after spending time with His word.

Drawing from my own experience, in this chapter, you will discover how your marriage arrived at its current state, and then together we will explore the root issues causing your marriage to fail.

Let's start by trying to identify where the arguments, disagreements, and misunderstandings came from. The Apostle Paul had this to say to the church in Galatia:

It is absolutely clear that God has called you to a free life. Just make sure that you don't use this freedom as an excuse to do whatever you want to do and destroy your freedom. Rather, use your freedom to serve one another in love; that's how freedom grows.

> *"For everything we know about God's Word is summed up in a single sentence: Love others as you love yourself. That's an act of true freedom. If you bite and ravage each other, watch out — in no time at all you will be annihilating each other, and where will your precious freedom be then?"*
> (GALATIANS 5:13-15 MSG)

When you first get married you live to be in the presence of the other person. Doing something for the sole benefit of your spouse is easy and enjoyable. With the passage of time, however, those loving acts start to wane and sometimes feel more like a chore. Then at some point, you begin to take stock of how your spouse reciprocates your acts of love.

Perhaps one of the following things have occurred: a) your spouse takes you for granted, b) your spouse doesn't acknowledgment you c) your spouse rejects you with negative words, or d) your spouse never reciprocates.

Not long after these incidents you begin to feel you are the one who must initiate love if there is to be any in your marriage. Not long after arriving at this realization, you decide to stop doing all the work and only provide expressions of love when your spouse does something loving first.

Lesson Learned #1 – Marriage is freedom.

Unfortunately, when you make that decision, the marriage stops growing. The Apostle Paul pointed out that a marriage in this state can no longer grow because the act of serving one another in love has ended. The world views marriage quite differently by concluding it is bondage. In fact, some people like to refer to their spouse as the old "ball and chain." Obviously, this is contrary to God's Word. Let us go back to Galatians Chapter 5 and visit Verse 1:

> *"Christ has set us free to live a free life. So take your stand!*
> *Never again let anyone put a harness of slavery on you."*
> (GALATIANS 5:1 MSG)

When Christ died for us and we accepted him as our Savior, we were set free from the bondage of sin and given the right to pursue living a free life. As marriage is a part of life, it was included in the gift of freedom paid for by Christ. This means for all of us who have been redeemed, our marriage is freedom, too. You should be free to express yourselves without fear that by showing your true self it will be later used against you. This is the service of loving the Apostle Paul described. It is the bond married people are meant to share with one another.

Each time you love your spouse as you love yourself, express your faith in love, or serve one another in love, your freedom grows. Why? Because the Bible says as you give your life away in the service of love, that same service of love will come back to you. Not only will it be returned, but it will not be in the same measure as you gave it. It will be given back with bonus. (Luke 6:38) This is good news! Who wouldn't want that freedom?

Regrettably, not all marriages experience this freedom. Instead, many face quite the opposite. If serving one another in love brings freedom, then the opposite is also true: not serving one another brings bondage.

Marriages in which couples have no covenant with God are not the only ones experiencing bondage in marriage. Many Christian couples are having the same experience.

If Christian couples and non-Christian couples are experiencing the same feeling of bondage in marriage when the Bible says there should be freedom for Christians, what is the barrier? Why can't couples serve each other in love like the Apostle Paul outlined in Galatians? To find that answer, we need to go back to Galatians chapter 5 and see what else the Apostle Paul had to say on the subject:

> *"My counsel is this: Live freely, animated and motivated by God's Spirit. Then you won't feed the compulsions of selfishness. For there is a root of sinful self-interest in us that is at odds with a free spirit, just as the free spirit is incompatible with selfishness. These two ways of life are antithetical, so that you cannot live at times one way and at times another way according to how you feel on any given day. So why don't you choose to be led by the Spirit and so escape the erratic compulsions of a law-dominated existence?"*
> (GALATIANS 5: 16-20 MSG)

The text very clearly indicates that the reason we stop serving one another in love is because of our selfishness. The Bible calls this "a root of sinful self-interest." This occurs every time that root causes us to give into the pressure of being, thinking, and acting self-centeredly. When we are selfish, we are only looking out for ourselves; the concern for others is completely lost or becomes secondary to our own desires. The Apostle Paul is also very forthright in stating a person can only live one way or the other, and each way of living is the result of a choice. He calls it being led by the Spirit or being led by the law.

Have you ever noticed what happens to a married couple when they first begin experiencing marital issues? Their first response to the issues is to set up rules and boundaries for each of them to curtail their behavior. Unbeknownst to the couple, they have taken their first step toward being led by the law and not the Spirit.

The systems of the world we live in respond to problems by trying to manage them. For people with anger issues, the resolution is to practice anger management. The solution for people who live in constant fear is to help the person better manage it. These thoughts and opinions contradict what the Word tells Christians about how they should handle these issues.

Instead of managing anger, the Bible says to be slow to anger (James 1:19) and to put anger away from you (Ephesians 5:31). Similarly, instead of managing fear, the Word tells us that perfect love casts out fear (1 John 4:18) and that God didn't give us a spirit of fear (2 Timothy 1:7). In both scenarios, the Bible tells us we have been empowered to get rid of anger and fear. Choosing to manage our emotions through self-imposed rules and boundaries is pointless and only gets in the way of true acceptance of God's will (Galatians 5: 23-24 MSG).

The Apostle Paul goes on in chapter 5 to explain what happens when we live this way.

> *"It is obvious what kind of life develops out of trying to get your own way all the time: repetitive, loveless, cheap sex, a stinking accumulation of mental and emotional garbage; frenzied and joyless grabs for happiness; trinket gods; magic-show religion; paranoid loneliness; cutthroat competition; all-consuming-yet-never-satisfying wants; a brutal temper; an impotence to love or be loved; divided homes and divided lives; small-minded and lopsided pursuits; the vicious habit of depersonalizing everyone into a rival; uncontrolled and uncontrollable addictions; ugly parodies of community. I could go on. This isn't the first time I have warned you, you know. If you use your freedom this way, you will not inherit God's kingdom."*
>
> (GALATIANS 5:19 – 21 MSG)

Do you recognize any of these—such as the world's way of living or other sinful qualities—in your marriage? Each time my wife and I separated, I reviewed this list and realized every time we had allowed one or several of these nasty characteristics outlined in Galatians Chapter 5:19-21 into our lives.

Isn't this behavior listed above just for non-Christians? The answer is no. When Paul wrote the letter that would eventually become known as the Book of Galatians, the letter was written to the church in Galatia, a church filled with individuals who had already accepted Christ.

People do not have to choose the behavior listed above because it is natural to them. Without Christ, people can only respond out of natural minds, feelings, and actions because the option to be led by the Spirit is not available. The privilege of living by the Spirit has been reserved to those who have been reborn through acceptance of the blood and work of Christ at Calvary.

PRINCIPLE #1:
Allowing the Holy Spirit to lead you
brings God's good gifts into our lives. (Galatians 5: 21-22 MSG)

Christians can continue to live out their natural tendencies or they let the Holy Spirit lead them. Once again, looking back in Galatians chapter 5, this is what Apostle Paul says happens when we live by the Spirit:

> *"But what happens when we live God's way? He brings gifts into our lives, much the same way that fruit appears in an*

orchard – things like affection for others, exuberance about life, serenity. We develop a willingness to stick with things, a sense of compassion in the heart, a conviction that a basic holiness permeates things and people. We find ourselves in loyal commitments, not needing to force our way in life, able to marshal and direct our energies wisely."

(GALATIANS 5: 21-22 MSG)

The ability to walk in loyalty, commitment, serenity, affection, and exuberance are qualities sought by Christians and non-Christians alike. The Apostle Paul, revealing these gifts in Galatians 5a;21-22, says they are like fruit growing in an orchard and they appear in a fruit-bearing process. According to Motherearthnews.com (Reich, 2008), growing a fruit bearing tree can be accomplished through a list of steps that are similar to how the Apostle Paul describes the way the fruit of the Holy Spirit grows in us.

Steps for Growing A Fruit Tree	Steps for Growing the Fruit of the Spirit	Scripture
Grow a seed from a great tasting specimen	Grow a seed from the Word God preached	Matthew 13:19
Drying the pit allows the seed to shrink, making it easier to exit	Determine the type of soil you need for your seed	Matthew 13:20-22
Soak the seed in room temperature water overnight, then put it in a jar of slightly moist potting soil	Mix the seed with your faith	Matthew 12:23
Close the jar and put it in your refrigerator where it won't get frozen or forgotten	The testing of your faith produces endurance (patience)	James 1:3
Check contents of the jar after about a month	Growth is a process; first the blade, then the ear, then full grain in the ear	Mark 4:28
Plant in fertile, well-drained soil	Solid food [of the Word] is for the mature	Hebrews 5:13-14
Prune as necessary	Be transformed by the renewing of your mind	Romans 12: 1-2
Protect tree from insects, diseases, weather conditions as well as fruit stealing and tree damaging creatures	Submit to God and resist the devil	James 4:7-10
Eat the fruit that grows from the tree	The word will transform your life	Psalms 128:2

By now it has become obvious, a couple who submits to being led by the Holy

Spirit will had a different kind of marriage than a couple who does not. Once again, we are talking about the couple where at least one spouse has made a decision to live this way. For the Christian couple where neither spouse chooses to be led by the Spirit or according to God's way of living, the marriage can run into the same problems as those experienced by a non-Christian couple.

After hearing this, you may have questions. Should Christians and non-Christians be experiencing the same type of marital problems? Do they respond the same way? Doesn't God promise to bless every couple that gets married since marriage is from God?

The answer to all of the questions is no. God has never promised to bless every married couple. In fact, biblical marriage isn't just between a man and a woman, but rather it is between a man and woman who have chosen to be in covenant with God. This nuance is very important because today we have lost great meaning and value in discussing the institution of marriage when we talk about it as the bond between any male and any female who decide to get married.

Here is an example to add more clarity. Imagine an atheist male and an atheist female decide to marry. They go to Las Vegas, apply for a marriage license, and get married at a wedding chapel next door to a casino. Is God obligated to bless or be in covenant with this married couple?

No. Why? Because this couple has not acknowledged God nor accepted his gift of grace offered through the redemptive work Jesus did as their Lord and Savior. Without Jesus, they are unable to have a covenant relationship with God. The key to God's recognition as a biblically married couple is to be in a union that he joined together. Look at what the Bible says in Mark:

> *"And the two shall become one flesh, so that they are no longer*
> *two but one flesh. Therefore, what God has joined together, let*
> *no one separate."*
>
> (MARK 10:8-9 NIV)

Principle # 2: God is only involved in marriages

Based on the scripture above, God literally takes credit for the union when a couple invites him to be an active participant in the bonds of holy matrimony by making a holy commitment to become one flesh. It is this commitment that sets a biblical marriage apart from any other marriage, including a marriage between a Christians male and female who make decisions in their marriage based on their natural minds instead of being led by the Spirit.

The Greek word for one flesh is sarkos, which can be translated as parts of the body (Zodhiates, 1991). To better understand its meaning, consider that the couple has committed to act as one heart, think as one mind, speak with one voice, and give as one hand within their marriage. This is just the beginning, because a couple could be of one heart, one mind, one voice, and one hand in robbing banks like Bonnie and Clyde.

We can all realize this cannot be the totality of God's intention. That is why verse 9 is important since it states the reason the male and female can become one flesh is because God joined them this way. It is God's responsibility to show an individual man and an individual woman that by submitting their ways to his direction they will become one flesh. The couple's commitment combined with God's commitment makes it a biblical marriage with three active partners—the husband, the wife, and God.

You can see confirmation God only considers marriage among those who are in covenant with Him. When Jesus spoke in Mark he was speaking to the people of Israel or God's chosen people and not to all marriages in the world. He was only talking to those who were already in a covenant with God.

Today, the word marriage has been reduced to mean any male or female who applied for a marriage license, held a marriage ceremony, and consummated the marriage with sexual intercourse. However, this is not God's definition. According to Mark, a marriage God has ordained is one he established by bringing together two covenant people. While the institution of marriage was established at creation, the word marriage has been hijacked by the world since the fall of man.

Taking the same liberty much of the world took when the word marriage was hijacked from meaning a covenant marriage to meaning a relationship between any man or woman, let's consider a new idea. Marriages not in covenant with God are actually nothing more than civil unions/marriages. According to Dictionary.com (Dictionary.com, 2016), a civil union is a relationship between a couple that is legally recognized by a governmental authority and has many of the same rights and responsibilities of legally married couples. A civil marriage is a marriage performed by anyone other than a member of the clergy.

For all the debate and energy expended on this issue, please know it has absolutely zero effect on the institution of marriage. Jesus himself indicated God is the author and creator of the institution of marriage.

> "But at the beginning of creation God made them male and female. For this reason, a man will leave his father and mother and be united to his wife, and the two will become one flesh. So they are no longer two, but one flesh. Therefore, what God has joined together, let no one separate."
>
> (MARK 10:9 NIV)

The institution of marriage is as strong today as it was at creation. At no time did God transfer His authority on the institution of marriage over to mankind. Governments can define marriage however they would like, and they can provide those legal rights to whomever they elect to subscribe those rights to, but

this doesn't impact or change the way God views or defines marriage.

> *Jesus himself indicated God knows how to separate that which*
> *belongs to God and that which belongs to any man-made govern-*
> *ment (Mark 12:17). When it comes to marriage, God is not look-*
> *ing at the outward appearance; instead He looks at the heart .*
> (1 SAMUEL 16:7)

Any marriage where God is not in fellowship with the union through covenant and at least one person in the couple maintains having a heart toward God by being led by the Spirit is nothing more than a civil union. To be a biblically based marriage, the couple must be in covenant with God and at least one member of the fellowship must let the Holy Spirit lead his or her life.

Quite a bit has been said about marriage in this chapter, but I promised to show you the root cause of problems in your marriage. Now that your thinking about marriage has been compared to what God thinks about marriage, it is time to ask yourself, "Where did I get my thoughts and understanding about marriage?"

That was a tough question for me the first two times my wife and I separated. After some soul searching, I had to admit my thoughts about marriage came from watching my parents, older siblings, friends, and even couples I saw in the media. It is amazing how much the images we capture from these groups have influenced how we think and approach our marriages and other relationships.

My parents were married for over 50 years. I understand when they met they were madly in love. That seemed to have lasted until just before I was born. By the time I, baby number six, came on the scene, my parents had begun acting more like roommates than lovers or friends. There was very little affection between them at home or outside the house, and they rarely spent time together. They seemed to have different schedules, interests, and friends. When all of my siblings left and my parents were left alone, that status didn't last very long. Soon grandchildren filled the void until their marriage ended when my father died.

Growing up in a household like this had a profound impact on my siblings and me. Out of the eight children born to my parents, only two of us have not been divorced, and my marriage came deadly close to it. Some of my brothers and sisters have been divorced more than once. In talking to some of them about this, I discovered one of the biggest concerns each of them have is the fear of becoming stuck in a loveless marriage.

My wife's parents divorced when she was nine years old. Like my siblings, most of her siblings also have also been divorced. Both of her parents were divorced more than once. Many of our closest friends—both inside and outside of the church—experienced divorces.

All of the failed relationships that surrounded us had an impact on our relationship. Every time we ran into marital issues, we would get loads of advice that led us away from being submitted to the Holy Spirit. We also found many marriage counselors, ministers, and therapists had gone through a divorce.

Deciding to have a marriage which resembles God's original plan for marriage means you are going to blaze a trail not traveled by many. It all begins when you set your views and decide about the issues of your marriage from the Word of God.

Unfortunately, if you are at all like I was, you do not always make life or marriage decisions solely based on what God has to say in his Word. Instead, sometimes you respond to your feelings and react to your spouse's actions. It is not long before you discover the interaction between you and your spouse becomes tit for tat, which often can be characterized as revenge.

The you-do-for-me-then-I-do-for-you attitude gets old really fast. It is likely soon one person in the relationship won't do his or her part, giving the other person nothing to respond to. If you respond and your spouse ignores you, the feeling of being unappreciated begins. On and on this goes until annoyance grow to irritation, which grows to frustration, which grows to retaliation. I cannot imagine anyone would willingly or knowingly decide to live this way, but it happens every day.

Individuals who do not know or fully understand what God's Word says about their situation or who are willfully disobedient will experience marital problems. When you realize God's promise to unite the couple into one flesh, you realize what went wrong. After the "I do's" at the altar, the couple stopped making God an active participant in the marriage and relegated his involvement to nothing more than a spectator.

Unfortunately, this describes the majority of Christian married couples. According to the State of the Bible survey produced by the Barna Group on the attitude and behaviors of Americans towards the Bible, only 37 percent of Americans report reading the Bible once a week or more (Barna Group, 2014). Among those who have read Scripture in the previous week, not quite six in 10 say they gave a lot of thought on how it might apply to their life. In 2015, the same survey saw that Bible reading among Christians didn't fare any better as one in seven adults say they read the Bible daily (14 percent); a similar portion spend time in Scripture several times per week (14 percent); eight percent read it once a week; nine percent read the Bible once a month; and six percent read it three to four times a year (Barna Group, 2015).

If Christians are not taking time to study the Bible, it is no wonder they do not know what God has to say about marriage. If they are open to hearing what He has to say, His words and wisdom can be available to shape their thoughts, actions, and decisions. Without this shaping, the couple cannot become one flesh and remain two independent persons. In this scenario, God remains on the sidelines instead of being an active participant in the relationship.

Having marital troubles is hard to admit, but realizing the problems are hap-

pening because you and your spouse failed to allow God to shape your responses to each other when the two of you could not find agreement or possibly facing infidelity is a tough reality to accept. The truth is if you had let God guide your responses, there would be forgiveness instead of condemnation, love instead of anger, long suffering instead of bitterness, patience instead of frustration. The list continues. Rather than you and your spouse having laundry lists of each other's faults, you would have those lists covered by the blood of Jesus and his comfort and care would have been available to help heal your heart wounds. It is a harsh reality but one I am confident we can explore together and find victory on the other side.

We can no longer live without God's wisdom because when we do, we subject ourselves to experiencing life however it comes our way. The Bible says in Hosea 4:6, "My people are destroyed from lack of knowledge."

The anger we feel, the wounds we suffer, and the utter exhaustion we are experiencing is the marriage destruction God's Word is bringing to our attention. Its origin is our lack of understanding and ability to apply God's Word in our married lives; it brings about our ignorance and immaturity. It is this spiritual immaturity which has become the root of our marital problems. The good news is we don't have to live this way. At any time, we can choose life instead of destruction, and in the next chapter, we will discuss some of the ways God can help turn failed marriages around.

Scripture:

> *"So Jesus said to those Jews who had believed in Him, "If you abide in My Word [hold fast to My teachings and live in accordance with them], you are truly My disciples. And you will know the Truth, and the Truth will set you free."*
>
> (JOHN 8:31-32 AMP)

CHAPTER 2

GIVE PEACE A CHANCE

God has multiple ways to turn
your failing or failed marriage around.

The quality of life you experience today is based on the decisions you made yesterday. This means you have complete influence over your quality of life today and tomorrow. Coming to this understanding really helped me realize if I wanted to experience something different in my life, I would have to start making new decisions. I also realized there was no better time to start than immediately.

The Bible supports this thinking with a number of verses that reminds me every day the power to change my life is in my hand. Here are just a few:

> *"Above all else, guard your heart, for everything you do flows from it."*
>
> (PROVERBS 4:23 NIV)

> *"Words kill, words give life; they're either poison or fruit – you choose."*
>
> (PROVERBS 18:21 MSG)

> *"I call Heaven and Earth to witness against you today: I place before you Life and Death, Blessing and Curse. Choose life so that you and your children will live."*
>
> (DEUTERONOMY 30:19 MSG"

While it is true you cannot change your past decisions, you do not have to continue allowing those decisions to rule your life. You have the power to make different and better choices than you have made in the past, and, by doing so, you will end up with a far much better future. The key is to make decisions today that will guarantee life, hope, and a blessed future tomorrow.

CHAPTER 2: GIVE PEACE A CHANCE

One of my favorite movie series is *Back to the Future*. In the first film, the main character, Marty McFly, uses time travel to transport himself 30 years into the past to prevent his children from making decisions which will devastate their lives.

Marty discovers a book that chronicles the winning scores for all the sporting events from his present day to 30 years into the future. He came up with a plan to buy the book, return to his present day, and start making bets on all the winners to change his future. With this book in hand, he knew he would never lose any bet; knowing the scores in advance meant he eliminated all the risk. What if you could get your hands on that book? Would you use it to place bets on the winners? Having this information would have the potential to make you extremely rich; your future would literally be in your own hands.

So what would you decide? Would you use the book? You're probably saying no such book exists, so why bother playing the "what if" game. However, what if a book that held all the answers to all the decisions you would ever need to make in your life really did exist and you would have no barrier to accessing it? Would you make the decision to use the book then? Once again, your ability to use all the book has to offer to change your future would depend on how committed you are to using it to address the issues of your life.

According to the Bible, in Deuteronomy 30:19, God said He has placed all of the answers that will give you life, hope, and a future in His book. God promises you His book contains answers to life. God left the decision up to you to take advantage of this opportunity. If you read the end of the verse, He strongly encourages you to choose life. There is no ambiguity where God stands on this. If you don't choose life, the Bible is clear you automatically choose death. It goes on to describe decisions which aren't life-producing bring death.

When you think of death, termination of life comes to mind. While the Bible does incorporate that thinking, there is a broader meaning. Think of death as life being taken away from you. When you receive a paycheck at work, you exchanged hours of your life for a salary. The paycheck can be considered life because you can purchase things you need to support life such a living space, food, utilities, transportation, and even recreation. Without these things or even having them in short supply, your quality of your life is diminished.

Now consider what it would be like working for two weeks without a paycheck. You would not be able to purchase the things you would need to sustain your life. Each passing two-week period without pay would lower your quality of life. Ultimately, without a reversal or assistance along the way, you would experience a physical death. In this scenario, the absence of the paychecks could be considered death and the paychecks, when they arrived, would be considered life.

In his scripture, God pleads with the us to make decisions that *enhance* the quality of our lives instead of making choices that *take away* from it. Either life or death is available to you. According to God's word, if you do not make a choice, by default you get death.

You have a decision in front of you right now that concerns God. The situation requiring a decision is, of course, your marriage. The fact that you have kept reading this book says your marriage or the marriage of someone you know may be in danger of failing, and it is in trouble because of all the decisions both spouses made up to this point.

In the previous chapter, we discovered together God's plan for marriage is for you and your spouse to experience freedom. To accomplish this freedom, you need to make choices that allow you to provide love and service to each other. The more love you offer your spouse, the more love you will have returned to you.

In Chapter 1, we also looked at the importance being led by the Holy Spirit has on your relationship. When the Spirit leads you, you and your spouse become one flesh, or as we discussed, you now are of one heart, one mind, one voice, and one hand. Being led by the Spirit will also help you grow, thus attacking the root causes of marital problems—lack of knowledge of God's Word or spiritual immaturity.

We will continue to build upon what we learned by discussing how God will become involved in turning your failing marriage around.

The good news is God has a plan! He could not tell you to choose life or death unless He could honor whichever choice you made. God has a multitude of ways to turn your marriage around, and you have already heard of at least one of them. As we present God's redemptive works in your marriage, I will introduce them to you as the Holy Spirit introduced them to me.

One of these redemptive works can be compared to a life vest, a device worn over your upper body and is designed to save you from drowning by holding you up when you are in water. (The American Heritage Dictionary, 2001). Similarly, what I am calling a "spiritual life vest" is a specific godly character or behavior found in the Word of God and helps a believer rise about storms when they apply the Word to their lives.

We see a spiritual life vest in the story of Jesus and Peter walking on the water in Matthew 14:22-33. You will recall Peter saw Jesus walking outside of the boat and above the water in the midst of a storm. Although they had spent much of their lives on the water as fishermen, the Bible says the disciples were afraid as the boat took on water and nearly capsized as a result of the storm. When the Lord agreed, Peter climbed out of the boat and joined Him. The storm was still raging, but that was no longer a problem for Peter; however, it still remained a problem for the rest of the disciples.

The difference between Peter and the other disciples is Peter made a decision to act on the Lord's presence while the rest continued to stay frightened by the storm. Peter's focus turned to the Lord while their focus remained on the storm. Peter's focus on the Lord got him to think and act upon what seemed illogical and improbable for the situation he was facing. The others continued to respond to

27

what they were experiencing. Once Peter got out of the boat, he was in a state where the storm and water were no longer a consideration to him.

Notice none of the other disciples ever asked to join Jesus or Peter even though, by staying in the boat, death was a real possibility. Remember, Peter turned his focus to the Lord, and the storm ceased its effect on his life.

On the water with the Lord some ways away, Peter went from standing on the water to walking across it. In all that time, Peter's physical body was above the water and the storm had no effect.

How could he do this? Simple. Peter made a decision to follow Jesus when Jesus said, "Come." In that one word, the Lord told Peter he could do what he saw Jesus doing.

Was it the presence of the Lord that allowed Peter to walk on the water? No. It was him exhibiting the same character that Jesus had at that moment. We find the answer in verse 30, which says when Peter once again recognized the existence of the storm, he grew frightened and his focus went away from the Lord and back onto the storm and the water. He was no longer exhibiting the godly character which caused him to walk on the water. Instead, he became subject again to the storm and water. He began to sink.

Sinking and afraid, he called out for help. Immediately, Jesus reached out his hand, caught him, and held him (Matthew 14:31 AMP). Peter was no longer sinking. Why? Because Jesus, who was still exhibiting the character that allowed him to walk along the water in the first place, grabbed Peter and stopped him from sinking. As long as Peter stayed connected to the Lord, he was not subject to the storm or its effects. During that time, Jesus became Peter's life vest.

Together, Peter and Jesus continue their walk. At last they returned to the boat and got back in. Before they enter the boat, the Lord asked Peter, "O you of little faith, why did you doubt?"

Now we have our answer. The godly character Jesus was exhibiting and Peter was emulating for a while was faith. As long as he exercised faith, Peter was not subject to the storm or the water. In fact, the end of verse 31 says when they got into the boat, the wind stopped. With the Lord on the scene and faith in operation, no one was adversely affected by the storm or the water.

When you exhibit the character found in the Word of God, the very presence of the Lord is with you. He brings his character and nature on the scene to join with yours. As long as you continue to conduct yourself according to his character, you will ride above the crisis or situation you were previously experiencing, denying its power to harm you.

The key is to keep your focus on the Lord and exhibit the godly character like Peter did during the storm. You will get positive results every time. Having godly character in operation becomes your life vest and brings the power and

nature of the Lord on the scene. As long as you keep your focus on the Lord you will ride above the storm, but if you turn your attention to anything else and respond out of your natural thinking, you will be like Peter and begin to sink under your circumstances. Exhibiting the same godly character Jesus exhibits will keep you above the storms of life as God's assistance arrives on the scene to change the circumstances.

So what does this have to do with marriage? Everything.

If a husband and wife reject God's life vests, they will begin drowning in the ocean of their marital problems. Drowning and with no sense of direction, the couple could find themselves desperate. If they are unable to agree on a course of action, it is possible they will decide to go their separate ways to secure their own survival. In these cases, the life vest isn't enough to keep the marriage afloat. This is where a spiritual lifeboat, another redemptive work, is needed.

A lifeboat is defined as a buoyant boat for use in an emergency and especially in saving lives at sea (Merriam-Webster, Inc., 2016). When God sends out his lifeboat, it always comes with a crew captained by Jesus and steered by the Holy Spirit. Their task is to answer the intercessory prayers of the saints who remain in fellowship to the covenant to bring life-restoring support to those who have broken fellowship. In this chapter, we will discuss in detail, God's life vests and lifeboats.

> *"But you shall live by your sword, and serve your brother; how-*
> *ever, it shall come to pass when you break loose [from your*
> *anger and hatred], That you will tear his yoke off your neck*
> *[and you will be free of him].""*
>
> (GENESIS 27:40 AMP)

Take the time to read the entire chapter of Genesis 27 and learn about how Jacob, the younger son, stole the blessing and inheritance his father Isaac had intended to give to Esau, his first born and rightful heir. Even though Jacob received the blessing, riches, and wealth through deception, God did not strike him down for stealing it but rather honored his father's prayer.

If you read the entire story, you find Esau did not put the proper value on his birthright because he sold it to Jacob for the price of a bowl of stew. He had not looked at the long-term implication of his actions, and this ending up hurting him.

The birthright determined the position when inheriting goods as part of an estate. Esau was first in line to receive the best and majority share of his father's inheritance. With what Isaac had accumulated and prepared to pass to the next generation, there were elements of the inheritance that would only be in the hands of the firstborn. Jacob understood the importance of being the first born and wanted to receive the inheritance for himself. He plotted multiple times to steal the birthright and succeeded in getting Esau to give it up for stew.

When Esau recognized he had been defrauded out of the blessing, he pleaded for Isaac to bless him as well. Verse 40 in the chapter is Isaac's response to Esau's pleading with this key message to his son: "But [the time shall come] when you will grow restive and break loose, and you shall tear his yoke from off your neck." The Hebrew meaning of the word restive is "to be restless" (Strong's, 1994). From the text, we can conclude sometime in the future he would grow restless from having to live without the blessing and below his potential. Only then would Esau be able to break loose and be free (Genesis 27:40 MSG).

We can relate this story to marriage by looking at what Issac told Esau the circumstances under which he would be able to act in a way to free himself from the bondage of not receiving the blessing. When we find ourselves restless or dissatisfied, this is not the time to give up. It is an indication that it is time to fully rely on God to bring positive change to your relationship.

 Life Vest – A Spirit of Restlessness

God didn't leave Esau without a lifeline after being robbed of the blessing. He told him whenever he decided he had enough, he would do whatever it took and break free from the situation. Reading between the lines, God was letting Esau know two things—first, he was responsible for when that time would come, and second, he was empowered to break the yoke and set himself free from the moment Isaac prayed. Esau didn't have to ask for it; no additional prayer was needed. If Esau wanted to live with the yoke around his neck one day or 30 years, that was his decision to make. God's gift to Esau was a spirit of restlessness; the sooner Esau accepted this gift, the better it would be for him.

One of God's ways to help you turn your marriage around is by giving you and/or your spouse a feeling of dissatisfaction or restlessness. That feeling will help you recognize the quality of your marriage is less than what God wants for you. Through restlessness, you will be stirred to do something. As with Esau, God will give you restlessness and empowerment to bring a good and lasting resolution to the bondage and emptiness in your lives.

 Life Vest – Bearing One Another's Burdens

Another gift from God to help you turn around your marriage is each other. That is correct—your spouse is God's gift to help you turn around your failing marriage. You may view this as impractical because right now your spouse may seem more like the enemy than someone able to help, but that is only because you don't have God's perspective on who they are.

Your spouse is your deliverer, and God has sent your spouse as the deliver. The dictionary defines the deliverer as someone who takes another to their proper place, sets them free, or produces what is expected (The American Heritage Dictionary, 2001).

You and your spouse are the ones who can release each other from bad decisions, faulty character, and a past that has anchored you from being all God designed for you to become.

Yes, I am talking about the same person you are married to right now, and no, it doesn't matter what has happened in your marriage to get you to your current state. You could tell me your spouse is an abuser, drug addict, gambler, prostitute, or has any other character flaw. The answer is still the same.

This idea is probably contrary to what you view on your favorite television drama, but it doesn't negate the truth. Here are some scriptures to validate the point:

"With complete lowliness of mind (humility) and meekness (unselfishness, gentleness, mildness), with patience, bearing with one another and making allowances because you love one another."

(EPHESIANS 4:2 AMP)

"Brethren, if any person is overtaken in misconduct or sin or any sort, you who are spiritual [who are responsive to and con-trolled by the Spirit] should set him right and restore and rein-state him, without any sense of superiority and with all gentle-ness, keeping an attentive eye on yourself, lest you should be tempted also."

(GALATIANS 6:1 AMP)

"Be gentle and forbearing with one another and, if one has a difference (a grievance or compliant) against another, readily pardoning reach other; even as the Lord [freely] forgiven you, so must you also [forgive]."

(COLOSSIANS 3:13 AMP)

God knew your spouse before you did. He knows what makes him or her happy or sad. He knows the wrongs done to your spouse and the wrongs he or she has done. Even at this very moment, God knows what is on your spouse's mind and what secrets and motives are harbored in their heart (Jeremiah 17:10). There is nothing hidden from the Lord. Believe it or not, if you are a Bible-believing, Holy

Spirit-led Christian, this is the very reason God sent you into your spouse's life. God is looking for you to be to them what Jesus was to the world, a deliverer.

> *"For God so greatly loved and dearly prized the world that He [even] gave up His only begotten (unique) Son, so that whoever believes in (trusts in, clings to, relies on) Him shall not perish (come to destruction, be lost) but* have eternal (everlasting) life."
>
> (JOHN 3:16 AMP)

Unlike Christ, God is not looking for you to die to save your spouse. That work has already been done at Calvary; it doesn't need to be done again. Instead, God is looking for you to be in your spouse's life and to do what someone did for you when they introduced Christ to you. Even though Jesus died on the cross over 2,000 years ago, his redemptive work would have done you no good unless someone brought the Gospel to you. Maybe you heard it at church. That church service happened because someone preached a sermon, sang in the choir, greeted you at the door, or in some other way paved the way for you to receive the good news of God's gospel message. All of these people were operating as an extension of God's love to you. That is exactly what God wants you to be for your spouse—an extension of his love. You do this by daily encouraging your spouse in the Lord and helping him or her without condemnation to walk through the process of repentance, forgiveness, and yielding to the leading of the Spirit.

 Life Vest – Confessing Our Faults One to Another

As we discussed, God knows all of your spouse's moral deficiencies. In fact, all of your moral deficiencies are also known by God. For your marriage to follow his design, God wants you and your spouse to create an intimate atmosphere within your marriage so that the two of you can be naked and unashamed before each other.

> *"And the man and his wife were both naked and were not embarrassed or ashamed in each other's presence."*
>
> (GENESIS 2:25 AMP)

Another meaning of nakedness is simply to be uncovered (Zodhiates S. T., 1994). You and your spouse should be able to completely expose yourselves to one another without fear of condemnation, without worry anything shared will be used against either of you. Instead, what each of you should find is commitment, understanding, and a willingness to carry the burden of whatever your spouse has hidden in his or her heart. In this environment, your spouse will be at ease confessing faults and sins to you, and you will serve in this role to your spouse as well.

"Confess to one another therefore your faults (your slips, your false steps, your offenses, your sins) and pray [also] for one another, that you may be healed and restored [to a spiritual tone of mind and heart]. The earnest (heartfelt, continued) prayer of a righteous man makes tremendous power available [dynamic in its working]."

(JAMES 5:16 AMP)

Being free to confess faults, you and your spouse are free to identify areas in your respective lives that are not aligned to God's way, and through prayers of healing and restoration, each of you can help restore Christ's lordship in your hearts and minds.

The freer the environment you and your spouse create, the more quickly and more often the faults will be confessed. Without the availability of faults and unconfessed sins lingering around, the devil will find nothing he could use against you or your spouse to condemn either of you. Ultimately, this will mean that the devil will not be able to find a foothold in you or your spouse as you continue to submit your lives to be led by the Holy Spirit (Ephesians 4:27).

 ## Life Vest – Spiritual Discernment

The next life vest we will discuss is spiritual discernment. Before defining it, let's take a look an example that should make it easier to understand.

Let's say your spouse—we will suppose in this case you are a woman and your spouse is a man—has a gambling problem that has come to your attention because you received a phone call from a casino demanding $10,000. You did not even know your husband had been going to the casino every Thursday because he told you he was going bowling.

First of all, if you were walking in the Spirit, long before you received that phone call, you would have gotten a feeling in your spirit every Thursday when your spouse misled you about going bowling. The feeling within your spirit is called spiritual discernment. In this case, the lack of peace you experienced every time your spouse said he intended to go bowling was the Spirit letting you know there was a spiritual matter needing your attention.

But the natural, nonspiritual man does not accept or welcome or admit into his heart the gifts and teachings and revelations of the Spirit of God, for they are folly (meaningless nonsense) to him; and he is incapable of knowing them [of progressively recognizing, understanding, and becoming better acquainted with them because they are spiritually discerned and estimated and appreciated].

But the spiritual man tries all things [he examines, investigates, inquiries into, questions, and discerns all things], yet is himself to be on trial and judged by no one [he can read the meaning of everything, but no one can properly discern or appraise or get an insight into him].

> *"For who has known or understood the mind (the counsels and purposes) of the Lord so as to guide and instruct Him and give Him knowledge? But we have the mind of Christ (the Messiah) and do hold the thoughts (feelings and purposes) of His heart."*
> (1 CORINTHIANS 2:14-16 AMP)

Spiritual discernment is when a believer calls on the aid of the Holy Spirit to lead or give direction and/or insight into a matter. Your spouse may think he is getting away with his lies, but if you are connected to the Spirit of God, you will get a sense of concern as a warning each time your spouse tells this lie.

By spending time with the Spirit through prayer and waiting on Spirit's insight, you will receive instructions about what needs your attention every time your spouse goes bowling. In this case, it is the fact he isn't going bowling but instead gambling without your knowledge. As you can imagine, gambling can lead you and your family into a bad situation. Before this happens, the Spirit is there to give you insight to avoid it or to be prepared to find the way out.

Even when your spouse believes he is carrying out clandestine gambling activities alone and completely devoid of your knowledge, if he is a believer, the Holy Spirit went with him whenever he went gambling. If your spouse is not a believer, the angel assigned to him knows where he is and what he is doing (Hebrews 1:14).

Either way your husband is never outside of God's sight. Taking advantage of spiritual discernment allows the Holy Spirit to let you know things that would not be readily picked up by your natural senses. Whether the Spirit who helps you discover the chip from the casino your spouse hid in his dresser drawer or the bank statements that shows the hidden cash withdrawals to fund his gambling runs, the Spirit will guide you to the trail to discover the truth. The Bible calls him the Spirit of Truth and, as you lend your ear to his guidance, he will share the truth he knows with you.

> *Then the evil desire, when it has conceived, gives birth to sin, and sin, when it is fully matured, brings forth death.*
> (JAMES 1:15 AMP)

Losing $10,000 from your bank account, even if you had the money, would be a serious blow to your finances. Obviously, you and your spouse were not saving the money for that purpose, or your spouse wouldn't have had to sneak around, so the first place the Spirit will do his work is with your spouse when the evil desire entered into his thinking. The Spirit will work against those enticing thoughts; however, if your spouse acts on his desire to go to the casino, his mind will be more open to accept the enticing thoughts rather than the thoughts of deliverance that were planted by the Holy Spirit.

God will not violate your spouse's will to choose between life and death. However, even before your spouse makes a bad choice, the Spirit will try to alert you to the potential enticement. But once your spouse makes the decision and lies to cover his tracks, the Holy Spirit realizes this is the work of the enemy attacking your marriage.

The Spirit knows if the gambling continues, it will be a hardship, so the Spirit gives you an inner witness to what is going on. The Spirit will also not let up on your bringing conviction to your spouse (John 16:8) and helping you to pray in a manner specific and effective for this situation (Romans 8:26). As you pray, your prayers will enable all of heaven's resources to be marshaled on your behalf (1 John 5:14-15).

By the time you get that phone call from the casino, the Spirit will have already instructed you how to respond and what actions to take. You will have fostered great love in your heart so that you can communicate with your spouse in meekness, love, and humility.

God is not looking for you to condemn your spouse for the lost money. The convictions come to your spouse's heart about how fellowship was broken with you and God with the lost money should drive repentance. This is what God wants to happen as you offer your spouse unconditional love to restore him. God sees this is a small price to pay to win your spouse back in fellowship with himself and with you.

God is always concerned with reaching believers and non-believers alike and having them make an eternal decision for Christ. That is not to say he isn't concerned about the money. If you listen to the Spirit, part of the instructions you will receive is that because of your obedience, Satan will have to pay you back at least two and possibly seven-fold (Proverbs 6:31). You may have had to give away $10,000, but God will have you reimbursed from the kingdom of darkness with as much as $70,000, depending on what you are willing to believe you'll receive. In the end, you will have a spouse who is very grateful for your love and forgiveness. He will be closer to God and you than before. You will have grown spiritually through the trial, and your bank account will be fatter than before. This started off as just the life vest of spiritual discernment, but by the time you were done with the trial, you will have also exercised the life vest of bearing each other's burden.

 ## Life Vest – Taking Spiritual Authority

Another tool married couples can use to turn their marriage around is to take spiritual authority. Apostle Paul explains it this way:

> *"For the wife does not have [exclusive] authority and control over her own body, but the husband [has his rights]; likewise, also the husband does not have [exclusive] authority and control over his body, but the wife [has her rights]."*
>
> (1 CORINTHIANS 7:4 AMP)

With each spouse having authority and rights of control over the other spouse's body, each one has an avenue to expect more, speak with words of faith, and facilitate a course correction to any troubling situation.

For example, my wife has had a long-term problem with hypertension. Despite taking medication, during our most recent separation, her blood pressure was out of control, and she ended up spending many days and nights in the hospital.

When God finally brought us back together, I reestablished my role as having authority and control over her body. Standing on 1 Corinthians 7:4, I spoke the Word of God over her body and took spiritual authority over her blood pressure. Speaking by faith, I commanded her blood pressure to get come back to normal levels. I set a specific target for it. Every evening I spoke to her body and reminded her blood pressure of the target set by faith.

We have seen tremendous results. The overnight hospital stays have ceased. Her blood pressure levels have gone from stroke levels down to near-normal ranges. We continue to believe that her blood pressure will meet the specific target.

The results show we are being tested to see if we will settle for her blood pressure out of our target range. We understand we are being challenged to see how committed we are to standing by faith on the word in 1 Corinthians 7:4. Every night we reaffirm our commitment and set our expectation to meet our target. This is the authority God has given to every believer, including Christian married couples! Don't be afraid to take authority and see God work miracles in your spouse's body on your behalf.

Spiritual discernment, bearing one another's burdens, taking spiritual authority, confessing our faults to each other, and a feeling of restlessness are God's life vests for your marriage. Life vests by themselves are not enough because if one spouse decides not to use these life-saving devices or departs from the shelter the marriage under the protection God provides, then the spouse could find himself or herself washed away by the flood waters of life.

Flood waters of life happen when a traumatic and unexpected event occurs. Two years ago I went to Los Angeles to attend a business meeting and to visit my daughter who had relocated to the area a few months before. As I exited the building after the business meeting ended, I noticed that my cell phone, which had been placed on silent, had a number of repeat calls.

Listening to one of the voicemails, I discovered one of my relatives was calling to tell me that my daughter had gone missing. If you are a parent, you know that a missing child, regardless of your child's age, is a traumatic event.

This horrifying situation lasted for three weeks. During that time neither my wife nor I lived a normal life. Praise be to God, the Lord intervened and our daughter returned to us and the healing process began.

This is an example of flood waters. From that phone call and until the exact moment we knew our daughter would be well again, we felt like we were in an ocean by ourselves. There were times we felt like we were drowning. Our friends and families prayed with us, and to the best of their abilities they felt our pain but they didn't feel they were drowning like we did. They could go home at night and hug and kiss their child or children. They could hear their child say, "I love you, Mom. I love you, Dad," whereas we had no idea where our child even was. As those days and nights went by, the more we put our trust in Jesus and hung on to his hand, the more that drowning feeling subsided.

In each of our lives, we will experience storms and flash floods. Jesus told us about this in one of his parables when he said the following:

> "Though the rain comes in torrents and the floodwaters rise and the winds beat against that house."
>
> (MATTHEW 7:25A NLT)

Throughout the four gospels (Matthew, Mark, Luke, and John),

Jesus used stories and analogies to help illustrate the spiritual concepts. As the Holy Spirit gave his revelation on marriage, he also used stories and analogies to convey the message to me.

A marriage can be compared to a car in that everyone and everything in the car must work toward the same purpose. If driven properly, the car will make sure the driver and all of its contents arrive to an appointed destination safely.

The car can only have one driver at a time, even if there are two or more persons in the car. The vehicle can only arrive at one destination at a time. The car will respond to the directions the driver provides. The driver and its passengers must agree on the desired route, otherwise whatever purpose they have for driving a particular route and to a particular place will be lost.

In marriage, the husband and wife are both drivers with varying skills, but only one driver can be behind the steering wheel at any given time. The other driver can help with navigation and watch out for hazards along the road.

God's intention is for the husband and wife to live together in harmony with the same mutual respect that occurs between a driver and passenger in a car. The marriage is supposed to offer shelter for the husband and wife. As the driver and passenger will travel to the same direction and may have different agendas for their reasons for going to the same destination, marriage should offer the same support and flexibility for the husband and wife. God's expectation is that the husband and wife would not only be in the marriage (car) actively performing their respective roles (driver and navigator), but while in the marriage (car) they would be wearing their life vests.

You probably do not wear life vests in your car, but you do wear seatbelts, which serve the same purpose. Having a life vest in your car takes safety one step further and is not a bad idea, though it is probably not something most people consider. You may do what I did and put a life vest in the context of a boat, not a car. As I thought deeper, though, I now understand that the Lord was trying to get me to do is think deeper about the importance of preparation in advance of unexpected situation, using the life boat as a metaphor for the flash floods one might face from time to time in marriage.

I researched a bit online and found story after story of individuals who were in their cars and got caught by a flash flood. There were mothers, fathers, brothers, sisters, and children in automobiles heading to normal activities like grocery shopping, church or Little League who never arrived at their destination because a flash flood hit their car.

An average of 127 people die every year from flood deaths according to the National Weather Service (National Weather Service, 2016). Most flash floods are caused by slow- moving thunderstorms that cause floods to develop in minutes or hours depending on the intensity and duration of the rain (National Weather Service, 2016). Flash floods can roll boulders, tear out trees, and destroy buildings. The rapidly rising water can reach heights of 30 feet or more (National Weather Service, 2016).

Those 127 people who made it out of flashfloods safely probably thought having a life vest in their car was a silly idea until they ran into a flash flood. Flash floods come with no warning and neither due the flash floods of life.

God warns us floods will come into our lives, yet very few Christians take his warning and prepare themselves and families with spiritual life vests. Instead, they think they have time or the storm will never come. Flash floods do happen, and when you do not prepare yourself with the same character you have witnessed Jesus prepare with in the Bible, you subject yourself to the storm and its desire to do destructive damage in your lives and families.

God tries to prevent you and your spouse from becoming a marital casualty. Using his life vests will keep you from drowning, but in the event one of you gets out of his protective fellowship with God, he will send a lifeboat.

 Lifeboat - Marriage Reconciliation

God will not abandon the married couple who needs to turn around their marriage. He will continue to extend his life vests, but he will also send a life boat to meet the couple where they in troubled waters.

That life boat is called marriage reconciliation. I am sure you have probably heard of marriage reconciliation, but just as the word marriage was hijacked by our culture, this term has met the same fate.

Here is one example of how the world defines marriage reconciliation— "Marriage reconciliation is where two people going through a divorce or separation decide to re-think their decisions about ending their marriage. Many times people make mistakes and over-react—they may say something and regret it later. Marriage reconciliation is just that. (Just Answer, LLC, 2016)."

While there are many similarities with our culture's definition of marriage reconciliation and the Bible's definition, God's definition goes much further in its approach and in the results.

> *Vs. 10 and 11 – "And if you are married, stay married. This is the Master's command, not mine. If a wife should leave her husband, she must either remain single or else come back and make things right with him. And a husband has no right to get rid of his wife. Vs. 16 - You never know, wife: The way you handle this might bring your husband not only back to you but to God. You never know, husband: The way you handle this might bring your wife not only back to you but to God."*
> (1 CORINTHIANS 7:10-11, 16 MSG)

With Western culture's definition of marriage reconciliation, after separating or while going through divorce, the couple rethinks their decisions about ending the marriage and decides to give the marriage another try. With God's definition, the reconciliation is not only between the couple. It is also a reconciliation of the couple back to God. What this implies is through the aid of the Holy Spirit, God continues to offer the couple life vests, but he will also involve others to aid the couple. It could be a pastor or minister, close friend, another brother or sister in the Lord, or a marriage counselor. Whomever God uses, the couple has the opportunity to re-examine being in fellowship with the marital covenant they entered into with God.

The couple will need to re-examine the covenant God extended to them for its terms, provisions, and benefits and honestly examine how many times they have rejected his efforts to honor the covenant. Through a minister, friend, family member, or spiritual counselor, the couple is able to hear what they could not hear from God directly. Conviction comes to the couple, and they decide to submit to it by seeking repentance and forgiveness.

As they go through this process, the couple re-enters into fellowship with God and each other. This re-commitment helps them grow spiritually, and they can start making a new commitment to allow the Spirit of God lead their marriage. Walking with the Spirit's leading, the couple once again—or for the first time—starts serving one another in love, becomes willing to bear one another's burdens, begins confessing their faults one to another, and continues by walking in the freedom that was given to them in Christ.

Unlike the couple who reconciles only because they rethought their decisions and have agreed to give the marriage a try again, the couple who embraces a marital reconciliation from God is now

aware God has given them the tools not only to identify the issues which caused them to ship wreck in the first place but also how to overcome them.

Coming close to being a marital casualty and being delivered by God's hand of grace brings a renewed effort for each spouse to share grace with each other. With each passing day, the couple understands they have the ability to see growth and happiness by pruning away those desires take them away from God and each other while fertilizing their hearts with the guidance of the Holy Spirit. They no longer need to fear their marriage will again need a turnaround.

God is in the turnaround business, and your marriage can go from failing to soaring by taking hold of God's many life vests and or his life boat. It is his desire to see all the dreams you and your spouse have for your each other and the marriage become reality. All you have to do is decide you don't want your marriage to fail and reach out to God for his help through prayer and faith. He is already on the scene and waiting for your decision to make a turnaround for you.

Scripture:

> *"Bear (endure, carry) one another's burdens and troublesome moral faults, and in this way fulfill and observe perfectly the law of Christ (the Messiah) and complete what is lacking [in your obedience to it]."*

(GALATIANS 6:2 AMP)

CHAPTER 3

WHERE DID WE GO WRONG?

When words cease, the door is open for divorce to enter and end the marriage.

A marriage doesn't go from good to dead overnight. It takes time to cultivate a divorce just as it does to build a marriage. If you want your marriage to continue, it is vitally important to identify the state of the relationship with your spouse. Picking up this book is a good indicator you are concerned about your marriage. The good news is at this stage your marriage is probably not dead, but you may be headed in that direction.

Before my marriage died, it was in a state similar to someone with a serious gunshot wound would be. Survival is dependent on receiving appropriate medical care before vital organs shutdown. The point of this chapter is to help you identify the state of your relationship by seeing the similarities in my marriage just before my wife filed for divorce. I am confident you will see parallels.

Our marriage began to take a turn toward divorce when communication ended. On the surface it seemed either we had found a way to co-exist with our problems or we were just taking a time out. Unfortunately, something much more fatal was happening behind the scenes. I wish I knew then what I'm sharing with you now, but if you take hold of the lessons learned, you can infuse new hope for your marriage. In fact, what my wife and I discovered is when your marriage hits this stage—the silent phase—you are in the best position to avoid divorce as long as you can correctly identify the signs and interrupt the process by getting the help your marriage needs.

Silence between the spouses is an important sign deadness has started to set in. Silence happens when a spouse hits the limit of the tension he or she can endure.

The phrase "I am talking to a brick wall" certainly applied in our situation. No amount of talking would change anything, so there was no point in continuing to talk. At least that's what I thought. When communication shuts down completely, there is probably no respect for each other's opinion or decisions. What is interesting is when silence takes over, the arguments don't actually end—they continue in the mind.

Having an argument in your head is an interesting experience. You are always right, the other one is always wrong, and you are never the one taking the other person for granted. It is easy to pursue a winning scenario when you are free to play the argument through your own imagination without constraints or boundaries.

A winning scenario happens when you have visualized all your opponent's objections to your point of view. Then you find a combination of arguments and tactics that make it inevitable your opponent will agree with what you would like to happen. Hence, you win.

I have been in sales for over 20 years, and it is common for sales leaders to help salespeople win an important customer by having them visualize the sales call before they talk to the customer. Visualizing a sales call and running various scenarios with an experienced peer or leader allows salespeople to work through all of their arguments that support the benefits of the products they are proposing while matching them up with the customer's perceived needs and wants. The salespeople continue to do this until they find the right pitch and way to position their product to gain the customer's agreement.

However, there is a flaw with visualization. To work properly, the visualization presupposes the salesperson fully understands the customer's wants and needs. If the salesperson did not fully undercover the customer's complete need for the product or concerns for their use of the product, then the visualization effort will not produce the correct set of arguments. The result could cost the salesperson the business.

When my wife was so unhappy in our marriage that something had to change, she, like the salesperson, would go through a myriad of virtual conversations in her head, playing out her argument and my supposed response. Instead of engaging in conversations with me, she would be silent for days, only surfacing to present the same argument in a different way in the hope that I would respond differently.

Unfortunately, unlike the salesperson she did not take time to really understand the reasons for my position. She only knew my likely responses, and she did not even really understand those. You can guess what the outcome was every time she emerged out of her head to present one of her arguments to me.

Unfortunately, mental simulation like visualization is not the same as real-time interaction. You are not held to the rules your spouse has established in his or her head. In addition, the environment is never as sterile as what develops inside the head. During face-to-face interactions, even the best laid plans get interrupted because of life's normal activities, such as a phone ringing or one of the kids needing attention.

Silence is pretty easy to recognize, but identifying you are being offered a mentally stimulated argument may slip past you. For a long time, I failed to recognize my wife was doing this. It wasn't until after we separated I figured out my wife had presented me with two of these scenarios. Neither of them helped solve problems in our marriage.

Understand if you reject the premise of the someone's argument, with each scenario, his or her willingness to present another potential suggestion significantly diminishes. When my wife presented both of her scenarios, I completely rejected them. I have since come to learn the same rules of persuasive communication and negotiation apply with simulated arguments when they are articulated, which include remaining open-minded and looking for common ground.

It is important to realize you are only going to get a few chances to get this right. Remember, the winning scenario is actually what your spouse is trying to achieve. Try showing you care by staying engaged in the discussion, and when your spouse presents his or her mentally simulated argument, look for something in the argument you are willing to accept. It does not have to be their entire argument, it could be a small part. Even agreeing there is a problem is validation gives the two of you a stepping stone to finding more common ground. That is a huge accomplishment compared to both of you wanting your arguments accepted in their entirety.

If a winning scenario is not achieved during the course of your dialogue, your spouse may shift to simulating how to make living with you bearable. Perhaps one of you could live upstairs and the other downstairs. What if you work the night shift, and she works during the day shift so you do not have to see each other? Over and over the spouse plays "what if" scenarios and sometimes, as in my wife's case, she was unable to find a winnable solution.

Because of the eating disorder she was dealing with, she entered an intensive outpatient treatment facility 75 miles away from home. For several weeks, she would come home on weekends only. I think these times of separation made it easy for her to depart.

> **Principle # 3 – When we get frustrated enough,
> we will seek to use our strength to break the yokes
> and burdens off our lives. (Genesis 27:40)**

We looked at this scripture in chapter 2 when we discussed the spirit of restlessness. Now we will further examine this scripture to draw an even greater meaning. In 18th and 19th Century America, a yoke was used to subjugate humans into slavery. Once the device was shackled around someone's neck, the person could be easily manipulated and forced to submit to the desires of another.

God did not make man with a yoke. Nor did he design man to be put into slavery or subjugation to another. Instead, in the garden,

God created man to be caretakers over the works that he created (Genesis 2). It was not until man fell in the garden he became subject to hardship, each other, and death (Genesis 3). In addition, part of the curse which entered as a result of the fall was the woman would be ruled by the man, which kicked off the battle between the sexes that remains today.

God didn't create any of us to be subject to one another or another person's property; each of us inherently knows freedom is part of our birthright. However, acquiring freedom may be harder in some cases than others. This is one of the reasons couples venture into silence that fuels their imaginations and heightens their desire for freedom.

In chapter 2, we looked at the story of Esau, Isaac, and Jacob and how Esau lost the blessing when he didn't properly value it as part of the inheritance. Here is part of the story in Genesis 27 again to refresh your mind:

> *Isaac trembled violently and said, "Who was it, then, that hunted game and brought it to me? I ate it just before you came and I blessed him – and indeed he will be blessed!" When Esau heard his father's words, he burst out with a loud and bitter cry and said to his father, "Blessed me – me too, my father!" But he said, "Your brother came deceitfully and took your blessing." Esau said, "Isn't he rightly name Jacob? This is the second time he has taken advantage of me: He took my birthright, and now he's taken my blessing!" Then he asked, "Haven't you reserved any blessing for me?" Isaac answered Esau, "I have made him lord over you and have made all his relatives his servants and I have sustained him with grain and new wine. So what can I possibly do for you, my son?" Esau said to his father, "Do you have only one blessing, my father? Bless me too, my father!" Then Esau wept aloud. His father Isaac answered him, "Your dwelling will be away from the earth's richness away from the dew of heaven above. You will live by the sword and you will serve your brother. But when you grow restless, you will throw his yoke from off your neck."*
>
> (GENESIS 27:33 – 40 NIV)

You and your spouse were able to walk down the aisle together because you were convinced you were meant to be togeth-

er. Vowing each would be there for the other no matter what, you said, "I do," and together you ventured into the life of your dreams. For a while, things were good, but at some point your spouse began to realize you were never going to live up to fulfilling your end of the dream. You probably felt the same way. Like Esau, your spouse pleaded with you for changes, and you did not make the changes that would put the blessing and good fortune back on course. What you are now experiencing is verse 40 of the story coming to pass, "But when you grow restless, you will throw his yoke from off your neck."

Lesson Learned #2 –
Divorce is an act of desperation.

People seek divorce when they feel they have run out of options and played their last move. Ending the marriage seems to be the next logical step to regain their freedom. Do not let those online ads of "$149 divorces" fool you. You and your spouse will suffer financially. Whether it is the cost to separate one household into two, child or spousal support, or legal bills, divorce is costly. You nor your spouse who will be winners when you choose divorce. It will be the retailers, landlords, utility providers, car dealers, and lawyers who, with your divorce, take more of both your incomes because you two could not stay together.

Another cost is the emotional toll. No one can really put a price on what you will go through emotionally. Extreme stress will affect your physical health. Moreover, a divorce can have devastating effects not only for the couple but also for immediate and extended family and friends.

Lesson Learned #3 –
The white flag of surrender is the final cry for help

No one chooses divorce without first raising a flag of surrender with the hopes of relinquishing fighting positions and reaching a peace accord. In our third and final separation, I remember going through all of our communication from past months to determine if my wife had raised a white flag. I looked for two months without finding anything. Then one day I found it. It happened to be the same day I committed to having our marriage restored. It was the Lord who led me to go further back in my search and this is when I found her email.

It was without a doubt her white flag. In her note she outlined how she felt. She shared her fears and concerns while expressing she no longer wished to be paralyzed by her greatest fear. My response to her email never even addressed her concerns and provided her with no hope our dreams together were still possible. It definitely did not mention her biggest fear.

Principle #4 – Whatever we greatly fear will come upon us.

"For the thing which I greatly feared is come upon me, and that which I was afraid of is come unto me."

(JOB 3:25 KJV)

Fear is something everyone eventually needs to address in their lives. Not all fears are alike. While some things we fear are trivial, there is usually at least one thing that causes us to have heightened fear. While we talk about the trivial ones (fear of spiders, snakes, or heights), we generally work hard keeping silent about the thing we fear the most.

I discovered my greatest fear a few years ago when my father was dying. I visited him in the hospital one month before he passed away. A WWII Navy veteran and heavy weight boxing title holder, I knew him to be a strong, hardworking man. I did not see much of him as I was growing up because he left for his first job before I got up in the morning and didn't come home from his second job until after I went to bed.

My father was 43 years old when I was born, and he had always dreamed of having his own business he could share with his five sons. When I was 10, the golden opportunity arrived, and he had an opportunity to buy the catering business he had worked in for nearly 20 years. He won the owner a lot of business because celebrities and very wealthy families would award the catering business all their parties and special events just so my father could cater them. This seemed perfect for both the owner and my father.

Though my father did not have enough money in the bank, after years of diligently managing his money and with the owner's endorsement, the bank was willing to approve a loan for my father if he could secure the loan with a lien on the family home. It seemed like a done deal, but then his dreams shattered with one word from my mother. When he purchased the house, he put her name on the deed alongside his, and her signature was necessary to secure the loan.

My mother's greatest fear was being without a home. Her father had passed away at a young age, leaving her mother with eight young children to raise. Growing up poor and black in the South, my mother had to move from house to house until her parents were finally able to buy a family home. When her father died, complications made it difficult for her mother to immediately take over the home, so the family shuttled from relative to relative until it was finally settled. Losing her father so young and then struggling with the possibility of losing her home made a lasting impression on my mother, and she vowed to never be without a home again. Consequently, my mother would not agree to sign the papers to refinance the family home.

As I spoke with Dad in the hospital, he was no longer the man I had loved and respected all my life. He was frail and extremely depressed. He opened up and shared with me how he felt. He was afraid—not of dying but of living. Exhausted, he shared with me his greatest fear— he would leave this world

without accomplishing his dreams.

Though it seemed my Dad had once had his dreams in the palm of his hand, he had not realized them because they crossed with my mother's greatest fear. This intersection could have found a resolution that satisfied them both. No solution was ever found because instead of the two of them turning to God and asking his direction on how to address this conflict, they each choose to stake an unchangeable position. My father died with his greatest fear intact. My mother has never ceased to have a home, but fear of losing her home is still present. As a couple, they did not put Christ first or make their marriage subject to his direction. Their relationship deteriorated as a result. By the time they retired, they were roommates, and by the time my father passed away, they barely spoke except to argue.

After seeing what my mother did to my father, I was determined not to let that happen to me. I vowed to myself I would never be in a position where my future or my dreams were at the mercy of my wife's approval.

Most of the time my wife and I were together, I had no knowledge of what she feared the most. Even though we separated twice, it never crossed my mind to address this with her. Looking back, I now realize each of the separations and even filing for divorce were motivated by her greatest fear.

Her parents divorced when she was young. Both of her parents remarried only to divorce again. My wife grew up living with her mother; for the most part her father was not part of her life. The impact of her parents' divorce changed everything, not only for her mother but also for my future wife.

Without her father's income, she and her mother had to move from the nice neighborhood and the house they had been living in into an apartment. Her mother had to work outside the home to support them. She became a latch-key kid and caretaker for her siblings while her mother worked. My wife's greatest fear was to end up in her mother's predicament—losing her livelihood and caring for young children alone.

The stories above illustrate your greatest fear will inevitably come upon you. Each time my wife and I disagreed, she interpreted our disharmony to mean our marriage was failing. She found it extremely difficult to see a pathway to restoration. After several years of marriage, I discovered she had vowed to herself she would not put herself at the mercy of losing her livelihood without a husband; and if we were going to split, she would be the first to leave. Each time my wife and I separated, she became ruthless and heartless, allowing her fears to dominate her thinking. Unable to see how devastating her actions had become, she did things that only benefitted herself, even if they came at a major cost to me.

To sum it up, my wife and I were both letting our fears destroy our marriage. On one hand, my wife feared to be at the mercy of a lifestyle change without a husband, and on the other hand, I feared my wife would sabotage my dreams by not supporting them. This was a powerful mixture of combustible fears waiting for the right spark to cause an explosion. Eventually, that day came with the appropriate amount kindling.

Like my father, I had found a business deal that would bring all my dreams to pass, yet the bank required my wife to guarantee the loan. Between my wife's fears of change and my feelings that she couldn't support me in my choices we were at an impasse. It made my wife feel that our relationship was dying, and she concluded the fulfillment of my dream would bankrupt the family.

Sound familiar? Well, the result was my wife decided there was nothing left but to file for a divorce. My dreams of owning my own business didn't materialize. All of our fears—my father and mother's, mine and my wife's, made it impossible to see what God had in store for us. Fear kept all of us in bondage.

> *"And also that He might deliver and completely set free all those who through the [haunting] fear of death were held in bondage throughout the whole course of their lives."*
> (HEBREWS 2:15 AMP)

Fear will keep you oppressed. When you think you are ready to take a step forward, it brings you back down. I am sure if you took time to really think about what is at the heart of the disagreement and ill feelings between you and your spouse, you will most likely find fear is at the center. When you don't allow God to help you and your spouse identify your fears, you never get rid of them, and they can show up at unexpected times.

When people experience fear, their bodies typically react with vocal changes, avoidance behaviors, a fast heartbeat, quick and shallow breathing, as well as feelings of anxiety which interfere with the ability to sleep, communicate, and process information. When disagreements with your spouse end up spilling into areas that resemble your greatest fear, you are probably not going to be able to show compassion, love, and empathy. God understands, which is why he doesn't tell us to walk in fear but instead walk in love.

> *"There is no fear in love [dread does not exist], but full grown (complete, perfect) love turns fear out of doors and expels every trace of terror! For fear brings with it thought of punishment, and [so] he who is afraid has not reached the full maturity of love [is not yet grown into love's complete perfection.]"*
> (1 JOHN 4:18 AMP)

Fear was at the root of the problems in my marriage and very likely the root of your problems. The silence that has probably grown between you is like the silence in my marriage. Where we went wrong was through these reactions, we stopped serving each other with God's love.

I propose it is highly likely the same thing happened in your marriage:

you and your spouse each stopped serving each other with God's love. That love would have caused fear to be flushed out of your system as well as your spouse's. Instead, those fears were allowed to linger, and eventually they consumed you both.

With the rest of this book, I am going to unveil to you God's wonderful redemptive work that will breathe life into your dead marriage even if you're in the middle of divorce. If you did not know what you had been doing wrong, even after God completed his work, you are bound to repeat yourself.

In addition, God's redemptive work will not be available to you if you're still responding to frustration, desperation, lack of communication, and fear in the same manner you have been throughout your marriage. Right now you must decide how bad you want to put a stop to your separation or divorce. How important is it to you to have your spouse come home again so your marriage will continue? If you don't want it with all of your heart, you will not make the necessary personal changes. You cannot afford to respond the way you always have responded if you want your marriage to live again.

In this chapter, we talked about frustration, desperation, lack of communication, and fear. Take time now to think about how you responded when you became frustrated. How did you feel when you needed to take what you believed was a desperate action? In God, desperate times never call for desperate measures; they call for the presence of God. It is time for you to consider how Christ would respond in your situation. Review the scriptures above and make a decision now to respond differently to the challenges you have been facing in your marriage. Making needed changes will be foundation for you to be able to see God move to save your dead marriage.

Scripture:

> *"So here's what I want you to do, God helping you: Take your everyday, ordinary life—your sleeping, eating, going-to-work, and walking around life—and place it before God as an offering. Embracing what God does for you is the best thing you can do for him. Don't become so well-adjusted to your culture that you fit into it without even thinking.*
>
> *Instead, fix your attention on God. You'll be changed from the inside out. Readily recognize what he wants from you, and quickly respond to it. Unlike the culture around you, always dragging you down to its level of immaturity, God brings the best out of you, develops well-formed maturity in you."*
>
> (ROMANS 12:2 MSG)

CHAPTER 4

IS IT REALLY OVER, WHEN IT'S OVER?

Is martial separation or divorce really what you want?

Despite the multitude of ways God provides married couples to turn their failing marriages around, many choose to reject his help and to pursue divorce. US statistics on separation and divorce show almost 87 percent of separated couples proceed to obtain a divorce.

This leaves a mere 13 percent choosing to reunite after separation (DivorceStatistics.Info, 2016). Statistics also show almost half of the couples who separate remain separated at least a year before divorcing and just 16 percent remain separated for three years or more (Rooks, 2016). The average length of a first separation is three years for those who end up divorcing and two years for those who reunite with their spouse (Rooks, 2016). With lopsided statistics such as this, one can draw the conclusion that marriage reconciliation doesn't work, separation is nothing more than a pass-through to divorce, and once a marriage is in trouble, divorce is inevitable.

A survey released a few years ago by Barna Group on marriage and divorce among adults who have been married, came to the following conclusion: "Americans have grown comfortable with divorce as a natural part of life. There no longer seems to be a stigma attached to divorce; it is now seen as an unavoidable rite of passage (Barna Group, 2008)." The research went on to show divorce occurs as often or more among married couples who self-identify as being Christian as does married couples who do not (Barna Group, 2008). Thirty percent of those who identify as atheist or agnostic have been divorced while about 33 percent of those who identify as born again or non-born again Christians have experienced divorce. Based on these statistics, a couple's racial, ethnic, social-economic, and religious identification are immaterial as it is clear all groups are selecting divorce as a means to address their marital problems.

It seems many Christians have comfortably answered the question "Can I get a divorce?" with a firm yes. Having recently gone through a contested divorce process, it is my opinion as Christians, we have been asking the wrong question. I believe it would be more advantageous to ask, "Why would I want a divorce?"

Every married couple always has the authority to exercise their legal rights to pursue a divorce. Divorce has been given to them by the government for which they have their citizenship. The Apostle Paul had this to say with regards to our legal rights versus our walk with the Lord.

> "All things are legitimate [permissible – and we are free to do anything we please], but not all things are helpful (expedient, profitable and wholesome). All things are legitimate, but not all things are constructive [to character] and edifying [to spiritual life]."
>
> (1 CORINTHIANS 10:23 AMP)

Clearly, Paul is suggesting even though we may have the legal right to pursue what has been given to us by the laws within society, we should consider the impact that decision would have on our spiritual lives. Paul encourages us to ask if what we are considering is expedient, profitable, wholesome, and constructive to increasing our spiritual lives or if it detracts from it. In this chapter, we are going to take Paul's suggestion and look at the potential impact separation and divorce have on the spiritual life of a Christian.

Lesson Learned #4 –
Divorce does not require faith.

When my wife filed for divorce, her action didn't require her to exercise her faith in God. Divorce never requires faith in God because it is a legal right. To get a divorce, one just needs to file the necessary paperwork with the court and the court will consider the petition. Secondly, the courts will not force anyone to stay in a marriage if it is not his or her desire. We enter into a marriage voluntarily, and each of us has the right to withdraw from the voluntarily commitment at any time. Divorce doesn't require us to believe in anything related to God and his kingdom; instead a person seeking to terminate a marriage has to want to do so. No belief of anything is required; just a desire for a specified outcome is all it takes.

Divorce has many unknowns, such as, "How will my spouse respond? Will I be able to keep the house? How will the children be affected? Will I be able to make it without my spouse's income?"

Of course, everyone hopes for favorable outcomes to those questions, but hope is the key word here. Hope alone is not faith. The book of Hebrews gives a definition of faith as follows:

*"Now is faith is the assurance (the confirmation, the title deed)
of the things [we] hope for being the proof of things [we] do
not see and the conviction of their reality [faith perceiving as
real fact what is not revealed to the senses."*

(HEBREWS 11:1 AMP)

While hope is a confident expectation with a positive attitude, it does not have the ability to bring to pass what is hoped for. Everyone who has hope in anything is holding onto a belief their desired outcome will materialize. For example, if we look at any sporting contest, whether it is football, baseball, boxing, tennis, drag racing, or swimming, every athlete hopes for victory. Some may have great hope because of their abilities and talents. Having this advantage may give them a very strong and positive hope. Having hope alone does not ensure victory because once the contest begins reality trumps hope.

This is why God gave us faith and not hope alone. We saw from the verse in Hebrews faith is the material that brings the confirmation and proof of the things we hope for to actually come to pass. In other words, faith makes tangible what is hoped for. Faith makes you the victor while hope gives you a positive attitude until it is matched against reality. For example, I might hope that in a half-court game of basketball game against LeBron James to be the first to score 21 points. However, once LeBron steps onto the court and the game begins, all of my hope will be wiped away with the reality I barely know how to play the game, and he is one of the best basketball players in the world.

Now, in this same scenario, if God spoke to my spirit and told me I would end up with the victory, then LeBron would be no match against me because God's ability would put me over. That is what happened when David faced Goliath. The fight was as mismatched as me facing LeBron, yet David came away the victor. The difference was David had God on his side, and God gave him the ability to become the victor.

To have faith, you must be anchored on the material that has the ability to change the realities and facts. For example, you may have an outstanding bill in the amount of one thousand dollars the bank has demanded you pay today or it will send your account into collections. You only have a hundred dollars in your bank account and cannot foresee getting your hands on the remaining nine hundred dollars. However, you do not panic because you have been praying about this situation for weeks, standing on the Word, knowing God will supply all of your needs according to his riches in glory (Philippians 4:19). In fact, you do not think any more about it because you have rolled the care onto the Lord (1 Peter 5:7). Near the end of that particular day, you pull into your driveway after work and discover an envelope in the mail containing a check in the amount of nine hundred dollars with a letter from a creditor saying it found you had been overcharged on your account, and they have enclosed a refund check. Your faith in God allowed him to work on your behalf, which prompted your creditor to conduct an audit and discover the error in your favor.

"So faith comes by hearing [what is told], and what is heard comes by the preaching [of the message that came from the lips] of Christ (the Messiah Himself)."

(ROMANS 10:17 AMP)

Based on this we can see faith's material is the Word of God. In thinking about your marriage in relationship to the lesson learned, you might ask, "What specific promises about divorce has God said to my spouse and me as believers?" The answer is, "None."

There is not one promise in the Bible about divorce that believers can connect with their faith. Someone can argue while there is no specific promise from God on divorce, there are other promises in the Bible that give us a hope, such as Philippians 4:19 when God commits to supplying all of our needs. The issue is the promise would have to be taken out of context and misapplied to marriage.

To exercise your legal right to divorce, you would have to overlook or violate many scriptures which have been given to us as guardrails for our conduct. Here are a couple we have already examined:

"Let me give you a new command: Love one another. In the same way I loved you, you love one another. This is how everyone will recognize that you are my disciples – when they see the love you have for each other."

(JOHN 13:34-35 MSG)

"Make a clean break with all cutting, backbiting, profane talk. Be gentle with one another, sensitive. Forgive one another as quickly and as thoroughly as God in Christ forgave you."

(EPHESIANS 4:31-32 MSG)

To proceed with a divorce, you would have to violate the commandment of love and forgiveness. Whether it is the husband, the wife, or both, it is impossible to be an active proponent of divorce and at the same time practice the love of Christ and his forgiveness. To be a proponent of divorce one would have to promote the concern for self over the concern of the spouse (others) and the marriage unit.

The definition for the love of Christ is to consider the needs of others before we think about ourselves. Divorce is about self-preservation; it doesn't leave room for the love of Christ to be displayed. That does not mean someone pursuing divorce cannot be kind and gentle. Both gentleness and kindness are attributes of the love of Christ. If a spouse even starts down the path considering divorce as an option, it will not be long before he or she starts re-thinking divorce. For a spouse to file a divorce and see it all the way through, he or she has to put his or her concern squarely on themselves.

Like me, someone could find him or herself as a defendant in a divorce proceeding. I had been served with divorce papers, and my wife shared with me she no longer wanted to continue in relationship with me. Additionally, she said and did things to me that hurt. All of this could have made me let offense arise in my heart and like my wife, I could have chosen to focus on my self-preservation. In my case, I decided to practice of the love of Christ by walking in forgiveness and staying in fellowship with the marriage covenant.

As a result, and despite the circumstance, I exhibited the same behavior Jesus displayed while he was on the cross when he said, "Father forgive them for they know not what they do (Luke 23:34)." In this way, Jesus showed love and forgiveness to those who felt they had the legal right and authorization to crucify him. Despite the horror, pain, and anguish he experienced, he still demonstrated the love of the Lord (Hosea 3:1).

You may be asking, "If divorce requires no faith, then what is it?" There are several answers to that question. The first can be found in Romans where it says,

> *"But the man who has doubts (misgivings, an uneasy conscience) about eating, and then eats [perhaps because of you], stands condemned [before God], because he is not true to his convictions and he does not act from faith. For whatever does not originate and proceed from faith is sin [whatever is done without a conviction of its approval by God is sinful]."*
> (ROMANS 14:23 AMP)

Notice how no Christian ever has to ask whether or not it is permissible to love one another or to forgive one another. This is because in each Christian is the Holy Spirit, which the Bible says has been given to teach us all things (John 14:26). Even if you were thrown into prison with no access to a Bible, as a newly born-again Christian who had accepted Christ, you would know this to be true. Why? Because in that state you would have the Holy Spirit with you, and he would give you an inner knowing which would teach you about love and forgiveness. While you could not confirm chapter and verse from the Bible, their very existence would be alive in your heart and by examining creation you would know of God's existence and discover his love and forgiveness (John 14:17).

The concept of divorce works the same way. Christians know before they ever ask where God lands on the subject of divorce because in their heart the Holy Spirit will let them know how God feels about it. Whether or not they accept the inner witness is a decision each person has to make. It is the inner witness given to the spouse who will choose to show the love of Christ and forgiveness despite how his or her spouse is treating them. Others who do not make this decision will look to find other sources among their friends, families, and even the church to help them hear and follow an answer other than the one the Holy Spirit gave them.

While it does not take faith to file for divorce or walk in self-preservation, it does take faith to show the love of Christ and walk in forgiveness, especially in the middle of divorce proceedings. Whether or not you believe God will save your marriage, to show the love of Christ, you will have to deny any feelings of anger or hurt and make a conscious decision to choose to respond as Christ would respond.

This is not easy when your flesh wants to scream and throw a tantrum. Your natural tendency will be to respond to every allegation or hurt the other spouse causes. Instead, the love of Christ thinks first of the spouse who has caused the pain. Walking in forgiveness means you will have to make a choice to release your spouse from the liability for each of the wrongs he or she has done to you, especially when your flesh is looking for justice. To choose to exhibit the character of God and please the Lord will take faith in his Word. Why would someone go through the effort of conducting themselves in a way not natural to them if there was no reward at the other end? Be a person of faith who values a reward from God over any reward that can come from your spouse or the courts.

If you are going to have faith to please God, why not go further and believe God will turn your marriage around? If having faith pleases God and faith is required to believe God will redeem your marriage, surely it pleases God when you have faith to believe your dead marriage will live again.

> *"But without faith it is impossible to please and be satisfactory to Him. For whoever would come near to God must [necessarily] believe that God exists and that He is a rewarded of those who earnestly and diligently seek Him [out]."*
> (HEBREWS 11:6 AMP)

There is a large section of the married Christian population who is not convinced pleasing the Lord is more important than satisfying their personal needs. As a result, when their marriage hits a rough patch and the struggles seem insurmountable, they seek relief in divorce.

God will never be pleased with divorce because it gives him nothing to work with. If one person is pursuing the divorce, that person has removed dependence from God to himself or herself and to the wisdom and resources of this world. It does not matter how many ways you try to slice this, there is no way to please God without faith.

Another attribute about divorce is you have to turn yourself into an accuser of the brethren. The minute someone sits down with a lawyer and begins to explain the reasons for seeking a divorce, that person potentially steps into the role of accuser. The dictionary defines an accuser as someone who brings charges against another (The American Heritage Dictionary, 2001).

To file a complaint, one of the spouses has to state the other spouse's character violated the marriage in some way allowable by law, and so the wronged spouse is seeking to terminate the relationship. This is called a "fault" divorce, and the allegations will be made part of the public record.

Many states have now have "no-fault" divorces, which means one spouse can file for divorce against another for incompatibility or voluntarily living separate for at least one year. Another type of marriage termination is a dissolution, which means the two parties agree to go their separate ways and agree about the division of issues and assets surrounding the marriage. Under a dissolution, there may be fewer accusations, but if you look at our earlier discussion about divorce, there is no faith required in this scenario either. In fact, with a dissolution, both spouses have chosen not to trust God to fix their marriage.

Both at-fault and no-fault divorces require some level of accusations for the marriage to be dissolved. At the beginning of the marriage, the couple agreed they have found the right person to spend their lives with. They also believed they were compatible. At some point in the relationship, though, something changed to the point they believed they were incompatible. What is really being said is the couple had major differing of opinions on how to conduct themselves or the decisions related to their marriage.

The Bible says "the two shall <u>become</u> one flesh (Mark 10:8)," not the two <u>became</u> one flesh. While each married couple should be working on becoming one flesh, when someone files for divorce, it means one or both became unwilling to serve the other, valuing their own opinions and ideas above the other spouse.

Even though a divorce petition may say no-fault on the court documents, the person who filed the complaint is basically saying because his or her spouse is unwilling to be flexible, considerate of his or her needs, and see life the way he or she sees life, the person petitioning for the divorce wants to terminate this relationship. While the accusation may not get much attention in the court room, in heaven this accusation gets a lot of attention because the accusation is not just against the other spouse, it is also against God.

The filing spouse is stating they believe God is either unable or unwilling to complete the marriage restoration work is necessary for them to become one flesh (Mark 10:8) with their spouse. With each argument requiring supporting evidence, the only thing the filing spouse can present before God is the other spouse's behavior. In that regard, they have again stepped into the role of being an accuser.

To accuse a brethren, the spouse must hold one person's sins against them. It is a stance which indicates once a wrong has been committed it cannot be forgiven. As Christians, God does not deal with us this way. Earlier, we read in Ephesians chapter 4 in verses 31 and 32 the Apostle Paul encouraged us to forgive as quickly and as thoroughly as the Lord forgives us. In 1 John, the Bible tells us that He always forgives us.

> *"If we confess our sins, he is faithful and just to forgive us our sins and to cleanse us from all unrighteousness."*
> (1 JOHN 1:9 ESV)

CHAPTER 4: IS IT REALLY OVER, WHEN IT'S OVER?

When someone publicly accuses another brother or sister in the Lord, as in a divorce, the person sets him or herself up as judge over that person. Both of these actions are condemned by God in the word when He said the following:

> *"Do not judge, and you will not be judge. Do not condemn,*
> *and you will not be condemned. Forgive, and you will be will*
> *be forgiven."*
>
> (LUKE 6:37 NIV)

A *Christianity Today* article entitled "Who Are We to Judge" had the following to say about judging others, "When a person judges, she also forms an opinion. But an opinion is not necessarily the same as a judgment. Opinions are often framed by our fears, pride, or ignorance. Judgments are opinions we form only after we have made a serious effort to know the facts, and, for those of us who are Christians, only after we have consulted the moral teachings of Scripture and prayed for Spirit-informed discernment. Any lazy or biased fool can have opinions; making judgments is the hard work of responsible and compassionate people." The issue is not everyone has made a commitment to forgo his or her opinion until he or she consults the moral guidance from the scriptures and through the Spirit. Instead, the person will settle with knowing the facts and then forming an opinion. Once the person forms an opinion, he or she condemns the person to a punishment.

Christ died to set us free from the punishment in the law. The purpose of his coming was not to punish us but to redeem us back to God. In this way, becoming an accuser does not redeem your spouse back to God but instead further alienates him or her from you and the creator.

When a spouse become the accuser, he or she takes on the characteristics of Satan who himself is called "The accuser of the brethren" in Revelations chapter 12 verse 10. The Bible also says that Satan stands in God's presence (Job 1:6) and is always ready to accuse us before him (Zechariah 3:1). This type of behavior among Christians doesn't bring us closer to God but rather has us following in the footsteps of the devil. Look at what Jesus had to say to Peter in Matthew's gospel:

> *"But he turned and said to Peter, "Get behind Me, Satan. You*
> *are a stumbling block to Me; you co nog have in mind the con-*
> *cerns of God, but merely human concerns."*
>
> (MATTHEW 16:23 NIV)

Jesus' comments are applicable in divorce because the spouse bringing up charges against the other in court is not mindful of the work God may be trying to do with the other spouse. God is always trying to do a work that fully restores each of us back to ourselves. Reminding others of their failures and cutting fellowship with them does not support the work God wants done.

Here is what the Apostle Paul said in his letter to the church in Corinth about taking believers to court:

> *"If any of you has a dispute with another, do you dare to take it before the ungodly for judgment instead of before the Lord's people? Or do you not know that the Lord's people will judge the world? And if you are to judge the world are you not competent to judge trivial cases? Do you know that we will judge angels? How much more the things of this life! Therefore, if you have disputes about such matters, do you ask for a ruling from those whose way of life is scorned in the church? I say this to shame you. Is it possible that there is nobody among you wise enough to judge a dispute between believers? But instead, one brother takes another to court – and this in front of unbelievers!*
>
> *The very fact that you have lawsuits among you means you have been completely defeated already. Why not rather be wronged? Why not rather be cheated? Instead, you yourselves cheat and do wrong, and you do this to your brothers and sisters. Or do you not know that wrongdoers will not inherit the kingdom of God?"*
> (1 CORINTHIANS 6: 1-9A NIV)

The Apostle Paul expressed strong disagreement with believers taking each other to court for many of the same reasons we have already explored. He suggested it would be better if we let ourselves be wronged or cheated than to swap places and bring wrong by taking our complaints before the court.

Now I realize for many Christians this is tough to accept, and it can be difficult to believe and accept a world in which you would have to be stuck in a relationship. The truth is you are not stuck. Instead you are honoring God by giving him time to work a change in you and your spouse's lives. Unfortunately, according to statistics, today many will not do that because of their fears.

> **Principle # 5:**
> **Where there is fear, there is no faith.**
> **(Matthew 8:26 NIV)**

Couples ultimately choose divorce because they are afraid. There may be a fear of being stuck in a dead marriage, fear of wasting time with the wrong person, fear of staying in a marriage that will cost them their health, finances, and peace of mind. The bottom line is the spouse believes he or she will grow more afraid remaining in the marriage. As we saw earlier, the Bible has quite a bit to say about fear, including where there is fear, faith cannot function. Review these comments made by the Lord in Matthew and Mark:

> *"He replied, "You of little faith, why are you so afraid?"*
>
> (MATTHEW 8:26 NIV)

> *"He said to his disciples, "Why are you so afraid? Do you still have no faith?"*
>
> (MARK 4:40 NIV)

Faith and fear cannot operate in the same environment simultaneously, just as hot and cold cannot exist together at the same time. In the context of our study, the entire process of divorce is fear based. The more the spouse thinks about his or her situation without turning it over to the Lord, the more he or she will continue to imagine limited choices that lead to beliefs in a bleak future. With God, however, he always has something much more positive and hopeful in store. He has this to say in the book of Jeremiah:

> *"For I know the plans I have for you," declares the Lord, "plans to prosper you and not to harm you, plans to give you hope and a future."*
>
> (JEREMIAH 29:11 NIV)

God's plans will give you hope and a future. You will prosper with his plans. The very nature of divorce doesn't promise a prosperous future.

Lesson Learned # 5:
Divorce is a destroyer of relationships
and a robber of God's plans for you.

It is very easy to see divorce as a destroyer of relationships. This essence of divorce is to terminate the legal relationship between a husband and wife. What may be difficult to ascertain is the impact divorce has on relationships other than the couple's. Activate a divorce in your life and you will quickly find out it can impact children, other family members, friends, acquaintances, and even employers. In the life of a Christian, the first and most important relationship that is impacted is fellowship with Christ.

> *"But if we walk in the light, as he is in the light, we have fellowship with one another, and the blood of Jesus, his Son, purifies us from all sin."*
>
> (1 JOHN 1: 7 NIV)

What happens when we take the opposite of this verse? Let's switch to the Amplified translation and look at how it reads in the opposing point of view:

> *"But if we [really aren't] living and walking in the Light, as He*
> *[Himself] is in the Light, we have [false, broken] fellowship with*
> *one another, and the blood of Jesus Christ His Son cleanses not*
> *(doesn't remove) from all sin and guilt [can't keep us cleansed*
> *from sin in all its forms and manifestations]."*
>
> (1 JOHN 1:7 AMP)

Though you may attempt to end the relationship only with your spouse, the Bible is very clear when you seek to break fellowship with another believer it causes a break in fellowship with Christ. The result of this is the cleansing power in the blood is not available to you. The good news is our Lord has made a way for you to restore your relationship with him through repentance. No one can predict how anyone in your life is going to respond once divorce enters the picture.

When my wife filed for divorce and I shared this with others, their attitudes toward both of us they had hidden in their hearts surprised me. It was as if the divorce gave everyone the freedom to divulge all the issues they were harboring about my wife, me, and our marriage. Some individuals I was sure would be kind to me made it clear when my wife exited a relationship with me, they went with her. Separately, my wife discovered the same thing. Now that we have reconciled, there are relationships which may never be the same, at least not without the blood of Jesus working on our behalf. Once the spirit of division is allowed access to your marriage, be prepared for it to destroy some relationships you thought were on solid ground.

When you were born, God already had a plan and purpose for your life (Jeremiah 1:5). His purpose and plans for your life were all inclusive. He knew who you would select as your spouse before you did, and he included your spouse in the plans and purposes he designed for you. What happens when you and your spouse go your separate ways? Here are God's thoughts about it:

> *"I hate divorce," says the God of Israel. God of the Angel Armies*
> *says, "I hate violent dismembering of the 'one flesh' of marriage."*
>
> (MALACHI 2:16A)

God hates divorce for the very reason we are discussing. When a couple tears from becoming one flesh, the plan God outlined for the two of them can no longer be attained. Who knows what is lost through the dismembering process? Only God can see what was planned for the couple and when the couple arrives before the King, they too will know what they have given up through divorce. God's declaration he hates divorce should cause each of us to pause and count the cost of what will be lost in the dismembering process.

**Principle #6:
God takes pleasure in the prosperity of his servant.
(Psalms 35:27 AMP)**

"Let those who favor my righteous cause and have pleasure in my uprightness shout for joy and be glad and say continually, let the Lord be magnified, who takes pleasure in the prosperity of His servant."

(PSALMS 35:27 AMP)

Let us say you have spent your life listening to God and following his guidance from high school to college. You consulted him on what to study in school, where to work, and even what to do with the money you earned. All the while, God took pleasure in your obedience and blessed you with more blessings. After you had been married, you looked back and remembered the days when you and your spouse had barely enough money to pay the rent on your small apartment and had to share Ramen noodles for dinner. God has been merciful, kind, and faithful and those days are long behind you.

Now with a pending divorce, the life you once knew is being ripped from you and your spouse. The lawyers will take their share, the IRS will take a bigger share of your income, the movers will take some, and the list seems endless.

God does not take pleasure in seeing the prosperity he has given taken away. The Lord said, "A house divided against itself, that house can't stand (Mark 3:25 NIV)." Even if you get a judge to equally split the assets, it doesn't work out to be an equal split because new hands have their palms out wanting their slices. Costs will increase as a result of having two households instead of one. This stretching of what God has blessed means the areas you supported previously may have to be cut back. As a couple you may have been supporting missionaries overseas, but when you divorce, you may not be able to continue to keep up with those offerings.

God works daily to get the prosperity away from the sinner and gives it to the righteous (Proverbs 13:22). His plan is to increase you more and more and for you to be a good steward over the increase by spreading the Gospel around the world. Divorce works in the opposite direction. Where God multiplies, divorce divides. The Bible says the devil steals, kills, and destroys. Divorce does the same thing.

"The thief comes only in order to steal and kill and destroy. I

came that they may have and enjoy life, and have it more in
abundance (to the full, till it overflows)."

(JOHN 10:10 AMP)

Examining the words of Jesus, the thief is the enemy or Satan. It is clear God wants you to have a life that can be enjoyed with unlimited abundance. That is not, however, what happens with divorce. As we have already discussed, divorce kills relationships, steals away prosperity, and can destroy relationships beyond the couple.

When we choose divorce, whose character and nature are we emulating? Divorce at its core is a work the devil promotes. In earlier chapters, we discussed how God has many ways to save your failed marriage. How could God be willing to save the marriage and at the same time be the instrument to bring termination to the marriage? He is not. God cannot bless and curse a relationship.

"How can I curse whom God has not cursed? How can I de-
nounce whom the Lord has not denounced?

Behold, I received a command to bless: he has blessed, and I
cannot revoke it."

(NUMBERS 23:8, 20 ESV)

Also, we learned in an earlier chapter when we studied Mark 10:9 that in a biblical marriage God takes credit for putting the union together. In this case, how could God put a union together and then later work to tear the union apart? Again, this is not God's nature nor his character. If divorce is not God's character or nature and we have seen God's work is to bring restoration and reconciliation, then the work of divorce must be a work of the devil. If divorce brings us closer to being of the nature of Satan than why any Christian would want any part of this? That is unthinkable. If divorce subtracts from you when God wants to multiply, why would you want to be a part of that equation?

The answer can be found in Hosea 4:6a AMP when God said, "My people are destroyed for lack of knowledge." Christian couples are choosing to separate and divorce because they have bought into the lies of the enemy. He has promised freedom and a brighter future. Not only is Satan a thief, a destroyer, and a killer, the Bible also calls him a "liar and the father of lies (John 8:44)." There is absolutely no truth in him. All he can sell you are lies, and, unfortunately, he is an expert salesperson. You do not have to labor to get his lies. Instead, it takes time, energy, and hard work to get in the word to find out what God's approved message is for you (2 Timothy 2:15). This is why so many Christians are fooled into believing divorce is a viable option, when in fact it is death being masked as life.

By now I can hear you saying, "Preacher, I hear you and I agree with you. But you don't understand, I'm not one bringing the divorce, it's my spouse."

Take heart, my brother or sister in the Lord. Didn't I tell you earlier that God has life preservers and life boats to turn your marriage around? He understands and knew your spouse would take this action before it happened. You are not powerless as a result of your spouse's decision to divorce. There is something you can do. God has a life boat for you that you are probably unaware of, and it is the very reason I have written this book. God has mercy and grace to meet you right where you are. Continue onward to find out about his life boat.

Scripture:

> "[So] if we say we are partakers together and enjoy fellowship with Him when we live and move and are walking about in darkness, we are [both] speaking falsely and do not live and practice the Truth [which the Gospel presents].
>
> But if we [really] are living and walking in the Light, as He [Himself] is in the Light, we have [true, unbroken] fellowship with one another, and the blood of Jesus Christ His Son cleanses (removes) us from all sin and guilt [keeps us cleansed from sin in all its forms and manifestations].
>
> If we say we have no sin [refusing to admit that we are sinners], we delude and lead ourselves astray, and the Truth [which the Gospel presents] is not in us [does not dwell in our hearts].
>
> If we [freely] admit that we have sinned and confess our sins, He is faithful and just (true to His own nature and promises) and will forgive our sins [dismiss our lawlessness] and [continuously] cleanse us from all unrighteousness [everything not in conformity to His will in purpose, thought, and action]."
>
> (1 JOHN 1:5-10 AMP)

CHAPTER 5

MARRIAGE RECONCILIATION IS NOT MARRIAGE RESURRECTION

When marriage reconciliation is not possible God has another lifeboat.

With all the actions that come with separation and potential divorce—dealing with lawyers, moving, and trying to settle into a single lifestyle, to name a few—you probably have not spent much time thinking about what you want for your marriage. When you decided to get married, you likely had great plans for the relationship and the family that might come from the union. Where are your plans, dreams, and visions now? Will you place them in a storage box marked "unfiled" and store them in the attic or basement like tax records you hold onto in case you're audited?

On your wedding day, you were not the only with grand plans. According to his Word, the plans God had for you and your spouse didn't have this ending in mind.

> *"For I know the plans I have for you," declares the Lord, "plans*
> *to prosper you and not to harm you, plans to give you hope*
> *and a future."*
>
> (JEREMIAH 29:11 NIV)

From this verse, you can see God has a future for your marriage quite different than the one you are experiencing. What does God do now? Does he update his plans for your marriage to reflect the new road map you and your spouse are now following? The answer is no. Unlike us, God does not change his mind (Numbers 23:19 NIV). If God has not changed his plans for your marriage, why should you?

These thoughts raced through my head after my wife moved out and filed for divorce. We aspired to accomplish many dreams in our marriage, and suddenly my wife was throwing the visions I had in my heart into the trash like stale bread.

In the quietness of my empty bedroom I thought to myself, "Do I really want to start a new life without my wife?" and "Is divorce what I want?" The answers to both questions were a resounding no. It was clear to me marriage reconciliation was not immediately possible since my wife had no interest in pursuing that option.

Could there be another solution to our problems I just was not seeing? There had to be or it would be impossible for God to continue having plans to "give me a hope and a future" (Jeremiah 29:11 NIV) when divorce is intended to abort all hope of a reconciliation and a future with us together.

I concluded God had some inside information about my life I had missed. I thought, "If I can get a hold of what God knows and understands about my situation that still has him believing in a good end for my marriage, then I do not have to settle with a divorce."

I am going to walk you step by step through what God shared with me that resulted (spoiler alert!) in our divorce filing being dismissed and my wife coming home.

In this chapter, we will examine what marriage reconciliation is, why it is not working for many failed marriages, and introduce you to God's lifeboat. We talked about the lifeboat in Chapter 2 and defined it as a husband and wife rethinking their decision to separate or end the marriage, then together seeking the Lord's help to bring the marriage back to his image. We also cited a statistic showing that of the couples who separate, 87 percent proceed on to divorce (Marriage in America, 2016). That is a huge number of couples who decide not to reconcile. Let us examine for a moment why this happening.

Becky Whetstone, Ph.D., LFMT, is a licensed marriage and family therapist who practices in the state of Texas and Arkansas. Her practice has helped hundreds of distressed married individuals considering divorce to find clarity in their decision-making process (Whetstone, 2016).

Known as Doctor Becky, this marriage therapist had the following to say about couples who separate: "One of the most amazing facts I have found as a marriage therapist is most couples who are unhappy and considering separation have NO criteria for making such a decision, and often do it without any rhyme or reason and with NO plan for getting back together. Under these circumstances, what usually happens is one of two things: 1) They miss each other and get back together too soon, without resolving the issues that got them separated in the first place, or 2) There is so much acrimony – or apathy –they consider repairing the marriage too big of a mountain to climb and they throw in the towel and divorce."

Marriage reconciliation is a great lifeboat if properly used by the marital couple. We are not seeing better results from the work because a couple could choose to reconcile with or without the Lord's intervention. The lifeboat does not automatically come with Christ and the Holy Spirit as captain and crew of the boat. If a couple wants the Lord's help, they will need to reach out by faith and ask for his

assistance. The Lord knows what is going on in the marriage, but God gives each of us the right to choose him in direction of our daily steps (Proverbs 16:9).

If the couple decides they would rather rely on their feelings and human reasoning, the Lord will allow them to do so. Even if the couple decides to use marriage reconciliation as a lifeboat to save their marriage, if each spouse does not submit their body, mind, will, and emotions over to the Spirit's leading, they will be the captain of their lifeboat instead of letting the Lord lead them his restorative work.

As Doctor Becky so pointedly articulated, the couple could reconcile and never address the very issues that caused the separation in the first place. This is just one of the things which happens when the couple chooses God's tool (marriage reconciliation) but doesn't select Christ as the captain and the Holy Spirit as the crew. Instead, the couple finds reasons to reconcile or believes promising each other to change will make the reconciliation work.

This happened to my wife and I the first couple of times we tried marriage reconciliation. With each separation, one of us would make a promise to change that went just far enough to satisfy the other spouse. Promises do not necessarily produce change. Once the pain and anxiety built up because of the separation subsided due to the reconciliation, it was pretty much back to normal with only minor changes. Why? Because without repentance there can be no heart change, and without conviction there can be no repentance.

Conviction and repentance are the sole work of the Lord and the Holy Spirit. The Bible tells us the Holy Spirit has be given to men for the task of convicting them of sin (John 16:18) and Jesus was given the authority to forgive sin (Mark 2:10). When a married couple leaves the Holy Spirit and Christ out of the marriage reconciliation, they do not have the capacity to truly recognize their errors in relationship or God's plan to restore the marriage and there is no true conviction.

They may reconcile, but the reconciliation back to God's restorative work for the marriage doesn't take place. During our first two reconciliations, my wife was able to maintain unforgiveness in her heart toward things I had done very early in our marriage. As a result, she was not really able to operate fully with God's life vests (bearing each other's burdens, confessing faults one to another, spirit of restlessness, and discernment). Her dissatisfaction in the marriage grew with each passing year.

Eventually, these feelings made her decide to separate a third time and file for divorce in hopes of finding a lasting solution to the nagging lack of peace in her heart. The lack of peace was the spirit of restlessness trying to get her to realize she was walking around with unforgiveness. Unfortunately, neither she nor I recognized its purpose until it was very late in the divorce process, and by that point we had paid very steep costs for our spiritual immaturity and unwillingness to submit to the Spirit's leading.

Another issue with marital reconciliation indirectly highlighted in our testimony above is the work requires both spouses to decide to get into the lifeboat or it does not work. A reconciliation implies both spouses are willing to work on improving the marriage and both are willing to remove all limits to the individual changes they are willing to make. However, if one of them decides he or she does not want to turn aside from the separation or divorce, then reconciliation is not an option for that couple.

REVIEW

In review of marriage reconciliation as a redemptive work God has available to failing marriages we find more couples are not experiencing turnaround because of the following reasons:

1. A reconciliation cannot be done without help from Christ and the Holy Spirit,

2. Effective personal change cannot take place without conviction and repentance, and/or

3. Both spouses must choose to reconcile or a reconciliation cannot occur.

Now that we have a good foundation for marriage reconciliation, take a quick evaluation of your specific situation to make sure it qualifies for the work God can and wants to do for you.

CHECK ALL THAT APPLY:

☐ You or your spouse has physically moved out of the home.

☐ Marriage reconciliation is not an option because your spouse has no interest in trying.

☐ Your family's life has been severely disrupted.

☐ A legal divorce case has been filed to terminate the marriage.

☐ Your spouse has told you that they don't love you anymore.

☐ Your marriage is effectively dead and just waiting on the death certificate.

☐ Do you still love your spouse? (Required condition, please answer carefully).

If you were able to put a check mark on any of the conditions listed above, then you are a candidate for God working on your behalf. The last item was not a condition but rather a question. The answer is a conditional requirement of the work God wants to do. Let's examine this in more detail by looking in Hosea:

> *"Then said the Lord unto me, go yet, love a woman beloved of her friend, yet an adulteress, according to the love of the Lord toward the children of Israel, who looks to other gods, and loves flagons of wine."*
>
> (HOSEA 3:1 KJV)

In this text, we see when God gave the prophet Hosea the command to go reclaim his wife, he took time to call out the fact Hosea still had love for her. In fact, God compares the love Hosea has toward Gomer to the love he has toward the children of Israel. He called it "the love of the Lord." This text goes on to outline "the love of the Lord" is a love that is not conditional on how the other party feels toward them because in both God and Hosea's cases their lovers were no longer pursuing a relationship with them. As you consider your answer to that question, recognize God understands what it is like to be rejected and to continue to have regard and concern for someone who isn't showing you those same considerations.

In case you are still encountering any heart resistance with the last question, review what Jesus says about love in your situation. Here are four verses with Christ's feelings on the subject:

> *"But I tell you, love your enemies and bless them that curse you, do good to those that hate you, and pray for them which despitefully use you, and persecute you."*
>
> (MATTHEW 5:44 KJV)

> *"Bless those who curse you. Pray for those who hurt you."*
>
> (LUKE 6:28 NIV)

> *"I am giving you a new commandment, that you love one another. Just as I have loved you, so that you too are to love one another. By this everyone will know that you are My disciples, if you love and unselfish concern for one another."*
>
> (JOHN 13: 34-35 AMP)

> *"This is my commandment: Love each other in the same way I have loved you."*
>
> (JOHN 15:12 NIV)

Regardless of which of the definitions—love of the Lord, love of Christ, love of enemies, or love for one another—you settle in your heart as the definition you will use to retain love in your heart for your spouse, the bottom line is God and Christ expect you to accomplish this. God has quite a bit of experience at loving people even when they do not reciprocate. The Word tells us Jesus, who is our great high priest, not only knows this but is also able to empathize with our feelings and weaknesses. Somehow you are going to have to find a way to muster up love because without it, God cannot work on your behalf.

If knowing God and Jesus understands the rejection you are feeling is not enough for you to make a decision, let me add my own experience for your consideration. When my wife separated from me, filed for divorce, and told me she no longer loved me, I struggled to find love in my heart. Initially, I could not find love because her treatment had hurt me, and I no longer felt romantic love for her. The Greek word for this type of love is eros and it is defined as the physical or sensual love between a husband and wife (About.com, 2016). This Greek word is not actually in the Bible (About.com, 2016). Instead, the Greek word used is agape. Vines Expository Dictionary had this to say about this type of love—"Christian love, whether exercised toward the brethren or toward men generally, is not an impulse from the feelings; it does not always run with the natural inclinations, nor does it spend itself only upon those for whom some affinity is discovered. Love seeks the welfare of all (Romans 15:2), and works no ill to any (Romans 13:8-10); love seeks opportunity to do good to 'all men, and especially toward them that are of the household of the faith'"(Galatians 6:10) (Vines and Hogg, 2016).

Once I was able to put out of my mind I was not being asked to love her with a sensual love but instead with Christian love, I found I could be in agreement with that. This changed my perspective from viewing her as my lover and mate to being my sister in the Lord, and with that I was able to be submit to God's love command.

Where can your heart be located at this moment? Based on where you were left by your spouse, friends, and family, I am sure your heart is somewhat hidden right now. Hopefully, you can remove the protective barriers around your heart so you, too, can find agape love.

> **Principle # 7 – The report you believe about your marriage will be the marriage you end up with.**
> **(Isaiah 53:1 NIV)**

At this moment, your spouse's report says terminating the marriage through divorce is the only viable solution to your problems. However, God has a completely opposing view on the situation. As we discovered earlier in Jeremiah 29:11, his view is for a future that brings you prosperity, hope, and help. Whether you realize it or not, there is a choice before you. Helping you make a decision that lines up with God's Word brings us to our first lesson learned for this chapter.

Lesson Learned # 6 – Despite my spouse's decision to divorce, that decision needs my agreement, silence, lack of resistance, or cooperation for it to become a reality.

You may not be residing with your spouse right now, but you are where you are because you reacted to the separation thrusted upon you. However, you have not lost all the decision making power. At this very moment, you can continue allowing your spouse to make all the moves and react to those decisions or you can make some decisions of your own. It does not even matter if you already had a conversation about divorce and agreed to cooperate with your spouse's decision to end the marriage. As Christians we have been called to be peacemakers and to live peaceably with all men (Romans 12:8 NIV).

If you take time to examine that passage in Romans, you will notice the Apostle Paul gave you a qualifier, "If it be possible." This means the Apostle himself recognized there were going to be times when being at peace (The American Heritage Dictionary, 2001) or in agreement to end all resistance is not possible. I submit for your consideration this is one of those times. Review what the following passage has to say:

> *"Jesus replied, "Moses permitted you to divorce your wives because your hearts were hard. But it was not this way from the beginning."*

(MATTHEW 19:8 NIV)

In a recent article on the hardness of hearts, Andrew Wommack, American TV evangelist and host of the The Gospel Truth, a broadcast viewed by millions worldwide on 20 networks and 500 broadcast stations, said, "God made us so that we can harden our hearts and literally shout out unwanted influences. It was meant to be a positive thing, but because we have not understood this, what God meant for good has actually worked against us...In Mark 8:17, the characteristics of a hard heart are 1) unable to perceive, 2) unable to understand, 3) unable to see, 4) unable to hear and 5) unable to remember...And when spiritual things are perceived, a hard heart will keep a person from understanding the few things they can perceive. They might see what the Lord is trying to show them, but they can't get a hold of it in a way that they can apply it to their life" (Wommack, 2016).

Basically, a person with a hard heart is insensitive and unyielding in spiritual matters. This can happen to a believer or a non-believer. In the context of divorce, Jesus indicates it was permitted by Moses because the people of that day couldn't perceive what God wanted to do in marriage. In fact, if you look at the very next verse (Mark 8:18), you will see both the disciples and the people respond as they considered marriage without any possibility of essential release to them to be a severe and unbearable connection (Pulpit Commentary, 2016). Jesus went on to say this was not the way from the beginning.

When God created the institution of marriage in the Garden of Eden, he did not include divorce as part of his original design. This is what Jesus eluded to with his comment regarding the way things were in the beginning (Matthew 19:8 NIV). Today, as believers, we are not under the old covenant with God the disciples and the people of Israel were under when Jesus spoke those words.

Instead, we are under a new covenant (Hebrews 8:13), and with this new covenant we see that according to Acts 3:20 NIV, God's design is to restore everything as he promised long ago through his holy prophets.

In other words, God's will for us is a long life and fulfilling marriage that does not include the path of divorce. This is what marriage restoration is today. **It is the work of each married couple that has fellowship with God through the covenant to conduct restorative work on their marriage to bring it in alignment with God's original purpose and plan for marriage as he established it with Adam and Eve (Genesis 2:24).**

With this in appropriate context, we can say believers who are pursuing divorce cannot perceive the grace work God wants to restore under the new covenant but instead have chosen to address their problems naturally and not according to God's plan.

With this understanding, how should you and I interact with spouses who have their hearts and minds fixed on divorce? The answer can be found in the following verses:

> "If your brother or sister sins, go and point out their fault, just between the two of you. If they listen to you, you have won them over. But they will not listen, take one or two others along, so that every matter may be established by the testimony of two or three witnesses. If they still refuse to listen, tell it to the church; and if they refuse to listen even to the church, treat them as you would a pagan or a tax collector."
>
> (MATTHEW 18:15-17 NIV)

> "But if the unbelieving departs, let him depart. A brother or sister is not under bondage in such cases: But God has called us to peace."
>
> (1 CORINTHIANS 7:15 KJV)

From these verses we can see we are directed to treat our spouses like unbelievers since they are fixed on a path leading them away from God's truth. Their decisions did not make them lose their salvation, but their actions and decisions caused them to break fellowship with the Lord (1 John 1:7-9). In the context of 1 Corinthians 7:15-16, we are to stop fighting their desire to depart and let them depart.

"Thank God, Apostle Paul did not leave it there but demon-strated a full grasp of the restorative work God wants to do in marriage like the one outlined in 1 Corinthians 7:15-16:

You never know, wife: The way you handle this might bring your husband not only back to you but to God. You never know, husband: The way you handle this might bring your wife not only back to you but to God."

(1 CORINTHIANS 7:15-16 MSG)

As the Apostle pointed out, by our conduct, you and I can open the door for our spouses to return home and rekindle their relationship to God. This is good news that has been promised to you. Let us now discuss how God intends to help you accomplish this.

The work begins by recognizing your marriage, as it stands now, is dead and it will need to be resurrected. Earlier, we discussed marriage reconciliation may not be an option for you because marriage reconciliation requires both you and your spouse to have an open mind, an open heart, and a willingness to find solutions to the problems which plague the marriage. But what if you have a spouse who has no interest in a reconciliation?

 Lifeboat – Marriage Resurrection

If your spouse is not interested in reconciling, do not despair because there is an additional restorative work of God that extends beyond marital reconciliation is available to you. To better understand how marital reconciliation is different than this other redemptive work, consider two piers separated by a vast river. When marital reconciliation is no longer possible it is as if the spouses start together on the same pier, yet one notices a single-person boat at the bottom of the pier. In the distance, on the other side of the river, your spouse recognizes a more attractive and inviting land than the scenery on the pier he or she shares with the spouse.

This spouse decides to walk down the stairs to the docked boat. The spouse then unties the boat and goes alone to the other side of the river, leaving the mate behind. Today, this is where traditional marital counseling and other supports leave couples when common ground for reconciliation cannot be found.

Thank God his Word doesn't leave us at the end of the pier with no hope. Instead, God has a restorative work that actually becomes the bridge between the two piers, making it possible for the couple to reunite. It's another one of his lifeboats called marriage resurrection.

Referring to the Apostle Paul's statements in 1 Corinthians 7:16, we can find some insight into what marriage resurrection is when he tells the husband and wife that through their conduct they may bring back the departed spouse.

A central characteristic of marriage resurrection is it only requires the participation of the spouse who is not seeking to depart the marriage but rather remains faithful and in fellowship with the covenant.

When the spouse who is not willing to depart decides to stay faithful to the marriage commitment they made before God on their wedding day, the door opens for God to do a work that redeems the departed spouse back to himself and back to the spouse who remains in fellowship.

The second characteristic of a marriage resurrection occurs when the spouse who remains in fellowship pleads to the Lord and those of the household of faith on behalf of the departed spouse and asks for help turning the departed aside from sin and intentions he or she made that caused the spouse to break fellowship (Hosea 2:1-2). **Marriage resurrection occurs when one spouse chooses divorce the other spouse remains in fellowship with the marital covenant, asking for the Lord's help to restore the marriage.**

We can find the scriptural basis for a marriage resurrection in the book of Hosea chapters 2 and 3. The story actually begins in Ezekiel 16:8 where God proposes and enters into a marriage covenant with the people of Israel:

> *"Later I passed by, and when I looked at you and saw that you were old enough for love, I spread the corner of my garment over you and covered your naked body. I gave you my solemn oath and entered into a covenant with you, declares the Sovereign Lord and you became mine."*
>
> (EZEKIEL 16:8 NIV)

By the time we get to the book of Hosea in chapter 2:2 NIV, we see God making a new declaration about His bride:

Haul your mother into court. Accuse her! She's no longer my wife. I'm no longer her   husband. Tell her to quite dressing like a whore, displaying her breasts for sale.

We see God declaring Israel is no longer his wife and he is no longer her husband. A divorce between the two has occurred. To put a visual behind his marriage with Israel in Chapter 1:2 AMP, God told the prophet Hosea to find himself a wife of harlotry (prostitution) and make her his wife. Together they were to have children, He made this request because the people of Israel behaved like a prostitute when they departed from the Lord. As you read through the account of Hosea and Gomer in Chapter 1 and compare it to the account of God and Israel, you will see the actions of both brides are identical. Even the names of the children born to Gomer are indicative of the behavior of Gomer to Hosea and Israel to God.

In Hosea, chapter 2, God declares his marriage with Israel is over and in Hosea we see his marriage to Gomer has also ended because in verse 7 she refers to him as her "first husband and she intends to go to him."

While Gomer was away from Hosea, things did not go well for her. She wanted to return to Hosea but not for the right reasons. Further in verse 7 she says, "I will go back to my husband as at first, for then I was better off than now."

Her reasons had nothing to do with the love she had for Hosea or even the acknowledgment of the love and concern he had for her. Instead, she focused on his ability to support her, which was greater than she could do without him in her life. Reviewing the rest of chapter 2, you will see that God not only rejects that motivation, but also decides to allow her to endure her life completely exposed to whatever whims and desires life would bring to her. By chapter 3, life's circumstances have become so difficult for Gomer she finds herself in slavery.

Despite the marriage status of the relationships between Hosea and Gomer and God and Israel, God does not abandon either of the brides forever. Instead, God promises by his hand and willingness he would allow calamities to come upon them both (Israel and Gomer) until they repent. Despite the declaration of doom, the brides will be pleasantly surprised when their circumstances have turned dire and all those with whom they played the harlot had forsaken them, and their husbands will still be in love with them and willing to restore them as their wives. That love has motivated them to stay informed of the welfare of their brides and at the time set by God, he and Hosea both move into redeem their brides from the pits they dug for themselves. Both husbands lovingly accept the repentant hearts of their brides, offer forgiveness, and begin to restore them to their covenant positions.

A marriage resurrection allows the spouse who departs the opportunity for God to guide life's circumstances to have the spouse naturally perceive what they could not perceive spiritually when their hearts became fixed on divorce as the only solution. God's resolution allows couples the opportunity to see divorce for what it really is—relationship abortion—and allows them to experience its effects. Only then can he have the opportunity to chart them through a path of repentance, forgiveness, marital reconciliation, and finally back on the road of marital restoration.

A study conducted by the University of Minnesota shows 40 percent of divorced people regretted their divorce and thought it was preventable (William J Doherty, 2016). Another survey shows 62 percent of ex-husbands and ex-wives said they wished their spouses had worked harder and 35 percent of the ex-husbands and 21 percent of ex-wives said they wished they, themselves, had worked harder (Marriage in America, 2016). Also, those who responded to the survey said that a "lack of commitment" was the most frequently reason given for the divorce (Marriage in America, 2016). Regret after divorce is not just limited to the United States. In a survey conducted in the United Kingdom in 2014, 50 percent of divorcees have regrets about their break-ups, with 54 percent experiencing second thoughts about whether they had made the right decision (UK Daily, 2014).

When God performed a marriage resurrection during my separation and pending divorce, I was completely shocked at the work he did in my spouse's life. One day my wife espoused how committed she was to us divorcing and that reconciling with me was not possible. After one night with Christ, she had a complete heart change. It was during that time my wife become convicted of her sins and desired to move toward the will of God for her life. She realized that she had fallen prey to the tricks of the enemy regarding her relationship with me and no longer wanted to follow his path. Because of the stronghold Satan had on my wife's mind, it took some time for her complete healing but the process started during one night when she was able to finally see the truth of what she had done and what she needed to do.

Like Hosea, the Lord put me in a position where I had to be the one to redeem her from life's circumstances while many of those who encouraged her down that path of divorce had forsaken her. Like Gomer, my wife's circumstances were extremely dire, and if I had not been ready and placed by God where I was when she needed me most, it is very possible she would not be with us today. The heart change she experienced is an understatement of what happened. Imagine having your spouse's eyes open to every argument the two of you had during the entire marriage and at the end of an encounter with God, your spouse is supernaturally able to understand and empathize with the positions you took during those arguments without you speaking a single word. Even as I write this, it is difficult to find the right words. My spouse's night with God was better than all the pre- and post-marital counseling, books, CDs, DVDs, and other aids we received during our nearly 30 years together.

Now you know what a marriage resurrection is and what God will do on your behalf, the decision is up to you whether or not you are going to allow him to bring new life to your dead marriage.

Scripture:

HOSEA CHAPTER 2: VS 14-23

> *"And now, here's what I'm going to do: I'm going to start all over again. I'm taking her back out into the wilderness where we had our first date, I'll court her. I'll give her bouquets of roses. I'll turn Heartbreak Valley into Acres of Hope. She'll respond like she did as a young girl, those days when she was fresh out of Egypt "At that time" - this is God's message still- "you'll address me, 'Dear husband!' Never again will address me, 'My slave-master!' I'll wash your mouth out with soap, get rid of all the dirty false-gods' names, not so much as a whisper of those names again. At the same time, I'll make a peace treaty between you and wild animals and birds and reptiles, and get*

rid of all weapons of war. Think of it! Safe from beasts and bullies! And then I'll marry you for good- forever! I'll marry you true and proper, in love and tenderness. Yes, I'll marry you and neither leave you nor let you go. You'll know me, God, for who I really am.

"On the very same day, I'll answer" – this is God's Message- "I'll answer the sky, sky will answer earth, Earth will answer grain and wine and olive oil, and they'll all answer Jezrell. I'll plant her in the good earth. I'll have mercy on No-Mercy. I'll say to No-body, 'You're my dear Somebody,' and he'll say 'You're my God!'"

HOSEA CHAPTER 3: 1 -3

"Then God ordered me, "Start all over. Love your wife again, your wife who's in bed with her latest boyfriend, your cheating wife. Love her the way I, God, love the Israelite people, even as they flirt and party with every god that takes their fancy."

I did it. I paid good money to get her back. It cost me the price of a slave. Then I told her, "From now on you're living with me. No more whoring, no more sleeping around. You're living with me and I'm living with you."

(HOSEA 2: 14-23, 3:1-3 MSG)

WIFE'S COMMENTARY

Initially I was hesitant to participate in this book because I thought it was going to be a discussion about me. I was sensitive about the subject because though our story has a happy ending, I had initiated our separation, I was the complainant in the divorce case, and I had violated our marriage covenant. I sarcastically said to my husband one day when we were discussing the concept, "I'm so glad to have been able to give you so much fodder for this book."

I was wrong. Though this book does mention our marital issues and how we overcame them, it's so much more than that. The book shows how my husband stood committed to the covenant he made with God concerning our marriage throughout the separation and divorce proceedings. It discusses how he helped me break through the enemy's lies and deceit to make my way back home. More than a testimony of one couple's victory over a dead marriage, this book is a revelation to the Body of Christ about how to reign as Kingdom people and resist today's common worldview on marriage, separation, and divorce. It is also a clear example of how Christ loves the Church.

When my husband and I got married, we were like most young couples, I suppose. We believed our married life wouldn't be any different from the way things were when we were dating. We had a motto, "It's better together," promising ourselves to each other and vowing never to mention the "D" word. Because my parents divorced when I was young and while growing up my husband saw his parents act more like roommates than a loving couple, neither of us wanted to end up in either of those situations. What I discovered three separations and a near divorce later is that just hoping you do not fall into a particular circumstance is not enough to keep you from going there, and as Christians, we have an adversary—the devil—whose sole purpose is to deceive and divide.

Tired is how I felt about my marriage after experiencing separation number three from my husband. I had no hope my marriage would survive another one. Why should it? We had already gone through two separations, albeit they each had lasted less than 30 days. With renewed commitments each time to "work on our relationship," our attempts had been only partially successful. Through the years, raising children, working big jobs, and participating in leadership positions at church kept us fully occupied and reasonably able to keep everything, including our relationship, afloat. Or so we thought.

The summer I turned 50 was an especially happy time for me. I hosted a party in which more than 50 of my colleagues and friends joined my husband and youngest daughter to celebrate. I had high expectations about the year ahead as I planned to recommit to some abandoned hobbies such as jogging and painting.

I didn't see any of it coming. A traumatic accident two months after my birthday sent me on a downward spiral that felt like I had fallen into a deep, dark hole. I had no way of imagining over the next 18 months, I would spend several days in a psychiatric hospital and would battle post-traumatic stress syndrome, an eating disorder, and severe depression.

Looking back on the first two separations, I realize they occurred because I was harboring unforgiveness. I was unable to release those feelings fully and brought this attitude into our relationship after each separation. I did not discover I had not released my ill feelings until disagreements brought them out. By the time my husband and I experienced our third separation, my heart was hardened toward him. My disobedience to God and unfaithfulness to my husband nearly cost us our marriage.

When I abandoned my marriage covenant, my husband stayed true to his. He applied Galatians 6:1 by helping me get back on track. Another one of the foundational scriptures he stood on was Ephesians 4:2 in which he was gentle and patient while I was transformed into the image of Christ. While I was in the hospital for an extended stay of 17 days, my husband came to visit me daily and brought me cards and letters to encourage me. We stood on many scriptures, including Isaiah 40:31, Isaiah 43:18-19, Proverbs 18:21, 2 Corinthians 2:14, Ephesians 6:10, 1 Thessalonians 5:15-24, and others to get through those difficult days.

When I think about the person I was before our last separation and the person I am now, I hardly recognize myself.

If you are contemplating standing in the gap for your spouse, you'll have to have a tough skin. Your spouse may not cooperate immediately. If your spouse is anything like me, that is a guarantee. I was deceived by the enemy and felt justified in my thoughts and behaviors. Thankfully, my husband is a relatively stubborn person normally, and this character served him well when he was praying and believing for me to come home.

If it was not for my husband having a willingness to fight for me, showing me love unconditionally and forgiving me completely, I honestly do not know where I would be today. He epitomizes Ephesians 3:19 by showing me what the love of Christ looks like. As our marriage rose from the dead, the Lord took my stony heart, opened my eyes, and showed me how to forgive, love, and respect my husband.

I would like to combine my faith with yours at this time as you make the decision to turn to God for your marriage and stand in faith for your spouse to rejoin the marriage covenant. Though your job may be difficult, it is not impossible. With man, it may seem impossible, but with God, anything is possible (Matthew 19:26).

Scripture

> *"So, let's not get tired of doing good. At just the right time we will reap a harvest of blessing if we don't give up."*
>
> (GALATIANS 6:9 NLT)

God's Help in Marriage Restoration

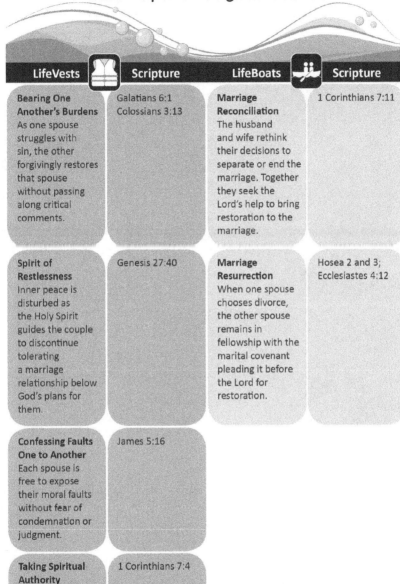

LifeVests	Scripture	LifeBoats	Scripture
Bearing One Another's Burdens As one spouse struggles with sin, the other forgivingly restores that spouse without passing along critical comments.	Galatians 6:1 Colossians 3:13	**Marriage Reconciliation** The husband and wife rethink their decisions to separate or end the marriage. Together they seek the Lord's help to bring restoration to the marriage.	1 Corinthians 7:11
Spirit of Restlessness Inner peace is disturbed as the Holy Spirit guides the couple to discontinue tolerating a marriage relationship below God's plans for them.	Genesis 27:40	**Marriage Resurrection** When one spouse chooses divorce, the other spouse remains in fellowship with the marital covenant pleading it before the Lord for restoration.	Hosea 2 and 3; Ecclesiastes 4:12
Confessing Faults One to Another Each spouse is free to expose their moral faults without fear of condemnation or judgment.	James 5:16		
Taking Spiritual Authority The couple recognizes that each spouse has spiritual authority over the other spouse's body.	1 Corinthians 7:4		

THE RESURRECTION PLAN

Ninety-eight percent. The number my lawyer provided as the percentage of divorce cases that conclude in divorce. From the very day I was served with divorce papers, it seemed as if my life went on auto pilot. I felt as if all decisions had already been made for me. Friends, family, and even neighbors dealt with me differently from the moment they learned about the pending divorce. Everyone was eager to share their negative opinions about my wife and/or their own horrific divorce story. It was as if once divorce proceedings began there was no way back.

Believing divorce is inevitable when your spouse files for divorce is the lie Satan hopes you will accept. God, on the other hand, wants you to believe your dead marriage can live again. Through a marriage resurrection you will find His amazing love and the spiritual tools He has given you to build a path that will bring your spouse back home. God has not left you alone. Divorce is not inevitable. As you explore the chapters in this section, you will identify the components of a marriage resurrection.

Marriage resurrection is about constructing a bridge from the love Jesus will use to cross into the enemy's camp to rescue your spouse from the enemy's grip. Once released, and as your spouse and the Lord start to make their way back across the bridge, the Lord will answer your prayers of intercession, addressing the many things that separated the two of you.

The way an individual marriage resurrection works is always up to the Holy Spirit who serves as the foreman on the job of building your love bridge. He will specifically teach you during those daily sessions of intercession which bridge component you will need to focus on that day. While you may not understand how your actions are lending themselves to the effort, you must keep faith the work is getting done.

SECTION 2 - THE RESURRECTION PLAN

As part of spiritual warfare during my marriage resurrecting, the Holy Spirit revealed to me ways to ensure my wife had access to the spoken and written Word. This was a very difficult task for me since I was not in communication with her. The Holy Spirit had me buy books to send to her. At the time, those purchases seemed like a waste of time and money. However, in the scheme of things, God knew my wife had cut off her access to the Word. Not only had she stopped coming to church, but she was no longer reading her Bible or getting the Word in any other form. Ultimately, God would use those purchases to get my wife's attention and to help her make decisions that brought her home.

Only through spending time in prayer and meditation with the Holy Spirit can you learn when to use each tool. In the next section, I will share all of the components of the marriage resurrection and how God will use each of them to build His love bridge. Your task is to believe God can bring new life to your dead marriage. You provide the labor through your intercessory prayer for your spouse. As you pray, the Holy Spirit will give you specific instructions to ensure the bridge will be built. You will need to love what seems unlovable, believe what seems impossible, stay patient when it appears that the circumstances aren't working, and maintain fellowship with other believers even if it is the last thing you feel like doing.

Following the Holy Spirit's direction will undoubtedly lead you to victory as the enemy is defeated—ultimately leading your spouse to reconcile with God and return home.

CHAPTER 6

DARE TO BELIEVE YOUR MARRIAGE CAN LIVE AGAIN

Choose to believe your dead marriage can be resurrected.

Now you realize the separation is real, take a moment and ask yourself whether or not a divorce is what you really want. What have you really gained from winning some arguments and losing others, breaking trust and destroying the relationship with your best friend? When one of you wins, both of you lose!

I did not like being single, and I surely did not like my life after my wife left. One day during our third and final separation I realized my wife was not bluffing about her departure, I asked myself, "If I had another shot at my marriage, what would I do differently?"

> **Lesson Learned#7 –**
> **Disagreements and misunderstandings in marriage indicate a lack of God's presence in your relationship.**

After spending time doodling on a piece of paper I came up with two images. While I had the concepts for what I wanted to eliminate, I had no idea how to change. What I am about to share is what I learned during my separation that changed our relationship, ended the divorce, and brought my spouse home.

The first thing I came to understand is all our disagreements and misunderstandings proved is God was not present in our marriage. We attended church regularly, participated in the ministry, gave our tithes and even held leadership positions, but there still were some very important aspects of our lives displeasing to God.

> "But I want you to know and realize that Christ is the Head of every man, the head of woman is her husband, and the Head of Christ is God."
>
> (1 CORINTHIANS 11:3 AMP)

What I am referring to is we did not make Christ the everyday head of our marriage. We embraced the principle the head of woman is the husband and the "Head of Christ is God," but we did not operate in the truth "Christ is the Head of every man."

Lesson Learned #8 –
A Christless marriage is a headless marriage,
and a headless marriage won't last very long.

The head serves the body in five primary ways.

☐ Nourishment

☐ Understanding of the world around us

☐ Protection

☐ Identity

☐ Guidance

Nourishment comes through the head and transfers to the body in the form of air, oxygen, food and water. When I thought about Jesus as the head of the church, I thought about how believers accept Him as food and breath. A marriage does not require physical things like these, rather its nourishment can be found in what is termed as the fruit of the Holy Spirit.

> "But the fruit of the [Holy] Spirit [the work which His presence within accomplishes] is love, joy (gladness), peace, patience (an even temper, forbearance), kindness, goodness (benevolence), faithfulness, gentleness (meekness, humility), self-control (self-restraint). Against such things there is no law [that can bring a charge]."
>
> (GALATIANS 5:22-23 AMP)

The way I interpreted this was as a husband, if I actively demonstrated these characteristics to my wife, I would not have found myself sitting in court charged with gross neglect of duty. Though I exhibited the fruits of the Spirit from time to time, I wasn't diligent with her. Being honest with myself, I figured within a week, I probably demonstrated these traits only one to two days out of seven. Using a calculator, two days out seven is only 28.5 percent, which is an "F" in any classroom I've ever been in.

The head is the body's ability to correctly acknowledge, interrupt and understand the world around it through the five senses. Though touch can be conducted through the hands, your hands have no idea what it has come in contact with until the data is passed to the brain and interpreted. Going back to Ephesians, I found how the Lord supports the Body of Christ while we are in the world. It reads –

> "That he might sanctify and cleanse it with the washing of the water by the word, that he might present it to himself a glorious church, not having spot, or wrinkle or any such thing but that it should be holy and without blemish."
>
> (EPHESIANS 5:26 -27)

The Lord doesn't just let us go into the world after accepting Him as Savior to live out His work to salvation alone. Instead, He has made provisions for us with His spoken and written word through His Spirit to guide us into all truth. Thus, as a husband, my job is to take the Word and share it daily with my wife so as she takes on her day, her fears, disappointments, anger, lack of understanding, hurts and other emotional pain will be washed away by the Word.

Instead, when I was not practicing selective hearing, I would listen to her issues or about her day and try to give my best pep speech, which sounded no different than a coach's locker room talk before a game. After a while she stopped coming to me. Truth is, what she really needed me to be was not her life coach but to lift her up with the Word of God.

The head also provides protection by identifying any attack, event or threat that would bring us harm. This activates the psychological response known as "fight or flight," which sends signals throughout the body to produce the appropriate reaction to the pending threat.

Ephesians 5:25 tells us Christ laid down His life for the church and by doing so, saved each of us from the second death, offering us everlasting life (Revelation 20:14). If Christ laid down his life for me, surely I could lay down my pride, stubbornness and selfishness that had resulted in being alone and separated from my life's partner.

The head also gives identity.

> "God knew what he was doing from the very beginning. He de-

cided from the outset to shape the lives of those who love him
along the same lines as the life of his Son. The Son stands first
in the line of humanity he restored. We see the original and
intended shape of our lives there in him."

(ROMANS 8:29-30 MSG)

How was the image of the Son reflecting in my life? Was that reflection enough to help mold and shape my wife into following that same image?

I had to admit is wasn't. More and more my wife had wanted to do things with her girlfriends at work and church. I thought she just needed that girl time, but when the divorce papers were served the scales fell from my eyes, and I realized that she was just choosing not to spend those times with me.

My life no longer reflected the fruit of the Spirit, and when I stopped pursuing Him, it left my wife anchorless. I no longer provided the security and benefit of a faithful life. Instead she filled her soul with worldly influences. When she felt she had a missing space in her heart, worldly sources readily filled the gap. Because our perspectives were different in several areas, we were faced with the truth in the Word that a house divided against itself is going to fall (Mark 3:25), and ours most certainly did.

Finally, the head guides our feelings at any given moment, which direction we should take, and which events we should forget, which things we should remember, and what we should believe.

You cannot spend time in the Word without running into scriptures that tell you to forgive one another (Ephesians 4:32), to cast down thoughts not lined up with God's Word (2 Corinthians 10:5) and which things you should focus on (Philippians 4: 8); yet, I did the complete opposite.

I could not let go of wrongs my wife had done, which meant I was not forgiving. I embraced every thought about her and feeling for her that came my way, including from deep concern, to suspicion, anger and even lack of interest, without filtering or challenging them. Instead of focusing on the 80 percent of the wonderful ways my wife blessed my life every day, I focused on the 20 percent of the time I felt unfulfilled. My displeasure rather than the overwhelmingly positive things she did every day dominated our conversations daily.

> **Lesson Learned #9 -**
> **A dead marriage is a headless marriage or**
> **marriage where Christ is a bystander and not the head.**

Each time my wife and I separated it proved we had failed at making Christ the head of our marriage. I was not pleased with this and did not want to accept the possibility of one day standing before the Lord to give account for the way I had performed in my marriage. What would I say about how I handled the great gift

He gave me—my wife? I could give him an answer like Adam and say it was the woman's fault for our predicament, but things did not fare out so well for Adam, so I decided against that. (Read Genesis Chapter 3.)

Keep in mind is God witnesses every moment of your marriage, and like the special features on a DVD, he has more than just the movie playback. He knows your spouse's and your thoughts, intentions and motives. Everything will be before Him, including His Word. God has something to say about every moment of your marriage. His influence is available through his written or spoken Word, in dreams or by the Holy Spirit. The bottom line is God is not silent. How many times has He influenced your pastor or another minister or teach about marriage when you were too preoccupied or disinterested to receive the Word?

The totality of God's Word on marriage has always been right before you, and He will hold you accountable in the courtroom of Heaven. If nothing changes, the best you will be able to present is what "he said" and "she said."

You may be saying right now, "Okay, so I will be found guilty. You have no idea what I had to put up with while marriage. Besides, I accepted Jesus as my Savior and that is all that matters."

Well, there is one thing you failed to take into consideration. First of all, accepting Jesus as your Savior punched your ticket to be with Him when this life is over. However, it is the decisions you make in this life that determine what eternity will be like for you. If accepting Christ was the end of your salvation, the moment you accepted Him you would have left this world and immediately been in His presence. That didn't happen.

Accepting Him is just the beginning of salvation. While our spirits are made new, our bodies and souls are not. It is our responsibility as individuals to use our lives to fulfill God's plan and purpose. It is how we conduct ourselves in every area of our lives that will determine the testimonies and victories over the enemy. What we achieve and who we impact for Him are the true value of our lives. With these results, each of us will be with our authority we will be given the right to rule and reign with Him (2 Timothy 2:12). These rewards are for eternity.

The Bible is clear marriage is an earthly institution, and when you arrive in heaven your spouse will no longer be tied to you in marriage (Matthew 22:30). Only now, in the present, do you have the opportunity to enjoy the beauty and the work associated with marriage.

The realization your marriage is failing because you and your spouse did not put God as the head of your marriage is a tough pill to swallow. For me, coming to this realization in the middle of a breaking marriage made me long for another opportunity for a fulfilling marriage.

My motive to reunite with my wife had little to do with the fact I loved her. Do not get me wrong, I still loved her, but my heart was full of wounds. My wife and I were separated, and she officially filed for divorce. She built up a wall of friends, family and fellow believers around her who made sure I stayed away from her.

She secluded herself, with her whereabouts closely guarded and supported by a legal order preventing us from having contact with one another.

It looked like my marriage was dead. Though I was ready to accept that the failure of the marriage was due to not allowing Christ to be the head of our relationship, it looked like I was never going to get another chance at reconciliation.

You, too, may be having second thoughts about going forward with the divorce, and you may be facing similar or even greater obstacles to reconciliation than me. Well, I have good news. If you are seriously interested in getting another opportunity to reunite and willing to let Christ be the head of your marriage, God has outlined a way in his Word that can bring your dead marriage back to life.

Lesson Learned #10:
Jesus is an expert in resurrecting the dead

Fruits that are bruised or damaged are often still edible; you may just have to go a few layers deep. For example, a severely bruised and brownish colored apple may not be edible but there still may be life in the seeds. Your marriage can be compared to an apple. As long as you or your spouse has a seed of love in your heart for the other spouse and a willingness to let the Lord guide you, your marriage can be saved.

Jesus is an expert in resurrecting the dead. Whether it is the son of the woman from Nain (Luke 7: 11-15); Jairus' daughter (Mark 5: 21-43), Lazarus (John 11) or himself (Matthew 27:52-53), death is not a barrier he cannot cross. In each of these stories, someone died but that did not stop Jesus from speaking to them and restoring their lives. No matter how long the person had been dead, he was able to do the resurrection work his father had send him to do. Take a look at this excerpt from Lazarus' story:

When Jesus finally got there, he found Lazarus already four days dead. Bethany was near Jerusalem, only a couple of miles away, and many of the Jews were visiting Martha and Mary, sympathizing with them over their brother. Martha heard Jesus was coming and went out to meet him. Mary remained in the house. Martha said, "Master if you'd been here my brother wouldn't have died. Even now, I know that whatever you ask God he will give you." Jesus said, "Your brother will be raised up." John 11 KJV

Jesus did not stop to take a poll to see what people thought He should do or to see if any believed whether or not Lazarus was really dead. He did not come by to drop off chicken or potato salad at the wake and to give Mary and Martha condolences. Instead, He came for one purpose. He said, "Your brother will rise again" (John 11:23 NIV).

Martha did not ask Jesus to raise her brother from the dead and He did not ask

her if that was what she wanted. Before Jesus spoke, Martha had done her part to acknowledge Jesus' manifested presence, goodness and power (glory) had arrived. She submitted herself to His will when she called Him "Master."

Her speech shows while she was not necessarily asking for or expecting resurrection, she was not ready to rule it out, which is why she said, "Even now, I know whatever you ask God, he will give you" (John 11:22).

While Martha's heart was in the right place, her theology was not quite on target. In the Book of John (John 6:38), Jesus clearly stated He did not come to do His own will but that of the Father's.

> *"Do you not believe that I am in the Father, and the Father is in Me? The words I say to you I do not say on My own initiative or authority, but the Father, abiding continually in Me, does His works [His attesting miracles and acts of power]."*
>
> (JOHN 14:10 AMP)

Jesus gave them this answer:

> *"Very truly I tell you, the Son can do nothing by Himself: He can do only what He sees His Father doing, because whatever the Father does the Son also does."*
>
> (JOHN 5:19 NIV)

Nowhere do you see Jesus turning aside to pray and ask God what He wants done. He simply told Martha, "Your brother will be raised up" (John 11:23). His mission and purpose for being there was to raise Lazarus out of the tomb. He already knew the will of the Father, otherwise He would have never shown up.

Jesus may have acted the same way when a man stopped him on the road to Jerusalem seeking to become a disciple. He asked Jesus for permission to first bury his father, and Jesus responded "Let the dead bury the dead."

Clearly, in the case of Lazarus and others, Jesus received specific instructions from the Father to raise them from the dead. If you read the whole story, you will see Jesus first heard about Lazarus when Lazarus was still alive—he was ill, but death had not yet come. The Bible says Jesus waited two more days before telling his disciples they needed to go back to Judea (John 11:6). While the Bible makes no mention of a messenger coming to tell Jesus that Lazarus has died during those two days, Jesus was aware he had died, and he told his disciples "Our friend Lazarus has fallen asleep; but I am going there to wake him up" (John 11:11). Clearly, Jesus received not only the approval from the Father to raise Lazarus from the dead, but he also received news this was His mission.

Returning back to Lazarus there are three more important points you must see:

CHAPTER 6: DARE TO BELIEVE YOUR MARRIAGE CAN LIVE AGAIN

But some of them said, "Could not he who opened the eyes of the blind man have kept this man from dying? "Jesus once more deeply moved, came to the tomb. It was a cave with a stone laid across the entrance. "Take away the stone," he said. "But, Lord," said Martha, the sister of the dead man, "by this time there is a bad odor, for he has been there four days." Then Jesus said, "Did I not tell you that if you believe, you will see the glory of God?" So they took away the stone. Then Jesus looked up and said, "Father, I thank you that you have heard me. I knew that you always hear me, but I said this for the benefit of the people standing here, that they may believe that you sent me." When he had said this, Jesus called in a loud voice, "Lazarus, come out!" The dead man came out, his hands and feet wrapped with strips of linen, and a cloth around his face. Jesus said to them, "Take off the grave clothes and let him go. (John 11: 37-44 MSG)

Notice the crowd asked crowd Jesus why he did not keep Lazarus from dying. They had a valid point. They had seen Jesus open the eyes of the blind man, so whatever illness Lazarus had, they assumed Jesus could have healed Lazarus, too, if He had been there. Martha felt this way as well.

In a similar vein, maybe you have been wondering why Jesus did not stop your spouse from leaving or filing for divorce. Those thoughts ran through my head as well, especially since I had been separated from my wife two other times.

While I do not know the specific circumstances behind your situation, in my case, I see the parallel between my divorce and Jesus' response when he was asked why he had not prevented Lazarus' death. Jesus said, "That for the benefit of the people standing here, that they may believe that you sent me." (John 11:42)

From the day we stood at the altar and said "I do" to the day our spouses walked out the door, we had our opportunity to acknowledge the presence of the Lord in our marriages and to let Him do His work of healing our sick marriages. In my case, I failed to do so because I just did not believe, and the Word tells us where there is the lack of belief, the Lord can do no mighty work (Mark 6:5).

Having faith in the Lord has a lot to do with what He is able to accomplish in your life. His will for you may be you stay married, but if your will overrides, He will allow your marriage to end in divorce. It might be God's plan through your testimony, once your marriage is resurrected, others will have faith they, too, can save their marriage.

That is what happened in my case. Other couples around us who separated and were headed toward divorce saw the depths of our despair and had front row tickets to the miraculous restorative work the Lord did in our marriage. The resurrection of our marriage led other couples to re-examine their relationships.

Another point from the story about Lazarus occurs when Martha tells Jesus that there was a strong odor from Lazarus since he has been dead four days. Lazarus' body had already started decomposing. After four days, there was absolutely no life in Lazarus' body and all of the organs had completely shut down.

This brings us to third and final point. Christ offers Life. Death is the curse started in Genesis Chapter 3. Divorce is the death of your marriage. It is on the way to its final resting place because you and your spouse made choices opened the door to death's power to choke the life out of the marriage. The Word tells us the administrator of the power of death is the devil (Hebrews 2:14 NIV).

> *"For wherever there is jealousy (envy) and contention (rivalry*
> *and selfish ambition), there will also be confusion (unrest, dis-*
> *harmony, rebellion) and all sorts of evil and vile practices."*
>
> (JAMES 3:16 AMP)

You and your spouse made the mistake of closing the door on the Lord's presence in your marriage, but you did not make sure the door for the devil was locked. Instead, you invited him in and when he accepted your invitation, he brought some gifts with him—jealousy, contention and unrest to name a few. This occurred because you lacked faith. Unfortunately, the Word is very clear "whatsoever is not of faith is sin; the wages (payment) for having sin is death" (Romans 6:23 AMP). The bottom-line is: you are experiencing a death in your marriage because you opened the door to the devil and accepted his evil works. Those works brought death.

There is good news. If you will close the door to the devil and reopen your heart to the Lord, you can see a turnaround in your marriage. Because unlike the devil, who comes to steal your joy and bring death, the Lord brings life (John 10:10).

Going back to the story of Lazarus, you will remember the key to resurrection was Jesus' mission to go and do that very work. Jesus would not have been able to do it if the Father did not want Him to speak words of life over Lazarus' lifeless body and bring him out of the tomb. The work could not be done unless it was the Father's will.

You may wonder if it is God's will to resurrect your dead marriage. Consider this:

> *"And here's a second offense: You fill the place of worship with*
> *your whining and sniveling because you don't get what you*
> *want from God. Do you know why? Simple. Because God was*
> *there as a witness when you spoke your marriage vows to your*
> *young bride, and now you've broken those vows, broken the*
> *faith-bond with your vow companion, your covenant wife. God,*
> *not you, made marriage. His Spirit inhibits even the smallest*
> *details of marriage. And what does he want from marriage?*
> *Children of God, that's what. So guard the spirit of marriage*
> *within you. Don't cheat on your spouse. "I hate divorce." Says*

the God of Israel. God of the-Angel-Armies says, "I hate the
violent dismembering of the 'one flesh' of marriage." So watch
yourselves. Don't let your guard down. Don't cheat."

(MALACHI 2:13-17 MSG)

From the above scripture, we can clearly walk away knowing God's feeling about divorce—He hates it.

"Therefore, what God has joined together, let no one separate."

(MARK 10:9 AMP)

With this verse we can rule out God is the one trying to bring separation and divorce to your marriage. Earlier, we identified the party behind your separation and pending divorce is the devil. There are two opposing forces. God has joined you and your spouse together, and the devil has brought his evil works to break you apart. So if God's will is for the union to continue, what instructions do you think He would relay to His Son about your situation? Here's the answer below:

"[But] he who commits sin (who practices evildoing) is of the
devil [takes his character from the evil one], for the devil has
sinned (violated the divine law) from the beginning. The rea-
son the Son of God was made manifest (visible) was to undo
(destroy, loosen, and dissolve) the works the devil [has done]."

(1 JOHN 3:8 AMP)

That is awesome news. The devil may have tricked you and your spouse by allowing contention and separation to enter your marriage, but Jesus said He was made manifest (visible) to destroy, loosen and dissolve the destructive work of divorce the devil has come to do. Sounds like marriage resurrection to me. Hallelujah!!!

My wife and I experienced God's awesome gift first-hand through a marriage resurrection.

There is something vitally important I need to tell you about a marriage resurrection. When Jesus, Lazarus, Jairus' daughter and anyone else was raised from the dead by the mighty power of God with life re-entering their bodies, what caused the death in the first place was not present. Otherwise, as soon as they came back to life they would have immediately died again. Their failed organs would not have been able to sustain the life-giving power because those organs had already shut down.

In Jesus' case, his cause of death was not the cross or even crucifixion but instead, the lack of oxygen to the lungs causing his lungs to collapse.[1] Therefore, when Jesus and the others were resurrected from the dead, they had the very

---

1   The American Heritage Dictionary, 4th Edition, Dell Publishing, New York, NY, 2001, page 211

thing that caused their death permanently removed, and any damage to their vital organs was totally restored.

This is what makes a marriage resurrection much different than a marriage reconciliation. My wife and I have experienced them both, and the differences are significant. When you experience a marriage resurrection, your marriage will go from a foul stench to a sweet scent rising to God, which will be recognized by all those suffer from marital discord (2 Corinthians 2:16 MSG). Your new marriage will give others hope where they have completely lost hope, and soon God will bring others to your doorstep who want to drink from the fountain of marital resurrection testimony. Because they are hurting, they will drive great distances to quench their thirst from the water of the Word that comes from your life's testimony. This is what God said He wanted in Malachi chapter 2.

A marriage resurrection is yours for the taking. You have to be crazy (bold) enough to believe what others will tell you it is not possible. While I have shared with you the theology behind a marriage resurrection, it is impossible for me to tell you the physics behind it. I also cannot tell you how a marriage resurrection is going to be accomplished in your life. I lived through one, and I am still in awe over the actual miracles the Lord performed to bring my wife and I back together again. God never asked me to know how He was going to do the work in my life, He just wanted to know if I believed He would do it.

Like Martha, I said I would, and I saw the glory (manifested presence, manifested power and manifested goodness) of God show up on my behalf. When it occurred suddenly for my wife and I, God gave me explicit instructions for my wife and me to go a dream vacation. For 30 years we dreamed of going to Italy to visit Tuscany, Venice, and Florence and to walk the streets of Rome. With four kids, college tuition, and a mortgage, this was no easy feat, especially because the separation and divorce proceeding had taken such a ravenous hit to our finances. Our savings were depleted, my retirement vanished, my wife was on disability and I was out of work for nine months. It didn't sound like we were going anywhere, but in seven days of my wife's discharge from the hospital and with the divorce officially dead at the courts, the two of us were walking the streets of Rome and floating in a gondola in Venice.

Psalms 126: 1-2 came true for us:

It seemed like a dream, too good to be true, when God returned Zion's exiles. We laughed, we sang, we couldn't believe our good fortune.

The Word says God is not a respecter of persons (Acts 10:34), but He did this for us, and He will be able to do the same for you. Believe and you shall receive. We have the photos to prove it.

Scripture:

> *"And if you are married, stay married. This is the Master's command, not mine. If a wife should leave her husband, she must*

either remain single or else come back and make things right with him. And a husband has no right to get rid of his wife.

For the rest of you who are in mixed marriages—Christian married to non-Christian—we have no explicit command from the Master. So this is what you must do. If you are a man with a wife who is not a believer but who still wants to live with you, hold on to her. If you are a woman with a husband who is not a believer but he wants to live with you, hold on to him.

The unbelieving husband shares to an extent in the holiness of his wife, and the unbelieving wife is likewise touched by the holiness of her husband. Otherwise, your children would be left out; as it is, they also are included in the spiritual purposes of God.

On the other hand, if the unbelieving spouse walks out, you've got to let him or her go. You don't have to hold on desperately. God has called us to make the best of it, as peacefully as we can. You never know, wife: The way you handle this might bring your husband not only back to you but to God. You never know, husband: The way you handle this might bring your wife not only back to you but to God."

(1 CORINTHIANS 7: 10-16 MSG)

CHAPTER 7

MAN IN THE MIRROR

Taking responsibility for your part when a marriage fails is the first step to resurrection.

Separating from my wife three times over the course of our 30 years together has given me plenty of opportunity to reflect on my own performance in the marriage. Something I learned with each separation is when I was the only occupant of our martial bed I could barely recall the disagreements, let alone have the same passion of my points of view as when she occupied the other side. What is it about us as humans that causes us to deflect or minimize our responsibility in a relationship?

Often, blaming becomes easy in a marriage because your partner is a ready-made escape goat. Our spouses are imperfect people and pointing out their faults is easy work for us (Philippians 3:12).

It also does not take much effort to act as if you and your spouse are sparring in a boxing ring. With each punch thrown, you feel yourself taking shots to the head, arms and across your jaw. Trying to keep from getting knocked out and knowing you cannot take much more, who would blame you for throwing a verbal punch that puts your spouse on his or her back? Is it your fault during all the years spent together you learned your spouse's most intimate thoughts, short comings and embarrassing moments? So you throw a punch below the belt, knowing it would be painful. Unfortunately, though, the last blow not only stopped the jabs but also knocked your spouse out of the ring. Each of us inherited a narcissistic attitude that puts the preservation of ourselves above the ones we love. According to scripture, you and I have our ancestors, Adam and Eve, to thank.

> *"Then the eyes of both of them were opened, and they realized*
> *they were naked: so they sewed fig leaves together and made*
> *coverings for themselves. Then the man and his wife heard the*
> *sound of the Lord God as he was walking in the garden in the*
> *cool of the day, and they hid from the Lord God among the trees*

of the garden. But the Lord God called to the man, "Where are you? He answered, "I heard you in the garden, and I was afraid because I was naked; so I hid?" And he said, "Who told you that you were naked? Have you eaten from the tree that I commanded you no to eat from?" The man said, "The woman you put here with me – she gave me some from fruit from the tree, and I ate it." Then the Lord God said to the woman, "What is this you have done?" The woman said, "The serpent deceived me, and I ate."

(GENESIS 3: 7-13 NIV)

Adam started by trying to deflect his responsibility for eating the forbidden fruit by blaming God for the woman. Then he indicted Eve as the real perpetrator because she gave him the fruit. Eve definitely didn't want to be the one holding the bag and felt it necessary to inform God she was deceived by the true culprit, the serpent. In the end, God rejects both of their excuses and makes them both culpable for their disobedience.

Lesson Learned #11 – There is no competition in marriage

In marriage there is no competition because there is always just one contestant. When you try to take advantage, you ultimately lose it yourself. On our wedding day, my wife and I began as individuals with different last names, histories and experiences but at the altar we exchanged all of that to become a whole new unit. My wife exchanged her last name for mine. We gave up our two separate living spaces and moved into a new residence called "our home." We wore rings to signify our union. From that moment forward, every single experience became part of our new collective. The Bible shows this coming together was an idea directly from God.

In the original creation, God made male and female to be together. Because of this, a man leaves father and mother, and in marriage he becomes one flesh with a woman – no longer two individuals, but forming a new unity. Because God created this organic union of the two sexes, no one should desecrate his art by cutting them apart. (Mark 10:6-8 MSG)

Every time my wife and I separated, I took stock of how I was conducting myself and found one common denominator—each time I had forgotten my wife and I were actually one unit and not two individual people. Regardless of the reasons behind each of the arguments which led to separation, at the heart of the matter was forgetting we had become one flesh.

In marriage, the concept of oneness should never mean he versus she to re-

solve a problem but rather he and she versus the problem. If the problem is the husband overspending on the credit cards, yelling and reprimanding the husband is a waste of time. Instead consider the two of you sitting down and discussing how the two of you can resolve the overspending together. If the topic is too difficult to handle together bring in a third party like a financial counselor who can provide practical insight on how to change the behavior in a way holds each of you accountable. Nothing is worse than trying to be the cop and the lover. It just doesn't work.

The responsibility for discipline in a marriage should always remain in God's hands. No matter what the wrong may be and even if the wrong was directed at you, turn the matter for evaluation and decision over to the Lord. As the Word states, the Lord desires to make your spouse into His image, and He will continue to do so until He calls your spouse home or comes backs for him or her as part of the gathering of the saints (Philippians 1:6 NIV).

Understanding the biblical concept of "being one flesh" also means there is no such thing as winning an argument. In marriage, the only way to accomplish this is to step away from being one flesh and act again as individuals. Becoming an individual means you and your spouse are no longer acting as one. Instead each of you individually wants to receive your own attention, affection, support, affirmation and anything you personally deem relevant to the world which revolves around you and your desires. In a word, you have become selfish.

> ## Lesson Learned #12 –
> ## To become selfish in marriage is
> ## to become a covenant breaker.

The word covenant is not used frequently today. Contract of agreement can be substituted. I am sure you are probably quite familiar with those words, since over the course of a lifetime we have all been asked to sign a number of different contracts from rental agreements to purchase agreements. Marriage is an agreement as well.

You and I made an agreement through our vows on our wedding day. We were so excited to spend the rest of our lives with our spouses we willingly gave a verbal agreement when we said "I do." Regardless of the specific words, when you entered into the institution of marriage as outlined in Mark chapter 10, you signed an agreement with God outlining how you would conduct yourselves in the marriage.

> ### Principle: # 8 –
> ### The man bears the responsibility as being the principle
> ### caretaker for the condition of the marriage
> ### (Mark 10:7 NIV).

From God's perspective, it is the man who becomes the initiator of the marriage transaction, though today women are just as empowered to ask a man for his hand. Despite how our societal norms have changed, God does not change. Because God sees the husband as the initiator, he has placed more responsibilities on the husband than on the wife. Those extended responsibilities include having the husband show love and leadership to his wife with the same measure and methods Christ uses to offer love, marked by giving, and leadership to the church (Ephesians 5: 23-28 MSG). Just in case the husband did not have good models while growing up, the Bible provides the standard for husbands to "love their wives as their own bodies." (Ephesians 5:28)

We label the behavior of individuals who have abused their own bodies as abnormal. Following this line of thinking, when a husband does not provide care to his wife they would treat themselves, it is as if he is abusing himself, which should be foreign behavior.

> ## Principle #9 –
> ## Our spouse has authority over our body
> ## (1 Corinthians 7:4 KJV).

As a husband, the authority over my physical body belongs to my wife and vice versa; and if there is something I desire or somewhere I want to take my body, I need to check with my spouse to make sure I have permission (1 Corinthians 7:4 KJV). Initially, I found this principle to be difficult to accept because I had been taught all my life I could choose to do anything and become anyone I wanted to be. The minute I went into covenant with my wife, it was not just about my life anymore. From that point on, I needed to take into account my spouse's needs, feelings and desires as I planned the activities which involved our bodies.

I learned in my marriage shared authority may start with our bodies, but the issue of authority starts to creep into other areas like time, roles, and of course, money. When the lines that govern issues of authority and responsibility start to get blurry, misunderstanding begins, and it will not be long arguments become the featured menu item for the day.

> ## Principle #10 –
> ## Forgiveness begins with you
> ## (Mark 5:23, Mark 11:25).

I was born in a family with five boys and three girls, making me baby number six. In our home, I was raised to believe if someone did wrong to another person then the person who caused the pain needed to go to the hurt individual to apologize and ask for forgiveness. What this behavior taught me was, from the moment the wrong was done until the time the perpetrator finally apologized, the person wronged could hold the transgression against the other. Otherwise there would be no wrong to forgive. That sounds okay when we are children and the parents make sure the offending child apologizes to their sibling the same day. Unfortunately, that practice does not lend itself well to every day adult life.

The Bible teaches us we are not to get offended, which means while we can and may want to get offended, we must choose not to allow offense to enter our hearts. (Proverbs 19:11) In fact, as I became an adult, I realized many adults do not apologize. When someone does something wrong or offensive, that person look for ways to move past it even if it means terminating any further engagement with the one who they offended.

For any one raised like I was, this left us being holders of a lot of wrongs never made right. These attitudes and behaviors can form a vicious cycle where we become not just the offended but also the offender by rationalizing if others are unwilling to make amends, there is no reason for us to go out of our way to forgive anyone. The problem is after a couple of rounds of this behavior in the marriage, it is not long before we become offended. If you picture each offense like adding a brick to a wall, soon the offended spouse has enough bricks to build a wall around his or her heart. The Bible offers a better way.

"And when you stand praying, forgive, if you have anything against any that your Father also which is I heaven may forgive you your trespasses."

(MARK 11:25 KJV)

Examining this scripture during one of our separations, I waited for my wife to pick up the telephone and apologize for all the various injustices she had done to me. As I realized this, I saw it was clear the need for initiating forgiveness was with me. I no longer had to wait on my spouse as God was looking for me to offer up to Him forgiveness on behalf of my spouse for each of the wrongs I felt she had done to me. As I started to consider this, I uncovered an amazing truth. The bricks I mentioned before were no longer a wall around my heart. The prayers of forgiveness removed my wall, making me free to feel love again.

Removal of the bricks causes some vulnerability, which makes it easier for God to work with you and through you. If you will let him, God will take away the hurts and bring healing to your wounded heart (Psalm 147:3). With God as my around-the-clock heart surgeon and nurse, I no longer have to be on guard to protect my heart from being hurt. With this support, I am free to take the next step, which is not to get offended at all. If I am empowered to give God my hurts and ask forgiveness for the offender, there is no reason for me to stay offended. If you re-read Mark 11:25, you will find there is a penalty for choosing not to forgive, which is God will not forgive you of your sins. Ouch!

I am sure as we went through this chapter together and you looked at yourselves in the mirror of God's Word, you probably saw a few areas where you contributed to the current state of your marriage. Just like you made deposits that brought deadness to your relationship, there are things I will discuss later that will help you bring new life to your marriage. First, it is time for you to take action with what you saw as you gazed at yourself in the mirror. Whom the Son sets free is free indeed and if you will take time to ask Him you shall receive your freedom today (John 8:36 KJV).

103

Scripture:

> *"Anyone who listens to the Word but does not do what it says is like someone who looks at his face in a mirror and, after looking at himself, goes away and immediately forgets what he looks like."*
>
> (JAMES 1:23-24 NIV)

CHAPTER 8

HOW MARRIAGE RESURRECTION WORKS

Part 1 – The Love Bridge

God will use you to build a bridge of love to bring your spouse home.

Let's review what you have learned so far as we examined God's work with married couples.

We discussed once a man and woman decide to marry and to do this in fellowship with God, he puts them on the road of marriage restoration to develop their marriage as he originally designed it to function at creation. During our study, we found out if the couple does not choose God's ways, decides to walk in self-preservation and denies the various redemptive works (life vests) God offered to them, the marriage will begin to fail. The failure the couple experiences will get them off the road to marriage restoration. Eventually the couple will face unexpected storms which will magnify the works of the flesh and the works of Satan, including unforgiveness, bitterness, strife, envy, adultery, hatred, and anger. Depending on the complexity, speed, intensity and duration of the storm, it could result in one or both considering termination of the relationship to gain some relief. However, if either of them rethinks the decision to separate or end the marriage, he or she will be able to take advantage of God's redemptive work in marriage reconcilation.

We also learned when a Christian couple arrives at the point one of the spouses seeks a divorce, this doesn't have to mean the end of the marriage. Instead, God made provision in another redemptive work in the form of a lifeboat. if one of the spouses decides to remain in fellowship with the marital covenant and intercede on behalf of the departed spouse, the Lord will work with that spouse to bring restoration. We called this life-boat marriage resurrection.

Chapter 8: HOW MARRIAGE RESURRECTION WORKS

In this chapter, you will learn how marriage resurrection works and your role in bringing this important redemptive work to completion. The goal of this chapter is to help you gain confidence and peace as you begin to believe your spouse will come home. Ask yourself the following three questions as you begin this work. Your answers will be vital.

☐ What will be required of me during this time?

☐ How long will it take before I see the results I am seeking?

☐ What will my spouse be doing while I'm believing God will restore our marriage?

When the Lord introduced the marriage resurrection concept to me, He did so by showing me two piers separated by a river. I introduced this to you in Chapter 5. Stairs lead down to a pier and an individual boat is tied there. There was no boat tied to the other pier. The Lord explained to me when my wife filed for divorce she could faintly see a city in the distance on the other side of the river and no longer wanted to be stuck on the road to nowhere with me. She climbed into the small boat and started off for a new life on the other side. Without a boat of my own, I was not able to follow her, and it was not long before she was out of communication range.

Soon she was out of sight as well. As time passed, it became clearer and clearer my wife's departure was not a bluff. She had not left just to get my attention. She wanted to get as far away from me as possible.

Alone and left without anything resembling our life together, I struggled with the idea of going forward with my life without her. The more her loss took hold inside of me, the more conviction gripped my heart. I became overwhelmed as I remembered all the chances to communicate that I had ignored. I saw how I let my love for her slip lower and lower on my list of priorities and how I failed at being the husband I knew I could be.

As I allowed the conviction to do whatever I needed to do to draw closer to the throne of God, I asked the Lord to forgive me and suddenly I was no longer alone at the end of the pier. Jesus, our Lord and King, had arrived to be by my side.

He asked me, "Would you like me to go to other side?" Instantly, I knew all he implied. In my heart, I knew He was asking if I wanted Him to get involved by going on the other side of the river and go after my wife. I had just repented and had no way of telling my wife of the heart change that had recently taken place and so I said, "Yes, Lord please."

His reply was unexpected. He said, "Then build me a love bridge."

Marriage resurrection involves building a bridge out of love so the Lord can walk across and redeem our loved one. The concept of the bridge illustration has been used extensively in evangelism to explain how a person can become a true

follower of Christ and receive the gift of eternal life (NavPress, 2016). The bridge illustrates through Jesus' death on the cross He became the bridge of lost man to be reconciled to God. It was the love God had for mankind and the love Jesus had in obedience to the Father that the price of redemption was paid on the cross.

> *"But God shows and clearly proves His [own] love for us by the*
> *fact that while we were still sinners, Christ (the Messiah, the*
> *Anointed One) died for us."*
>
> (ROMANS 5:8 AMP)

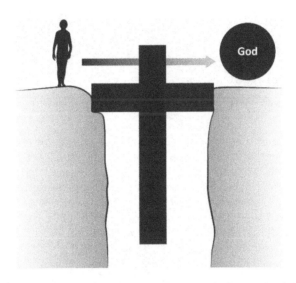

In this same manner, the Lord is asking us through the work of marriage resurrection to build a love bridge to reconcile our spouses back to God and to ourselves. Jesus has already paid the ultimate price to redeem each of us back to God. It is when we decide to walk in the flesh or sin, the Lord has left the work of restoring one who has already been redeemed and is not a believer who has gone astray. We have seen this before during our examination of Galatians 6:1:

> *"Brothers and sisters, if someone is caught in a sin, you who*
> *live by the Spirit should restore that person gently. But watch*
> *yourselves, or you also may be tempted."*
>
> (GALATIANS 6:1 AMP)

It is the very person your spouse has decided to leave behind God wants to use to build a bridge out of love will be the catalyst to redeem your spouse back to God and to you. It should not seem strange to us as believers because this is what God did for us. To redeem man back to Him, He sent Himself in the form of His Son. Now he is sending you to be the extension of his love to your spouse. The entire work you will do is to build this love bridge. Once it is built, Jesus will do the redemptive work. The bridge comprises eight different components that include:

Exterior Components	Interior Components
Parapet	Walkway
Joints	Fasteners
Labor	Foundation
Pillars	Blueprints
Handrails	

Without each of these components, the bridge could not exist. Each has its own special place in the formation of the bridge. We will separate the bridge components into two sections—exterior components and interior components. In your life, the difference between the two types are exterior components can be observed by anyone around you while interior components can only be seen by those who are connected with you via the Holy Spirit. While you are working on developing your external components, you may find those around you, especially Christians, will understand the actions you take in this area.

If your experience is anything like mine, those around you will initially see your decision to build this bridge of love as proof you are a good, brave Christian who is holding up the banner to walk as Christ would in a very difficult life situation. As you build your external components, there will be some who will walk with you because they believe it to be the right thing to do, and they will be proud of you for having the courage to believe God.

When you complete the external components and shift to the internal components you will find the work to be very lonely. Unless the people around you connect with you in the Spirit, they will not understand what you are doing because the work will be spiritual in nature.

Expect some will question your motives while others will think you have lost your control of your senses. As a result, the number of people you can rely on for support as you work on interior components will likely drop dramatically. In addition to experiencing a difference in the relationship with those around you, know also the answers you receive to the three vital questions we are exploring will be different when working on the exterior than those you will find when working on the interior components.

In the remainder of this chapter, we will examine the exterior components and pick up the interior components in the following chapter.

Exterior Components

Repentance – The Parapets of the Bridge

The parapets are the low protective walls at both ends of the bridge connecting the bridge to the pier or land (Merriam-Webster, Inc, 2016). In this work, they will be the first effort you undertake as they represent the work of repentance that occurs as you respond to conviction from the Holy Spirit. In the illustration discussed earlier in the chapter about my separation from my wife, it was not until I responded with repentance Christ joined me at the end of the pier. Once you allow conviction to change your mind about the decisions you have made thus far in your marriage, you can then embrace the love and forgiveness God has awaiting you.

> *"So repent (change your mind and purpose); turn around and return [to God], that your sins may be erased (blotted out, wiped clean), that times of refreshing (of recovering from the effects of heat, of reviving with fresh air) may come from the presence of the Lord."*
>
> (ACTS 3:19 AMP)

You would not be facing all that is happening to you and your spouse in your marriage if you had stayed on the road of marriage restoration by living according to God's ways of operating in your union. Though it is easy to look at your mate's faults, at this moment the Lord wants to have a conversation with you. Never once will He allow a conversation about your marriage to become validated with comments from you about your spouse's behavior. It is you he is having the conversation with, and it is you he has on His mind.

Take the time to let God soften your heart and recognize that his ways are always higher than our ways (Isaiah 55:8-9). When you allow repentance to come, you build the first component of the bridge. As the parapets take form, they will provide a wall of protection from condemnation, grief, anger and accusations that may be thrown your way as people react to the news your marriage has died. Let your first conversation be with God, and He will fortify you with His strength and surround you with His grace.

Intercession – The Labor of the Bridge

"And I sought a man among them who should build up the wall

and stand in the gap before Me for the land, that I should not
destroy it, but I found none."

(EZEKIEL 22:30 AM)

God is looking for you to be a person of prayer, willing to stand before Him and make petitions before his throne on behalf of your spouse. This is known as intercessory prayer, which is the act of praying on behalf of others.

Though God is infinite in power, is able and willing to bring to pass the promises of His word in our lives, he is looking for someone to bring him into remembrance of his Word in your situation (Isaiah 43:26, Ephesians 3:20, 2 Peter 3:9).

Without you interceding on behalf of your spouse, his or her case is being argued before the Lord. The Bible teaches us Satan is ever before the Lord accusing us (Revelations 12:10). God's mercy is long, and He desires to bring to past the desires of your heart, but you can't discount the desires of your spouse. God is obligated because of free will to accept your spouse's decision even if those decisions lead him or her away from God and expose him or her to destruction. When you pray and remind God of His word over your spouse, you give God something to work with.

You may feel uncomfortable or maybe you do not know where to begin. There are a number of books on the market today you can pick up at any Christian bookstore full of prayers. In fact, some of the books contain prayers specifically for the husband or the wife. Spending just 10 to 15 minutes a day, with diligence you can cover every issue concerning your spouse. If you will let the Spirit lead you, you will pray the necessary prayers for the hour.

I, too, was not sure how to begin this step while we were separated. Daily, as I sought the throne of God on my wife's behalf, I would take a moment or two to ask the Holy Spirit's guidance what I should pray for on that day. I had no earthly idea if my prayers were on target or even working, yet I continued to pray. One day the Holy Spirit would have me pray for her protection then the next day the focus was on her fears. The selection seemed arbitrary to me, but it turned out the selections were perfect for what she was experiencing each day.

When my wife and I reconciled she began telling me about the events in her life while we were apart. It really shocked me to learn how many times she came close to serious injury or even death. Yet in the middle of those situations, the prayers I daily laid before the Lord became the catalyst for His angels to give her protection. Over and over again as we compared her stories to the prayers I had been praying, it was clear to me the intercessory prayers that He had me pray had made a tremendous difference in her life.

Some would say my wife returning home and the cancellation of the divorce was a miracle. What I have found is it is God being faithful to His Word. The intercessory prayer in the marriage resurrection process is labor. Day in and day out you show up in your prayer closet to give God the spiritual matter, His word, to work with.

Recently, my wife and I built a new home. Each day I would drive by the land where our home was being built. There were days we drove up and neither the builder nor any of the contractors showed up. No labor was expended that day and as a result, we were no closer to our home becoming a reality. There were days we would show up and a bull dozer was digging out the space in the ground to lay a foundation. The next day a truck showed up and the concrete was poured for the foundation of the house. With each passing day, if there was progress on our home it was because the builder sent a contractor to the site with the explicit instructions to expend their time and energy laboring on our home.

The time in prayer you spend is the labor needed to fuel your marriage resurrection. Each day just listen to the Holy Spirit, and he will tell you the time needed to spend in prayer and what to pray. There were days I would spend only 10-15 minutes praying for my wife and then there were days I spent most of the day praying for her an hour here and an hour there. There may not be a set routine, but incline your ear to the Holy Spirit, and he will ensure your labor will not be in vain (1 Corinthians 15:58).

Pillars of the Bridge

Faith – The Pillar of the Bridge

"For God is not unjust so as to overlook your work and love that you have shown for his name in serving the saints, as you still do. And we desire each one of you to show the same earnestness to have the full assurance of hope until the end, so that you may not be sluggish, but imitators of those who through faith and patience inherit the promises."

(HEBREW 6:10-12 ESV)

Hebrews 11:1 gives us a definition of faith when it reads, "Now faith is the assurance of things hoped for, the conviction of things not seen." Do you believe the divorce is dead and your separation is over? Do you believe your spouse will come home? Do you believe your marriage will live again and be stronger than it ever was? If you cannot empathically say a resounding, "Yes" to all of these questions, then you seriously need to consider your beliefs may be based on hope and not on faith.

We discussed the difference between hope and faith in an earlier chapter. Hope is to have a positive attitude about an expected outcome will be subject to the results of reality. You can hope for a certain outcome until the cows come home, as they say, but hope will not make what you desire a reality.

Hope is a component of faith, but faith goes beyond hope. Faith can bring what is hoped for into existence because of God's Word. Faith can change facts and make them come into alignment of the truth of God's Word. In the context of your marriage resurrection, you must set your heart to believe God's word. You have to believe when the Bible tells you in Galatians 6:1 to "restore such a one in a spirit of gentleness," if you indeed set your heart to restore a brother or sister in the Lord and to walk in the spirit of gentleness, then restoration is a real possibility despite what the circumstances suggest. At the end of the day, your spouse is still your brother and sister in the Lord, and as we have already pointed out, because they are being deceived by Satan, they will need to be restored back into the fellowship with God. This cannot happen if you do not believe it.

Walking by faith means you set your heart to bringing God's word to pass in your life. First, you must choose to believe God and when doubt comes to tell you something other than what God has said, it will have to be an act of your personal will to firmly stay connected to the belief you have hidden in your heart (Psalms 119:11).

Through each chapter in this book, we have gone through great effort to provide scriptures to support each of the concepts presented about marriage resurrection and the characteristics of a believer walking by the Spirit of God. Look up the scriptures on your own. Take time to study them and read them to yourself out loud. When you read them aloud, the Bible teaches us that faith comes. More directly in Romans 10:17 it reads that, "So faith comes from hearing, and hearing through the word of Christ."

Even if you are struggling to believe through God your spouse will come home or the divorce is dead, you do not have to stay there. You can drive out lack of belief and fear by taking these verses from the Word of God and repeating them over and over to yourself aloud. As you hear the Word coming out of your mouth, the Bible says the faith in heart will increase.

Faith is a pillar of the bridge. The bridge cannot be finished if you do not believe God will do the work and resurrect your dead marriage when you build Him a bridge of love. Without this bridge, your spouse may never return, and your marriage will be terminated by the finalization of the divorce case. You can stop all of that by believing God. Putting your faith in God adds a critical component on the bridge. A bridge would collapse if the pillars were weakened or removed. Your bridge requires two pillars with the first being faith. You must allow faith to grow in your heart and you stand on the Word of God to believe those things He has said will come to past.

Patience – The Stabilizing Pillar of the Bridge

Patience is one of those Christian attributes which causes many to grunt or frown in disapproval when they are asked to be patient, not realizing by their stance they are failing to make the exact change in their behavior is necessary.

The dictionary defines patience as having the habit or capacity to remain calm and not be annoyed when waiting for a long time or when dealing with a problem or difficult people (Merriam-Webster, Inc., 2016). This reminds me of a time I was a teenager and I had a conversation about patience with my mother. I told her I was going to ask God to make me patient and her response was, "Oh no, you do not want to pray for patience because you will definitely get that prayer answered with something you are going to have to wait a long time for."

As I have gotten older and spent time in the Word, I have learned a lot about patience, and my conclusion is many Christians don't understand it. Going beyond the dictionary definition, let us explore some key attributes about patience and how to get it.

Patience is a fruit of the Holy Spirit (Galatians 5:22)

> "But the fruit of the Spirit is love, joy, peace, patience, kindness, goodness, faithfulness, gentleness, self-control, against such things there is no law and those who belong to Christ Jesus have crucified the flesh with its passions and desires."
>
> (GALATIANS 5:22-23 ESV)

If Jesus Christ is your Savior and Lord, then His Spirit is inside you. With the new birth and the entrance of the Holy Spirit into your life, he brings with him 12 fruits or virtues that reside inside you.

Patience is one of those virtues. You do not need to ask God for it because you already have it. You just need to believe you have been given patience and start developing fruit inside of you. An apple is nutritious and good for your body, but it will bring you no added energy if it is never eaten. In fact, if the apple is never eaten, it will eventually become rotten.

Patience is a fruit from the Holy Spirit sitting inside of you just waiting for you to begin exercising it. Like a muscle, every time you pick up a weight that produces sufficient resistance for the muscle, strength comes. The more weight, the greater the resistance and the greater the strength. Patience operates in the same way.

The opposite of patience is impatience, which means an unwillingness to wait. Looking at Galatians 5:22-23 again, it is clear if patience is a fruit of the Spirit, then impatience is a work of the flesh. While it is natural to be impatient, once you accepted Jesus Christ you should work on developing the fruit of patience. Every time a situation arises in your life and you decide to respond by not being willing to wait, you have signaled to God, yourself and even the world of darkness that you are more interested in continuing to develop the works of your flesh than to develop the fruit of the Spirit.

Every one of us as a child of God has been given this fruit. No one was anyone given this fruit in greater measure than anyone else. Instead, we all received the same fruit, because there is one Holy Spirit and he is does not favor one person over another. Some may be walking in greater measure of the fruit because that person decided to accept the fruit and exercise it. We cannot be upset with or discouraged by another person because he has worked his body and muscles to the point he looks like Mr. Universe. He has spent countless hours in the gym exercising, crafting his body with the proper weights and consuming a diet so he would the results he was looking for. It is the same with us in the Spirit. Just like the bodybuilder gives me comfort achieving that type of body is possible, recognizing someone walking in a greater measure of patience is an indicator it can be done.

The Bible tells us to "be patient" in Ephesians 4:2 NIV. You must decide you are going to be patient every time you have an opportunity to wait for a long time, deal with a problem or face a difficult person. Life will present you with plenty of opportunities to be patient. Every time you feel impatience rising, just remember you have patience inside of you and continue your resolve to respond with patience. When you do this, the Holy Spirit is required to aid you in response. The more you exercise being patient, the greater measure of patience you will walk in.

Patience – A Chosen Response

Now you have chosen to respond with patience instead of impatience, it is important to identify the times God wants you to respond in this manner.

☐ **When You're Afflicted -** *Be joyful in hope, patient in affliction, faithful in prayer (Romans 12:12 NIV).*

☐ **When You're Feeling Like You're Falling Behind –** *Be still before the Lord and wait patiently for him; do not fret when people succeed in their ways, when they carry out their wicked schemes (Psalm 37:7 NIV).*

☐ **When You Need an Answer from God –** *Wait for the Lord; be strong and take heart and wait for the Lord (Psalm 27:14 NIV).*

☐ **When You're Believing for a Promise to Manifest –** *The Lord is not slow in keeping his promise, as some understand slowness. Instead he is patient with you, no wanting anyone to perish, but everyone to come to repentance (2 Peter 3:9 NIV).*

☐ **When You Pray -** In *the morning, Lord you hear my voice; in the morning I lay my requests before you and wait expectantly (Psalm 5:*3 NIV).

☐ **When Love is Required –** *Be completely humble and gentle; be patient, bearing with one another in love (Ephesians 4:2 NIV).*

☐ **When Doing Good –** *Let us not become weary in doing good, for at proper time we will reap if we do not give up (Galatians 6:9 NIV).*

When Mercy is Needed – *But for that very reason I was shown mercy so that in me, the worst of sinners, Christ Jesus might display his immense patience as an example for those who believe in him and receive eternal life (1 Timothy 1: 16 NIV).*

When Justice is Needed – *Yet the Lord longs to be gracious to you; therefore, he will rise up to show you compassion. For the Lord is a God of justice. Blessed are all who wait for him (Isaiah 30:18 NIV)!*

When You Have Hope – *But if we hope for what we do not yet have, we wait for it patiently (Romans 8:25 NIV).*

When You Need God to Fight for You – *The Lord will fight for you; you need only be to still (Exodus 14:14 NIV).*

While this is not by any means an exhaustive list of when we will be required to walk in patience, it does cover several situations we are all bound to face. We just need to realize patience is a chosen response, and it will be up to us to recognize to be led by the Spirit of God, the patience will come from us.

It is incredibly important as part of your marriage resurrection to walk in patience. In answering the question, how long will this take? However long it takes.

Gloria Copeland has reported Kenneth Hagins said, "If you are determined to stand forever, it won't take very long" (Pearsons & Copeland, 2013). You will need to make raising your dead marriage one of your highest priorities—one you are willing to go as many rounds as it will take to get you the victory.

There are many issues God will have to address to bring to pass your marriage resurrection. God will need to get you to position yourself and get your spouse to release their hardened heart. Both take time, and you need to be patient.

I can attest it didn't take forever for me to experience my marriage resurrection when my wife filed for divorce. It took 104 days or three months and 12 days from the day she moved out until she had change of heart as a result of the Lord's intervention.

At the time, I had no idea how long I was going to be standing and so as the Hagin quote goes, I was prepared to stand forever. Trust me when I say it felt like a lifetime during those 104 days, and there were many days I felt like quitting. Instead of quitting, I made a fresh decision every day I would walk in patience. You can do it, too.

Will yours take 104 days? I had two separations from my wife and each lasted about 30 days. With the final separation going well beyond the 30-day mark, I knew it was going to be a test of my endurance. My point is you will not necessarily have to wait 104 days. Yours could be shorter. Yours could be longer. Regardless of the number of days it takes for your miracle of marriage resurrection to manifest, set your heart right now to patiently endure, and the Word says you will receive the promise (Hebrews 6:15).

Fellowship with Other Believers – The Joints of the Bridge

"From him the whole body, joined and held together by every supporting ligament, grows and builds itself up in love, as each part does it work."

(EPHESIANS 4:16 NIV)

There is absolutely no way I could have been successful in my marriage resurrection if I had to walk alone. At first, I was alone until my two adult daughters decided to do something most adult children do not do when their parents are in the midst of a divorce. They encouraged my wife and I to act like Christians throughout the entire process. There was a time very early in the separation when my daughters became disheartened with the actions of their mother and the pain that ensued from those actions. They decided to become like Samaritans, caring for the injured man on the road. In their care, we began to fellowship, not as father and daughters but instead as brother and sisters in Christ. We would encourage each other in the Word, uphold each other and their mother in prayer and go to church together.

They were not the only ones. Our pastor and my mother became integral members of my fellowship band to help me to stay strong in the Lord. To be successful in your marriage resurrection effort, you will need to lean on brothers and sisters in Christ. Your flesh probably will want to do this, but you need to be in fellowship with other believers. There are five blessings fellowshipping with other believers will bring to your life. The enemy is trying to keep you from gaining these gifts:

1. **Encouragement** – Therefore encourage one another and build each other up, just as in fact you are doing (1 Thessalonians 5:11 NIV).

2. **Toiling Together** – Two are better than one, because they have a good reward for their toil. For if they fall, one will lift up his fellow. But woe to him who is alone when he falls and has not another to lift him up! Again, if two lie together, they keep warm, but how can one keep warm alone? And though a man might prevail against one who is alone, two will withstand him – a threefold cord is not quickly broken (Ecclesiastes 4:9-12 ESV).

3. **Getting Sharpened** – Iron sharpens iron, and one man sharpens another (Proverbs 27:17 ESV).

4. **Getting Stirred Up** – And let us consider how to stir up one another to love and good works, not neglecting to meet together, as is the habit of

some, but encouraging one another, and all the more as you see the Day drawing near (Hebrews 10:24 and 25 ESV).

5. **Being in the Presence of the Lord** - For where two or three are gathered in my name there am I among them (Matthew 18:20 ESV).

Fellowshipping with other believers is not the same as hanging out with friends and family. You might have a large group of people you identify as friends, and you may have a large family. Neither of these constitutes what we are discussing here. Your heavenly relationships are higher relationships because they are eternal and established by the blood of Jesus. Your earthly relationships are founded by a commonness such as bloodlines, neighborhoods, schools and other earthly elements that will cease at death. To limit yourself to your earthbound relationships will hamper your marriage resurrection effort unless these individuals are willing to respond to you based on their relationship with Jesus. Being earth bound is the same as walking by your flesh because that is what will be the basis of their opinions, feelings and decisions. You need to limit these. When you create fellowship with other believers, especially those of like precious faith, you should be able to access God's mercy and grace extended through them.

If you never took the time to cultivate relationships with other believers, now is the time to begin. It may be difficult because you are hurting as a result of your marriage, but it is not impossible. Be brave and share with others how you are hurting. Let them know you are looking for other believers to undergird you.

The Bible says a man who has friends must show himself friendly (Proverbs 18:24). The best way to make a friend is by making yourself available to be someone else. While your marriage may be your area of struggle, it may be a strength for someone else. Be willing to open up and let them share with you what they have learned while you share with them what God has shown you. In doing so, you will have earned yourself a brother or sister in the Lord.

Love – The Handrails of the Bridge

Throughout this book we have been talking about how critical love is to the marriage resurrection effort. Love has a special work, and it is the bridge's handrails. A handrail is a narrow bar placed on the side of the walkway for grasping with the hand as support (Merriam-Webster, Inc., 2016).

> *"So do not fear, for I am with you; do not be dismayed, for I am*
> *your God. I will strengthen you and help you; I will uphold you*
> *with my righteous right hand."*
>
> (ISAIAH 41:10 NIV)

We discussed earlier faith is the opposite of fear and vice versa. You have to remember while you have decided to believe God and through a marriage res-urrection are expecting God to bring your spouse home, your spouse is being deceived by the devil.

The devil has no intention of watching you build this beautiful love bridge only to see Jesus walk across it with the purpose of redeeming your spouse. The dev-il's goal has always been to destroy your marriage and make you and your spouse ill witnesses for Christ. He is not going to give up without a fight.

The obstacle he intends to put in your way is fear. If the bridge is completed and your spouse begins to journey across it back to you, the devil intends to bring fear to your spouse's heart so he or she will not finish the journey across the love bridge. This is why the handrails must be made of love.

Your spouse will not have seen you labor through each of the components of the bridge. Your spouse won't know that you have forgiven them. Your spouse will not know you are walking in patience and gentleness. The last interaction with you may not have been comforting from their perspective. The handrails have a great importance because they will be made out perfect love.

> *"There is no fear in love. But perfect love drives out fear, be-cause fear has to do with punishment. The one who fears is not made perfect in love."*
>
> (1 JOHN 4:18 NIV)

As your spouse begins to journey across the love bridge, the devil will be telling him or her the entire time nothing has changed with you and once you learn about all he or she did while you were separated, you are going to retal-iate. When you allow love to get perfected, which is a specialized and higher level of love, you offer your love unconditionally. No matter how your spouse returns, you know your love and the love of Christ is more than enough to cover the situation.

You have to have an "I don't care" attitude when it comes to learning about the things your spouse may have done and be willing to cast those cares on the Lord (1 Peter 5:7). If you can achieve perfected love when your spouse starts journey home from his or her days of deception and separation, he or she will make it home.

Imagine, if you will, that while your spouse is crossing the bridge he or she is bombarded by accusations from the devil. With each accusation, however, pic-ture Jesus saying to your spouse, "That is not true, look they made this handrail for you so you would not slip and fall off the bridge." Without the handrail of perfected love, your spouse may only see the raging river of life-related issues as he or she crosses the bridge. That alone is enough to re-grip your spouse's heart with the same fear that caused him or her to cross the river originally. Having your handrails of perfected love gives your husband or wife the assurance of pro-tection and love. No message will have any greater importance to your spouse

at that moment than the silent message of perfected love you have signaled to them with your handrails.

When my wife and I reconciled we met up at a hospital. The police brought her there after her encounter in a hotel room with the Lord. From the very moment we saw each other, I knew how extremely important it was to walk in perfected love. She spent hours in the hospital and for about the first six or eight hours of her stay, I was not allowed to see her or visit with her. The police notified her divorce attorney of her hospitalization, and when the attorney arrived, she barred me and my daughters from visiting her.

When the attorney left, she told the nurses and other hospital staff not to let us visit. During the hours of waiting in the lobby, walking outside or being on the telephone informing her family of her hospitalization, I could have been offended. I knew if I did, whatever God was doing would cease.

As a result of not allowing offense to come, God worked it out when the nurses and doctors changed shift, the new group did not get the divorce attorney's instructions. The first group of nurses did not tell my wife my daughters and I were waiting in the lobby but the new group of nurses informed her.

My wife then gave them permission to allow us to see her. Even with us finally connecting after spending months apart, I had to really emphasize there would no judgment from me on what happened during the separation. I showered her with love and a gentle spirit. I recognized during our meeting in the emergency room she was still on that bridge.

That evening my wife was transferred to a psychiatric hospital nearly 100 miles away where she spent 17 days. Every day I traveled 200 miles' roundtrip to spend one-and-a half hours with her during visiting hours. During that time, the Lord specifically told me how to minister to her every day. Whether it was a song, a card, scripture, a meal, clothing or just a smile, I made sure my focus was love and encouragement. My wife had to battle major fear, and it took her three weeks to cross the length of that love bridge. Because God showed me how to walk in perfect love, she was able to make it to the other side.

Her journey across that bridge was no piece of cake, and the enemy pulled many tricks during her hospital stay. It was clear to see it was spiritual warfare and with each attack from the enemy, more and more fear gripped my wife's heart. Just as 1 John 4:18 states perfect love casts out fear, this is what happened in our situation. Ultimately, God brought us an attorney whom God used mightily to get my wife released from the hospital.

ANSWERS TO THE VITAL QUESTIONS

Now you have had the opportunity to learn about the love bridge and examine the components of the bridge, it is time to answer the three questions in reference to the exterior components.

- ❦ What will be required of me during this time?

    You will be required to build a bridge of love for Jesus Christ to cross over and redeem your spouse from the enemy's camp. Your love bridge will be made of both exterior and interior components. Of the exterior components, you will be required to build pillars of faith and patience, parapets of repentance, join fellowship with other believers and handrails of perfected love all from labor consisting of intercessory prayer.

- ❦ How long will it take before I see the results I am expecting?

    You may not see any positive results until your miracle manifests. You must be prepared to stand in patience for forever and as a result you won't be standing very long.

- ❦ What will my spouse be doing while I am believing God for restoration of our marriage?

    Staying separated from you and possibly proceeding with the divorce. All of this may continue while the Lord does his work. It will seem like nothing has changed in your spouse until the day of the Lord's visitation. That will probably be the first time you see your spouse begins the journey of crossing over that bridge of love you made. Remember the journey across that bridge could last a single day or multiple days. Be prepared to continue walking in love as your spouse makes their way home.

In the next chapter, we will examine the interior components of the love bridge and help you move your bridge towards completion. Today, begin the work of building the exterior components. You cannot begin work on the interior components until all of the exterior components are underway. There will come a time when you will work on both exterior components and interior components simultaneously, and as a result, while you are working on one component it will accelerate your progress on another component.

Scripture:

"But love your enemies and be kind and do good [doing favors so that someone derives benefit from them] and lend, expecting and hoping for nothing in return but considering nothing as lost and despairing of no one; and then your recompense (your reward) will be great (rich, strong, intense and abundant), and you will be sons of the Most High, for He is kind and charitable and good to the ungrateful and the selfish and wicked."

(LUKE 6:35 AMP)

CHAPTER 9

HOW MARRIAGE RESURRECTION WORKS

Part 2 – The Love Bridge

God will use you to build a bridge of love to bring your spouse home again.

There is no greater work a believer can do for another human than to help that person come into or return to a relationship with Jesus Christ. The Bible tells us when one sinner repents there is great joy in the presence of God's angels (Luke 15:10). It is a great feeling to know we had something to do a brother or sister repenting from sin and coming back to the Lord. Seeing conversion strengthens our faith and brings delight to our hearts knowing God used us to bring another soul into His kingdom.

Imagine how many times these feelings are magnified when the sinner coming home is your husband or wife. This is what is you have before you as you build this bridge out of love to bring your spouse home.

Do not forget, though, as we discussed in the previous chapter, the enemy will not stand by and watch you build this bridge without some form of retaliation. Satan and his forces will most definitely respond, but you do not need to be concerned about being outmatched or outflanked. Jesus told us in Luke 10:19 He has given us authority to overcome all the enemy's power. If you hold to this promise, you will find the enemy is no real match for you.

Being outmatched, however, has never stopped the devil from attacking. We see several instances in the Bible when Jesus was subject to Satan's attacks. Beginning in Luke 4:28, it says all the people in the synagogue were so furious they got up, drove Jesus out of town and took him to the brow of the hill on which the town was built to throw him off the cliff. In verse 30, we see the promise of Luke 10:19 come to pass as it says, "But he walked right through the crowd and went on his way."

Hallelujah! This is the promise God has provided for each of us who undertake any work on His behalf. You must be ready and prepared to go through the devil's attacks just as Jesus went through that crowd.

Interior Components

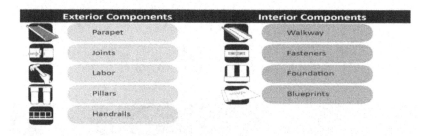

Looking at the interior components of the love bridge you must be ready to undergo an increased and more intense set of battles with the enemy.

You must keep three things in mind at all times:

1) You have been given the power to overcome all the works of the enemy (Luke 10:19).

2) God has already given you the victory through Jesus Christ (1 Corinthians 15:57).

3) You have been chosen as the one to bring God's deliverance to your spouse (John 17:18).

No matter how outmatched you may feel, your role of standing in the gap on behalf of your spouse is the critical component God needs to deliver your spouse. Without you, God may not have another opportunity to deliver your spouse for many years to come.

When I realized this during the middle of my divorce, it transformed my thinking from trying to reunite with my wife to helping a sister in the Lord from falling prey to the enemy's attacks.

As you investigate with faith to add these interior components to your love bridge, know you are signaling to the enemy you mean business. These interior components are aggressive weapons in the Spirit, which will take you into the enemy's territory. In His Word, 2 Corinthians 10: 3-5 says, "For though we walk in the flesh, we do not war according to the flesh. For the weapons of our warfare are not carnal but mighty in God for pulling down strongholds, casting down arguments and every high thing that exalts itself against the knowledge of God, bringing every thought into captivity to the obedience of Christ (NKJV) ."

As you enter enemy territory, you must realize the fight will be intense as you uncover the enemy's land mines, embankments, ambushes and sniper positions. In this chapter, we are going to discover God's weapons, and we will review how the interior components address the three vital questions we saw in Chapter 6.

Once again, the three vital questions are:

- ❦ What will be required of me during this time?

- ❦ How long will it take before I see the results I'm seeking?

- ❦ What will my spouse be doing while I am believing God for restoration of our marriage?

Let us begin by examining what makes the interior components unique. As we learned in the previous chapter, the interior components have three unique characteristics. First, the work of the components cannot be observed by the human eye. Second, others will have to be spiritual and seeking the Spirit's leading to properly understand your character and behavior. Third, you may be ridiculed and others may discourage you as they question your motives and actions when you display Christ's character.

The way these components work will intensify the enemy's attacks. You must realize that many individuals, including Christians, live by what they see with their natural eye and understand with their human intellect and reasoning. As long as someone is able to wrap his or her mind around what you are saying and doing they will be okay with you. However, when you start operating in the Spirit, unless others also live by faith, they will not be able to understand what you are doing as you put enter this part of building the love bridge.

The Bible says it this way:

> *"The person without the Spirit does not accept the things that come from the Spirit of God but considers them foolishness, and cannot understand them because they are discerned only through the Spirit."*
>
> (1 CORINTHIANS 2:14 NIV)

It is important to remember the ridicule, discouragement and opposition you face will not be because anyone has a problem with you but rather because he or she is unable to perceive the work the components are doing in the Spirit. If they are not walking in the Spirit to discern His work, your actions will seem foolish. Do not be surprised or alarmed by this. Having this understanding will help you realize you are not fighting with the individuals but against the ignorance which brought spiritual blindness to them from Satan (2 Corinthians 4:3-4). Your task will be to pray for their spiritual eyes to be opened without taking your attention off of building the love bridge. You will need to be like Nehemiah and not let distractions, opposition, and ridicule take away from the task God has for you (Nehemiah 3, 4).

The purpose of the enemy's attacks is to distract you from building the love bridge by impeding the progress or by frustrating you to the point that you give up. Either is a win for the enemy. If he can distract you, then he knows he can slow you down. Slowing the construction of the love bridge can mean its work will not be done before the devil completes his work of completely destroying your marriage.

It is a race against time, and the enemy is acutely aware of this fact. He knows that even the smallest delay causing you to give into one his distractions will benefit his evil and destructive work. Time turned against you the moment your spouse separated from you whether or not divorce has been filed. The longer you and your spouse stay separated, the easier it will become to justify divorce.

In section one, we discussed the statistic that 87 percent of married couples who go through a marital separation ultimately divorce (Marriage in America, 2016). That is why you can't afford to allow the enemy's attack to cause you to get distracted for even one day.   Beyond distraction is just all out quitting, which is the devil's ultimate goal. If he can cause you to get distracted once, he will continue to try to distract you in the hope the distractions will pile up on you to the point that you become discouraged. He knows that you will lose heart and ultimately quit if you feel enough despair. Galatians 6:9 tells us we will receive the promise if we do not lose heart. You must see the devil's attacks for what they really are—attempts to make you quit. With this knowledge, you can counter them with benefits from using the interior components, and soon God's promise will be yours.

Now that you understand what you are up against, let's look at the interior components, which are forgiveness (walkway), obedience (fasteners), spiritual warfare (foundation) and praise (blue prints). Before we dive into each of these individual parts, there are few additional things you need to know.

Lesson Learned #13 -
There is no specific order
to enact the interior parts.

You will need to be led by the Spirit of God every day to understand when and how to operate with each of these parts. The operation of forgiveness, obedience, spiritual warfare and praise can work independently or in tandem with

another component. For example, you might be giving God praise in faith for the victory you expect and in another situation, you may need to add obedience to allow forgiveness to really take root in your heart.

If the hurt done against you is committed by someone close to you, it may be more difficult to have forgiveness than if it was done by a total stranger. This is when you may find yourself making a commitment to walk in obedience to the Lord so you are able to forgive. If you begin to forgive and find your flesh remembering the hurts you spouse did, take to a moment to give God praise for putting your flesh secondary to your decision to walk in forgiveness.

Lesson Learned #14 – You must walk in each of these interior components every day.

You must walk in most of the bridge components every day. You must have the fruit of the Spirit operating in your life daily. Fellowship with other believers, intercessory prayer or repentance are not characteristics one would normally experience every day of their walk with Christ. That is why this lesson is mentioned to you with the interior components instead of the exterior components. Don't be surprised some days you will be really focused on operating in all four and on other days the time spent in operation with these will be limited. Only the Holy Spirit can properly lead you when it comes to how and when to operate in these each day.

Forgiveness – The Walkway of the Bridge

"Bear with each other and forgive one another if any of you has

a grievance against someone. Forgive as the Lord forgave you."
(COLOSSIANS 3:13 NIV)

Forgiving others is absolutely critical in your walk with the Lord. Building the love bridge, cannot be done without it. Forgiveness is the walkway of the bridge. Without the walkway, there will be nothing for Jesus to walk across when he arrives to redeem your spouse from the enemy. It is absolutely critical you start forgiving your spouse immediately for any and all things the Holy Spirit brings to your attention. This could take some time to complete because there may be things in your heart you have completely forgotten. Only the Holy Spirit knows what you have on the shelf of your heart and only when you turn your ear to Him will you regain knowledge of those unforgiven hurts that reside within you. You need to take them before the Lord in prayer and forgive your spouse for whatever he or she did. In addition, it may not be the things done in the immediate past alone that led to the separation. It may be things done many years ago. The Holy Spirit will share those things with you. Harboring those hurts in your heart instead of releasing them through forgiveness is the very definition of unforgiveness. Walking in unforgiveness impacts your life in two ways: your prayers will be hindered and your sins will not be forgiven.

> *"Therefore, I tell you, whatever you ask for in prayer, believe that you have received it, and it will be yours. And when you stand praying, if you hold anything against anyone, forgive them, so that your Father in heaven may forgive you your sins."*
>
> (MARK 11:24, 25 NIV)

These are words from Jesus himself and in this verse He gives us two warnings about unforgiveness. To receive answers to our prayers, when we pray we must: 1) believe we have received it and 2) forgive others.

We could choose to believe until we are blue in the face, but if we choose not to forgive, our prayer cannot be answered. That is how our prayer gets hindered; it gets put on hold waiting for us to remove the unforgiveness.

This reminds me of a situation in my personal life when my wife and I were awaiting a very sizable refund check from our tax return one year. The government owed us a very large income tax refund. It was large enough to pay off some debts, put a down payment on a new car, cover one of our children's college tuition bill and put aside money for our annual vacation.

You can imagine from the day I learned refund was coming, I anticipated its arrival. A week or so after the Internal Revenue Service (IRS) electronically accepted our filing I received an email stating there was information missing from my return. My refund was placed on hold awaiting my response. Until I responded to the correspondence I had received and the information met the IRS requirements, my refund would remain on hold. That meant for as long as the hold remained in effect, we had to live with the debts that would have been paid off, we would not be able to buy a new car, the tuition bill would still be due and there would be no family vacation that year.

I am sure you can imagine I was sufficiently motivated to provide the IRS the information they wanted right away. In fact, I do not believe a whole day transpired from the time I received that email to when I sent the information to the IRS. I was extremely motivated to get the refund and as soon as I got the email, I cleared commitments off my calendar and locked myself into my home office until I had prepared everything the IRS wanted. I did not let my wife, kids, television, phone calls or other emails distract me from completing the response as quickly as I could.

Imagine if I had never received that email. Days, weeks, months or even years could have transpired without receiving my refund. Whose fault would it have been? Of course, it would have been my fault. It was my tax return. and it was my responsibility for its timely submission and contents even if the email went into my spam or trash folder.

However, if I believed the IRS does not actually pay out every refund they accept or if I did not want the refund, I never would have checked on my refund because I did not trust they would pay. Either way I would have deprived myself of my refund. All along the refund was mine, the IRS expected to pay it, yet I did not have it. Why? Because I effectively walked away from it and the benefits the refund would have brought my family.

This is what happens when our prayers are hindered. It may be because we choose not to forgive our spouses or someone else over some transgression, and as a result we live without what we have asked of God. The responsibility of prayer is still ours. God expects to answer it with exactly what we expect to receive from Him. However, a prayer may be put on hold because of unforgiveness. God is not at fault if we fail to check with the Holy Spirit to see what may have hindered our prayers. Unfortunately, too many believers walk away believing the reason they do not receive an answer to their prayer is because they were in some way unworthy of receiving blessing. All along the prayer was on hold, waiting for them to forgive.

When you do not forgive others, then God will not forgive your sins. Now, you may be saying, "I do not need forgiveness because I do not sin." That is a very dangerous position you have taken because the Word of God is against you.

> *"If we claim to be without sin, we deceive ourselves and the truth is not in us. If we confess our sins, he is faithful and just and will forgive us our sins and purify us from all unrighteousness. If we claim we have not sinned, we make him out to be a liar and his word is not in us."*
>
> (JOHN 1:8 – 10 NIV)

When you think you cannot forgive someone of their sin, you are telling God you do not want or need your sins forgiven. Neither are true. You can release others from their sins and God will release you from yours.

The love bridge cannot be built without forgiveness, and I know I may have made it sound easier than I know it can be. It will take active submission to allow forgiveness to come to your heart. In this marital separation or even divorce, I am sure you have a laundry list of wrongs your spouse has done to you. To walk with the Lord in this marriage resurrection, you are going to have to turn the hurts over to the Lord and ask the Lord to forgive your spouse for all the wrongs done.

Learn to walk in forgiveness daily. As you go through this marriage resurrection and get to the other side, you have no idea what state you will find your spouse in when they come home. Training yourself to walk in forgiveness while your spouse is not in your presence is going to go a long way when you must do this when your spouse returns home. Forgiving only gets harder when your spouse is in your presence. Practicing while your spouse is gone will help you train your mind, body and spirit to respond with forgiveness consistently.

The next thing you need to know is once you have begun to walk in forgiveness, you must hold this stance no matter what new information you learn or how the situation changes. In this respect, you need to be like God and not keep an active log of our sins after we confess them. In fact, the Word teaches us once we confess our sins, He blots them out (Acts 3:19) and promises to remember them no longer (Hebrews 10:17). This is vital because when your spouse returns home, you may find some of the decisions he or she made while the two of you were separated will take time to heal. You will need to remember in those times you have forgiven them and you walk in forgiveness daily.

Throughout the chapters I have given some glimpses into the state of my life after our marriage resurrection was completed and my wife returned home. During our separation and divorce proceedings, my wife betrayed my confidence, destroyed my reputation, took away my livelihood, brought division between my son and me, killed a dream of mine, erased my earthly wealth, and generated mountains of new debt for herself and her former boyfriend.

Some of you may be reading this list and either think I am lying or doubting your ability to forgive under these circumstances. I do not blame you for feeling that way, because there are days when I find it hard to bare under this weight with love, forgiveness, and patience. Yet I do each day—not because of the love I have for my wife but rather for the love I have for Christ. I know Christ paid this price and more for me. Recalling this truth daily helps me get through those days when I feel like I cannot walk in forgiveness any longer.

You are stronger than you think. Inside of you is the Holy Spirit, and He comes bearing an endless supply of His fruit. Each day your task will be to choose to walk in forgiveness. Because there is no limit to His love, joy, peace, forbearance, kindness, goodness, faithfulness, gentleness or self-control, you have an abundant supply to properly maintain forgiveness.

As I write this chapter, I take comfort in knowing I can tell you with confidence you can bear under these weights because I am bearing under these weights. God is doing it for me, and He will definitely do it for you. In fact, I believe my situation is as messy as it is so I can testify to you to the goodness of the Lord. God gave me this message about marriage resurrection and the responsibility of sharing it with the Body of Christ.

While I am sure circumstances of our situation could be worse, the point is not how bad things could be; the heart of the matter is God is able and willing to heal your broken relationship. So, whether you are reading this book and it has been brought to your attention your separated spouse is having an affair or the divorce has caused your son or daughter to stop speaking to you, take heart and know God is faithful by learning from our testimony. My wife and I faced these things and more, yet we are here to tell you God is faithful.

It has been almost a year since I received a paycheck, yet all of my bills are paid. My son and I have started the process of reconciliation, which is a far cry from the email he sent me promising I would not be invited to his wedding or

get a chance to meet my future grandchildren. God has turned that around. I still have ongoing communication with my wife's former boyfriend. We communicate monthly or whenever he is going through challenges. God has used this situation so I can become his big brother in the Lord, and I am actively working to help him get restored to Christ.

No, I am not working on earning sainthood from the pope. Instead, I had to realize my wife's former boyfriend is just as much a victim in all of this as I am. Remember, our enemy is not each other but Satan and his forces. In the short time my wife and her former boyfriend were together, he really fell in love with my wife. He thought he had found his soul mate. The two of them talked about getting married after our divorce was finalized. They could not wait to comingle their lives, which is where a lot of the new debt I spoke about earlier occurred. I am sharing all of this with you to help you understand what wonderful work Christ can do and will do on your behalf in your marriage resurrection. Now the marriage resurrection is over for us, God is firmly putting us back on the road of marriage restoration.

It is on that road things like the new debt, unreconciled relationships, unemployment, loss of savings or whatever else the devil has stolen from you will get restored. Remember, it all begins with forgiveness. As a result, I am able to counsel with my wife's ex-boyfriend each month. I am honored to serve the Lord in this way. When our monthly calls last one, two or even three hours, I know I am doing it unto the Lord. My wife gets angry sometimes when we talk, because it reminds her of the bad choices she made. I remind her there is no commendation to those who are in Christ Jesus (Romans 1:8) and there is no commendation coming from me because I choose to walk in forgiveness.

Remember we found in Mark 11:24-25 you can ask God for whatever you want, and he will do for you. Forgiveness is no exception. All you have to do is believe you receive and then forgive. I do not forgive my spouse for what I can get from her in return. When you dwell on what you have or had in the past, it makes you want to walk in unforgiveness. When you realize you can have everything by just asking your Heavenly Father then you will not sweat what you lost. Instead, you focus on walking in forgiveness and putting your trust about all those things that need to be restored in Him. Casting your hurts, concerns and cares on Him will free your heart so you can walk In forgiveness.

Obedience – The Fasteners of the Bridge

Fasteners come in many shapes, sizes and packaging. Generally, you do not buy a single fastener; you buy a box of 10, 20, 50 or 100. When I used to work for the largest industrial supply distributor in the United States, we supplied fasteners in packages of 10,000 or 20,000. In those cases, the cost of a single fastener would cost less than a penny. As I walked through the manufacturing floors of some of America's biggest companies, I would see barrels and barrels of various fasteners. The different fastener types were stored in bins overflowing with a variety of sizes and shapes.

With fasteners so common and inexpensive, it is very easy to underestimate the important work fasteners do. Imagine trying to close your shirt or blouse without a zipper or buttons. Imagine trying to lock your front door without the nuts and bolts holding the lock in place. Better yet, imagine the chair you are sitting on right now without fasteners to hold it together. You would be flat on the floor. Our world is held together by fasteners, and without them the world you know today would be vastly different.

Obedience operates as a fastener in the Spirit world. Fasteners hold everything together. When you decide to obey God's Word, you give him something to hang promise, deliverance, blessing or even his presence on. The Bible has a lot to say about walking in obedience. Here are just a few for you to study:

Obedience Brings Our Inheritance

> "And that you may love the Lord your God, listen to his voice, and hold fast to him. For the Lord is your life, and he will you many years in the land he swore to give to your fathers Abraham, Isaac and Jacob."
>
> (DEUTERONOMY 30:20 NIV)

Obedience Brings the Blessing

> "He replied, "Blessed rather are those who hear the word of God and obey it."
>
> (LUKE 11:28 NIV)

Obedience Enables God to Take the Fight to Your Enemies

> "If you listen carefully to what he says and do all that I say, I will be an enemy to your enemies and will oppose those who oppose you."
>
> (EXODUS 23:22 NIV)

Obedience Lets You Eat the Best of the Land

> "If you are willing and obedient, you will eat the good things of the land."
>
> (ISAIAH 1:19 NIV)

Obedience Makes Things Go Well in Your Life

*"Obey, I beg of you, the voice of the Lord, Who speaks through
me. Then it will be well with you, and you will live."*

(JEREMIAH 38:20 AMP)

Obedience Brings Deliverance

*"So Samuel said to all the Israelites, "If y you are returning to
the Lord with all your hearts, then rid yourselves of the foreign
gods and the Ashtoreths and commit yourselves to the Lord
and serve him only, and he will deliver you out of the hands of
the Philistines."*

(1 SAMUEL 7:3 NIV)

From these scriptures we can see how obedience to God's word brings the inheritance, blessing, victory over your enemies, good of the land, a good life and deliverance. Several of these blessings will be particularly important in your marriage resurrection. It will be important for God to show up and fight your enemies. You cannot touch Satan in the natural world, but you can but in the spirit world.

Your obedience to God's Word puts God on your side against the devil. This matchup is like challenging all your neighbors and their sons to a backyard football game. You bring Tom Brady and the entire lineup of the Patriot's offense and defense as your team members. You know the neighborhood dads and sons would be grossly outmatched. A game like this might take place in Tom Brady's neighborhood, but for it to happen in your backyard would be amazing. That is God's point. No matter the purpose for the battle, the odds against you or the battle conditions, he will always tip the scale in your favor because of your obedience.

If your spouse is still being deceived, your spouse is in the enemy's camp. Your obedience brings deliverance. The enemy is not going to be able to retreat from the battle and take you with them. Just like when our Commander in Chief sends in America's special forces in to retrieve American citizens or assets that have come under enemy control, the mission is not complete until, "the package has been secured." God becomes your very own Navy Seals Team or Delta Force parachuting right in the middle of where the devil has captured you or your family and takes on the enemy until your freedom is secured. When God says it is secure, He means it as described in 1 John 5 when it reads:

*"We know that anyone born of God does not continue to sin;
the One who was born of God keeps them safe, and the evil one
cannot harm them."*

(1 JOHN 5:18 NIV)

Obedience to God's commands is the true sign of your love for God. The only way you can know if you are obeying Him is by knowing his Word (Salem Com-mmunications Corporation, 2016). In John 14 verse 15, Jesus tells us that if we love Him, we will keep His commandments. It does not stop there because our obedience brings a promise. It can be found in verse 21, which reads like this (author's paraphrase)—if you have Jesus' commandments and obey them, then you are the ones who love Him. If you love Jesus, then God will love you. Jesus promises to love that person also and show Himself to him.

Obedience is not obedience, though, unless it is tied to God's Word. Obeying the laws of the land may keep the police at bay, but it does not bring God on the scene. You can obey the policies at your job, the instructions of a recipe or even follow the laws of nature, which by themselves are great things, but in regards to bringing God on the scene, the laws of the land do nothing for you.

The opposite is also true—if you do not obey these rules, there will be natural consequences. For example, if you stick a metal fork into a live electrical socket, you can expect a current of electricity to follow that connection from the out-let through the metal fork and into your body. You will probably end up in the emergency room. If you decide to steal newspapers in front of the police station during the middle of the day with several police officers standing in front of the station, you can expect to receive a citation or possibly a night in jail.

It is the same in the Spirit. When you disobey God, there are consequences. For one thing, God will not be on the scene to outmatch the enemy. Instead of God taking the fight to your enemy, your enemy will be taking the fight to you without God. Both are avoidable situations simply obeying God.

Obedience, like fasteners, gets overlooked in the things we do in the Spirit. Because fasteners are usually small and plentiful, and their tasks so mundane, their importance can be easily overlooked until their presence is missed. If the barrel of fasteners is empty and the production line has to be halted until a re-placement barrel can be secured, everyone in the factory suddenly realizes how important those inexpensive fasteners are to the production of the end product.

When the barrel of fasteners runs out, stopping the production line, chaos breaks out not only on manufacturing floor but also in the executive offices. Those executives know that they cannot afford to get behind by even a single hour if they are going to meet their production quotas. If the quotas are not met, there will not be enough product for customers to buy. Without an adequate quantity of product for the customers to buy, there will not be enough sales to meet sales projections. If sales projections are not met, profitability will suffer. If probability suffers, then the owners of the company, called the shareholders, will want to make changes among the top leaders to find individuals who are better in tune with the business operations and can be on top of decisions to ensure the barrel of the fasteners do not run out.

Obedience is the same way. Many Christians overlook the importance of at-tending church services, weekly Bible study, praying, fasting, loving one another, forgiving one another, tithing and so many other matters the Word commands us

to do daily. Instead, like the barrel of fasteners, they have deceived themselves into thinking they can go on with their daily lives without paying attention to their level of obedience to God's commandments.

Allowing your obedience to run out will have a similar impact as it will weaken your patience. Being impatient means you will not be able to stand in faith very long. If you are not standing in faith very long, then you are going to faint. If you faint, then you cannot receive what you asked for from God for and what He promised to give you. If the thing God has promised you is not received, then God cannot stand by your side. If God is not by your side, then your enemy is not outmatched. Without resistance, your enemy runs past your human defenses and spoils your house, steals your goods and looks for ways to destroy you. All along, God, who you have dismissed from the scene, is watching everything, displeased at your decision not to tag Him.

Do not take lightly the things you do every day to build the bridge of love. Whether it is to rise before dawn to give Him praise, intercede on behalf of your spouse, or spend most of your day bathing in his Word, each action is critical in the eyes of God. Lean your ear to the Holy Spirit to derive what is on your calendar for the day instead of just following a predesigned script, because it is the act of hearing and doing what you heard from the Holy Spirit that is the obedience God is looking for from you. Doing this keeps your barrel of fasteners full and keeps the production of the love bridge in full operation.

Spiritual Warfare – The Bridge Foundation

"For our struggle is not against flesh and blood, but against the rulers, against the authorities, against the powers of this dark world and against the spiritual forces of evil in the heavenly realms."

(EPHESIANS 6:12 NIV)

Robert Sims, a 20-year former U.S. Army infantry sergeant and now missionary evangelist to soldiers, defines spiritual warfare as, "The cosmic war of good versus evil: its battles are fought daily between God and Satan; between the Christian Church and the world system ruled by our spiritual enemy; and within every child of God, between the Holy Spirit and the lusts of the carnal flesh. The clear meanings of good and evil, as defined by God rather than man, are revealed within the verses of the Holy Bible and the life of Jesus Christ (Sims, 2008)." There are at least 40 verses in the King James translation of the Bible that reference spiritual war or conflict between the forces of God and Satan, flesh versus the spirit or good versus evil. Here are just a few for your personal study:

"For though we live in the world, we do not wage war as the world does. The weapons we fight with are not the weapons of the world. On the contrary, they have divine power to demolish strongholds."

(CORINTHIANS 10:3-4 NIV)

"Dear friends, I urge you, as foreigners and exiles, to abstain from sinful desires, which wage war against your soul."

(1 PETER 2:11 NIV)

"I see another law at work in me, waging war against the law of my mind and making me a prisoner of the law of sin at work within me."

(ROMANS 7:23 NIV)

"Therefore, put on the full armor of God, so that when the day of evil comes, you may be able to stand your ground, and after you have done everything, to stand. Stand firm then."

(EPHESIANS 6:13, 14A NIV)

"Be alert and of sober mind. Your enemy the devil prowls around like a roaring lion looking for someone to devour."

(1 PETER 5:8 NIV)

Despite these and other biblical scriptures that clearly teach Satan is real, he is our spiritual enemy, he has demons as his forces, and we are to fight against them in the Spirit, many American Christians struggle to believe in their existence.

In 2009, the Barna Group conducted a survey among a group of 1,871 self-described American Christians about their beliefs in God, Jesus Christ, the Holy Spirit, Satan and demons (The Barna Group, 2009). The following excerpts from the research show what this group believes (The Barna Group, 2009):

- Four out of 10 Christians or 40 percent strongly agreed that Satan "is not a living being but is a symbol of evil." An additional two out of 10 Christians—19 percent, said they "agree somewhat" with that perspective. A minority of Christians indicated that they believe Satan is real by disagreeing with the statement: one-quarter (26%) disagreed strongly and about one-tenth (9%) disagreed somewhat. The remaining eight percent were not sure what they believe about the existence of Satan.

- Much like their perceptions of Satan, most Christians do not believe that the Holy Spirit is a living force, either. Overall, 38 percent strongly

agreed and 20 percent agreed somewhat that the Holy Spirit is "a symbol of God's power or presence but is not a living entity." Just one-third of Christians disagreed that the Holy Spirit is not a living force (9% disagreed somewhat, 25% disagreed strongly) while nine percent were not sure.

- A majority of Christians believe that a person can be under the influence of spiritual forces, such as demons or evil spirits. Two out of three Christians agreed that such influence is real (39% agreed strongly, 25% agreed somewhat), while just three out of 10 rejected the influence of supernatural forces (18% disagreed strongly, 10% disagreed somewhat). The remaining eight % were undecided on this matter.

Inconsistencies Noted from the Research

The conclusions from the research identified a number of instances in which people's beliefs seemed inconsistent. Here are a couple from the research that are relevant to our study of spiritual warfare (The Barna Group, 2009).

- About half (47%) of the Christians who believed that Satan is merely a symbol of evil nevertheless agreed that a person can be under the influence of spiritual forces such as demons.

- About half (49%) of those who agreed that the Holy Spirit is only a symbol but not a living entity also agreed that the Bible is totally accurate in all of the principles it teaches, even though the Bible clearly describes the Holy Spirit as more than a symbolic reference to God's power or presence.

George Barna, the founder of The Barna Group and author of nearly four dozen books that analyzing research concerning America's faith, made the following observations (The Barna Group, 2009):

> "Most Americans, even those who say they are Christian, have
>
> doubts about the intrusion of the supernatural into the natural
>
> world. Hollywood has made evil accessible and tame, making
>
> Satan and demons less worrisome than the Bible suggests they
>
> really are. It's hard for achievement-driven, self-reliant, inde-
>
> pendent people to believe that their lives can be impacted by
>
> unseen forces. At the same time, through sheer force of repeti-

CHAPTER 9: HOW MARRIAGE RESURRECTION WORKS

tion, many Americans intellectually accept some ideas – such as the fact that you either side with God or Satan, there's no in-between – that do not get translated into practice."

GEORGE BARNA
REPORT: MOST AMERICANS DON'T BELIEVE
SATAN OR THE HOLY SPIRIT EXIST
APRIL 2009

It is important to the success of your marriage resurrection you take time to examine your heart and know exactly what you believe in reference to the existence of Satan, his demonic forces and the work Christians are taught from the Word regarding spiritual warfare. Many of the things I shared with you in this book are founded upon my presumption you believe in the existence of Satan and the Holy Spirit and you accept spiritual warfare is conducted between these forces.

If you are not firm in this belief, then the probability for success with a marriage resurrection drops to nearly zero, because marital problems occur because of spiritual immaturity. We introduced this concept in Chapter 1 and built on this concept in subsequent chapters in which we showed if you're experiencing a marital separation or facing the possibly of a divorce it is because of spiritual deception on the part of Satan and his forces.

If you do not believe in the existence of Satan, demons and the lot of them, it will be impossible for you to have faith your spouse is being spiritually deceived. You may believe your spouse is deceived, but unless you believe in external influences of spiritual origin whose intent is to bring evil and calamity into your life, then you can only attribute your spouse's deception to his or her own ignorance, lack of access to good quality information or barriers (mental, emotional and others) which are stumbling blocks preventing him or her to process this information.

You will have to decide whether you believe there are outside influences impacting your marriage positively or negatively. Because at the end of the day, both God's and Satan's influences into your marriage will have external consequences. The only difference is God will not intervene unless invited, but Satan does not require an invitation to mettle in your marriage, and his influence will persist unless he is resisted.

If you do not believe your spouse is spiritually deceived, then you are convinced your response to conflict, because marital separation and divorce are marital conflicts, should be aimed squarely at your spouse. That is what the most married couples, Christian and non-Christian alike, are already doing. The results of married couples who do not believe their marriage is being influenced by external spiritual forces are all around us.

I suspect since you are reading this book, you are looking for a different outcome in your marriage than what almost everyone else is getting. If that is the case, then you really need to examine what you believe in this area because having a belief in the existence of spiritual warfare is foundational to the operation of your marriage resurrection and the building of your love bridge. Without this belief you have no basis to begin your campaign.

I have repeatedly said in this book your spouse is being spiritually deceived. He or she is not only being influenced by the enemy, but his or her decisions in the natural means your spouse is spiritually located in the midst of the enemy's camp. The whole purpose of building a love bridge is to give Jesus the pathway to complete the redemptive work by rescuing your spouse from the enemy and bringing him or her back across the bridge to be reunited with God and you. It is vital your belief is in direct alignment with this biblical teaching, otherwise there is no reason to build the love bridge, and there is no work for the Lord to do on your behalf.

As we were reviewing the research from the Barna Group, you may have identified where you stand in your belief on the existence of Satan and the Holy Spirit. Regardless of what you discovered, the fact you understand what you believe is a good first step. You believe what you believe because of the time you may have spent learning about what the Bible teaches about your spiritual defensive and offensive weapons. It is highly likely your beliefs have been influenced by the media, churches who preach and teach against Satan's existence and a culture emphasizing humanistic dominance over spiritual submission to God.

Despite your current belief, you have an opportunity to change what you believe. Take time to study what the Bible says about the existence of Satan and about the importance of spiritual warfare. There are plenty of great books and study guides that you give the ability to clear away the deceptions that may have masked and contaminated your belief until now. Doing this will increase the probability of bringing life to your dead marriage from zero to as successful as it can be due to your level of commitment.

Praise (Shout, Dance and Sing) – The Bridge Blueprints

"As they began to sing and praise, the Lord set ambushes against the men of Ammon and Moab and Mount Seir who were invading Judah, and they were defeated."
(2 CHRONICLES 20: 22 NIV)

Praise and worship is a very big topic and too expansive to be exhausted in this small section of one chapter. There are entire series of books and other materials can give you fuller understanding of the reason for and the importance of praise and worship. For our study, we will look at how praise and worship operate as the blueprints God uses to orchestrate warfare against our enemy and bring deliverance to God's people. Below are five stories in the Bible to validate this point and are worthy of your additional exploration. I will at least introduce them and show you how praise and worship impacts your marriage resurrection effort.

A Shout Brings Down the Walls of Jericho – Joshua 5: 13 -6:27

"Now when Joshua was near Jericho, he looked up and saw a man with a drawn sword in his hand. Joshua went up to him and asked, "Are you for us or for our enemies?" "Neither," he replied, "but as commander of the army of the Lord I have now come." Then Joshua fell facedown to the ground in reverence, and asked him, "What message does my Lord have for his servant?" The commander of the Lord's army replied, "Take off your sandals, for the place where you are standing is holy." And Joshua did so.

Now the gates of Jericho were securely barred because of the Israelites. No one went out and no one came in. Then the Lord said to Joshua, "See, I have delivered Jericho into your hands, along with its king and its fighting men. March around the city once with all the armed men. Do this for six days. Have seven priests carry trumpets of rams' horns in front of the ark. One the seventh day, march around the city seven times, with the priests blowing the trumpets. When you hear them sound a long blast on the trumpets, have the whole army give a loud shout; then the wall of the city will collapse and the army will go up, everyone straight in."

(JOSHUA 5:13 – 6:4 NIV)

Singing Sets Up Ambushes for the Enemy – 2 Chronicles 20

"Some people came and told Jehoshaphat, "A vast army is coming against you from Edom, from the other side of the Dead Sea. It is already in Hazezon Tamar," Alarmed Jehoshaphat resolved to inquire of the Lord and he proclaimed a fast for all Judah. The people of Judah came together to seek help from the Lord; indeed, they came

from every town, in Judah to seek him.

Then the Spirit of the Lord came on Jahaziel son of Zechariah, the son of Benaiah, the son of Jeiel, the son of Mattaniah, a Levite and descendant of Asaph, as he stood in the assembly. He said, "Listen, King Jehoshaphat and all who live in Judah and Jerusalem! This is what the Lord says to you: 'Do not be afraid or discouraged because of this vast army. For the battle is not yours, but God's. Tomorrow march down against them. They will be climbing up by the Pass of Ziz, and you will find them at the end of the gorge in the Desert of Jeruel. You will not have to fight this battle. Take up your positions; stand firm and see the deliverance the Lord will give you, Judah and Jerusalem. Do not be afraid; do not be discouraged. Go out to face them tomorrow and the Lord will be with you."

After consulting the people, Jehoshaphat appointed men to sing to the Lord and to praise him for the splendor of his holiness as they went out at the head of the army, saying "Give thanks to the Lord, for his love endures forever." As they began to sing and praise, the Lord set ambushes against the men of Ammon and Moab and Mount Seir who were invading Judah and they were defeated."

(2 CHRONICLES 20: 2-4, 15-17, 21-22 NIV)

David's Dancing Before God Brings Blessing to the City– 2 Samuel 6

"Now King David was told, "The Lord has blessed the household of Obed-Edom and everything he has, because of the ark of God." So David went to bring up the ark of God from the house of Obed-Edom to the City of David with rejoicing. When those who were carrying the ark of the Lord had taken six steps, he sacrificed a bull and a fattened calf. Wearing a linen ephod, David was dancing before the Lord with all his might, while he and all Israel were bringing up the ark of the Lord with shouts and sounds of trumpets."

(2 SAMUEL 6:12 -15 NIV)

Praise Opens the Prison Doors – Acts 16:25-34

> "After they had been severely flogged, they were thrown in
> prison, and the jailer was commanded to guard them carefully.
> When he received these orders, he put them in the inner cell
> and fastened their feet in the stocks.
> About midnight Paul and Silas were praying and singing hymns
> to God, and the other prisoners were listening to them. Sud-
> denly there was such a violent earthquake that the foundations
> of the prison where shaken. At once all the prison doors flew
> open, and everyone's chains came loose."
>
> (ACTS 16:23-26 NIV)

What ties each of these biblical stories together is when God's people need His protection, presence or provision, praise became Israel's battle plan to give them the city, set ambushes for the enemy, usher in God's presence or open the jail doors. Too often Christians overlook the importance of praise as a key to getting God's help. You can see every Sunday morning as most Christian churches start their services with worship and praise, the number of church attendance is lower at the beginning of the worship and praise portion of service. As worship and praise begins to wind down, you can look around most church buildings and notice the sanctuary begins to fill. It is as if we believe worship and praise is optional.

It is not. It is this vital tool God uses to bring deliverance. So many times we rush to the altar to pray, but we get up off our knees failing to give God praise to let Him know of our confidence in Him.

This is what opened the jail doors. Though their backs were bloodied and raw from the flogging, Paul and Silas lifted their voices to sing praises to God in the midst of their pain. As a result, their praise ushered in God's presence and those prison doors could not stay closed. It will be praise and worship added to your marriage resurrection effort that will bring the execution of the love bridge coming to together.

When my wife and I separated, praise and worship became a tool to bring reconciliation to our marriage. The first time we separated the Holy Spirit had me study the story of Joshua and the walls of Jericho. That was almost 20 years ago. One Sunday morning, my wife took our children while we were at church. She left without letting me know she was leaving me. I came out of the church service unaware my wife had decided to end our marriage and had taken our children. Over the next couple of days, she and the children boarded a plane with one-way tickets to fly across the country with no intention of returning. I was left to deal with our residence, our debt and our belongings, without a job, savings or knowledge of their whereabouts. I was heartbroken, but the Holy Spirit did not allow me time to have a pity party.

Within a day or two after she left with the kids, the Lord had gotten my attention on a plan of action. I was to complete a Jericho march around the city block that comprised our apartment complex over the next week. I followed the same instructions that the Lord gave to Joshua for each of those seven days. On the seventh day, I walked around the block seven times, and on the seventh time at a certain spot the Holy Spirit had brought to my attention, I gave out the shout of my life. I remember yelling and screaming as cars drove by. It startled some people in cars and individuals waiting at the light. Some drivers honked their horns. Right after I did that, the Lord dropped a plan into my spirit I followed, and it brought my wife and children home in 30 days. I had sold all of our possessions. People lined up outside my apartment to give me money, debts were supernaturally cancelled, and I received a new job with a great salary that came with a furnished apartment the employer paid for two months.

During our last separation, the Lord used a different form of praise. Since the first separation, I learned to become a worshipper. Raising my hands, singing and getting involved with praise and worship was normal for me. But one type of worship I did not regularly incorporate into my praise and worship before the Lord was dancing. Like David dancing to bring the ark of God to the City of David, I found myself rushing to the front of the sanctuary during every praise and worship service to dance before the Lord with all my might.

Since my wife has returned home, my heart yearns for those moments when it was me and the Lord before the whole congregation. When I danced, I could feel myself zoning out and becoming oblivious to anything or anyone around me. As wild as I danced, the Holy Spirit never let me hurt myself or even touch anyone around me. Since our church only had service on Sundays mornings and Wednesday evenings, I found any open church doors on the other days.

One particular Wednesday, our church was fellowshipping with another church in a city about 20 or so miles away. Somehow I got the name of the church wrong. Church began at 7 p.m., and I had driven around for about 20 minutes and could not find a church with any name close to where I was supposed to be.

At 7:05 p.m., I was panicking because I did not want to miss praise and worship. I was at a red light and across the street was a Pentecostal church whose sign showed that Wednesday services started at 7 p.m.

I drove across the street, quickly parked my car, and ran inside church. Bursting through the doors, I heard the sounds of praise and worship. I threw my belongings into the first open pew and ran down front dancing like my hair was on fire. Thank God they were Pentecostal and seeing me seemed to light up the place. That song must have lasted 30 minutes, and I danced every bit of it.

After the song service, the preachers pounced on me, laying their hands on me and believing God for whatever I was seeking I would receive. As the service ended, many people in the congregation came up to me to shake my hand and to say they would be praying for me. The pastor and a deacon asked who I was and what was I believing God for. When I told them I was believing God for my wife to be in her right mind again and to be reconciled back to God and me, they were thrilled. They even made me promise to come back when my wife came home. About six weeks later I did come back to that little small Pentecostal church on a Wednesday night with my wife in tow.

It was during all those praise and worship times with the Lord dropped the blueprints for the book you are now reading into my spirit. Take the time to add praise and worship to your marriage resurrection effort, and watch God drop into your spirit a blueprint of what to do. Do not be afraid your mind will have trouble comprehending; trust God and the direction from the Holy Spirit.

Before closing this chapter, it is important we revisit our three vital questions while taking into consideration their relationship to the interior components of the love bridge.

❦ What will be required of me during this time?

As you begin to incorporate the interior components of your bridge building, you must have spiritual courage and trust in the Lord. You will need to recognize that what you are believing from God is not an everyday type of request. Most Christians have never even heard of a marriage resurrection, let alone successfully see one completed. This is going to take spiritual courage on your part to believe God and operate your trust in Him doing this redemptive work on your behalf. You will be like a maverick, and so you will be believing God for something others will consider foolish. But, you will get results that others only wish they had.

❦ How long will it take before I see the results I'm seeking?

The answer given for the external components is exactly the same here. You have to be prepared to wait forever and you won't be waiting very long.

❦ What will my spouse be doing while I'm believing God for restoration of our marriage?

Be prepared for your spouse to do everything in his or her pow-er to confirm they have no interest in reconciling with you and they have no love for you. Do not believe it. It will be the en-emy's attempt to discourage you and cause you to quit. The

enemy sees the progress you are making on the love bridge, so his tactic is to use deception to discourage you from continuing to build. Stay the course, ignore the distraction and soon you will see God's miracle manifest right before your eyes.

Scripture:

"Brothers and sisters, think of what you were when you were called. Not many of you were wise by human standards; not many were influential; not many were of noble birth.

But God chose the foolish things of the world to shame the wise; God chose the weak things of the world to shame the strong.

God chose the lowly things of this world and the despised things—and the things that are not—to nullify the things that are—so that no one may boast before him."

(1 CORINTHIANS 1: 26-29 NIV)

CHAPTER 10

DOMESTIC VIOLENCE AND MARRIAGE RESURRECTION

God will not allow his lifeboat to be used by an abusive spouse to bring back a spouse.

Will God send an abused spouse back to his or her abusive spouse? That is a question that bears addressing because unfortunately, there are a number of husbands and wives who are looking to divorce their spouse for the issue of preservation and safety. Joe Beam's organization has guided over 200,000 people through the process of failing in love, growing in love and rescuing lost love. He wrote an article that spells out the reasons why married couples separate (Marriage Helper, Inc., 2016). In the article, Beam explains a couple separates for fatigue, facilitation or fear (Beam, 2007). The article goes on to describe each of these reasons (Beam, 2007):

- ❦ **Fatigue** – The spouse who wants to leave feels he or she cannot take it any longer. Browbeating, arguing, accusations, and criticisms eat into the individual to the point that he or she primarily thinks of escaping the relationship rather than healing it.

- ❦ **Facilitation** – The spouse who wants to leave desires separation to make it easier to pursue a relationship with someone else or a lifestyle the current marriage prohibits.

- ❦ **Fear** – The spouse who seeks to leave does so because he or she fears for the emotional, physical, or spiritual safety of self or children.

There seems to be a fairly recognizable path for how God's marriage resurrection lifeboat can be a redemptive tool to help the couple wanting to separate or divorce for the reasons of fatigue or facilitation. What about the couple separating or divorcing because of fear? Will God require the abused spouse to put him or herself or the children in harm's way again for the sake of keeping

147

the marriage together? Can an abusive spouse use marriage resurrection as a means of getting a spouse to return home? We will explore these and other questions to see how domestic violence fits within the redemptive work of marriage resurrection.

Without any suspense or delay, let me immediately answer the above questions by simply saying the marriage resurrection cannot be used to return an abused spouse back to an abusive husband or wife. This is a subject in which God has spoken very directly and often in the Bible. In each of the following verses, God's position is very clear. He is absolutely against violence. When it comes to marriage resurrection, there are five very specific reasons why the lifeboat is unavailable to the abuser:

> **Reason #1 –**
> **A marriage resurrection is approved by the Father,**
> **advocated by the Son and executed by the Holy Spirit;**
> **all three hate those who love violence.**

> *"The Lord tests the righteous, but his soul hates the wicked and*
> *the one who loves violence."*
> (PSALMS 11:5 ESV)

In a marriage resurrection, it is the Lord who does the work. The spouse who stayed in fellowship with the covenant has to be aware when a resurrection request is presented before the throne of God, the Lord is going to weigh his or her heart. Though a person can repent before God and have past faults removed, this only happens because true repentance takes place in the heart. Man looks on the outside and can be fooled by words, tears and good acting, but God cannot be fooled (Galatians 6:7 CEV). While man looks at the outside appearance, the Bible tells us God tests the heart (1 Samuel 6:7). If the husband or wife is praying for a marriage resurrection but there has been no real heart change, God will not answer that prayer.

> *"You do ask [God for them] and yet fail to receive, because you*
> *ask with wrong purpose and evil, selfish motives. Your intention*
> *is [when you get what you desire] to spend it in sensual plea-*
> *sures. So whoever chooses to be a friend of the world takes his*
> *stand as an enemy of God."*
> (JAMES 4:3 AND 4B)

> **Reason #2 –**
> **God cannot send the abused spouse home**
> **because it would violate his Word.**

"But understand this that in the last days there will come times of difficulty. For people will be lovers of self, lovers of money, proud, arrogant, abusive, disobedient to their parents, ungrateful, unholy, heartless, unappeasable, slanderous, without self-control, brutal, not loving good, treacherous, reckless, swollen with conceit, lovers of pleasure rather than lovers of God, having the appearance of godliness but denying its power. Avoid such people."

(2 TIMOTHY 3:1-5 ESV)

It is very clear God wants us to avoid abusive people. Avoiding does not mean we are to have no contact with people who struggle in this area. As Christians we are called to be the light to the world (Matthew 5:14), which means from time to time, our lives will connect with those who are in the world and practice evil. They may be struggling with being with one or any combination of the kind or person outlined in the verses above, but for the purpose of ministry we make ourselves available to these individuals to share the good news of the Gospel and win them for Christ.

Timothy tells us people who struggle in the ways cited in the passage above should not be a part of our inner circle. Our time with them should be limited to advancing the cause of Christ in their lives. Otherwise, we open ourselves to having their worldly ways negatively impact our spiritual walk (Galatians 5:11). For God to require a spouse to return to an abusive husband or wife would violate all the other scriptures that warn us to stay away.

Reason #3 –
Abuse violates God's command to love one another.

"Husbands, go all out in love for your wives. Don't take advantage of them."

(COLOSSIANS 3:19 MSG)

"Wives, submit to your husbands as is fitting in the Lord. Husbands, love your wives, and do not be harsh with them."

(COLOSSIANS 3:18, 19 ESV)

"What wife would not submit to a gentle and loving husband who, as Colossians says, goes all out in love for his wife? That is why the Bible does not tell the wife to love because it is implied and considered to be the only appropriate response when you are experiencing love, gentleness from someone who goes out

of their way to give preferential treatment. To the husband, the command is loud and strong to love our wives. The love in a marriage starts with the husband, that is why the commandment is directed to the husband. From the moment of creation, the wife was created to be a companion to the man, which means she is specifically gifted to response to the needs, wants and desires of her husband. In Colossians, God gave the man the command to love, and if the man has chosen to walk with God, he knows to be obedient he must love his wife. God does not call the wife to be submissive and give a man a pass to not walk in love with his wife. That is what God would be doing if he asked, compelled or used circumstances to encourage the wife to return to her abusive and unloving husband. This is would violate his Word and God will not violate his Word."

(PSALM 89:34)

Reason #4 –
Abuse and fits of anger are works of the flesh.

"Now the works of the flesh are evident: sexual immorality, impurity, sensuality, idolatry, sorcery, enmity, strife, jealousy, fits of anger, rivalries, dissension, divisions, envy, drunkenness, orgies, and things like these. I warned you before, that those who do such things will not inherit the kingdom of God."

(GALATIANS 5: 19-21 ESV)

Marriage resurrection is a redemptive work God wants to do when a married couple seeks to terminate the relationship. The work is done by God; it is spiritual. Any man or woman who chooses to walk in the flesh will not be permitted at the same time to walk in the spirit. In fact, the Bible tells us in Galatians 5:16 when we walk by the Spirit we will not have the desire to fulfill the lusts that come from our flesh. Therefore, if a person is doing the works of the flesh, though he gets a hold of the concept of marriage resurrection, he will not be able to activate God to work on his behalf. (1 Corinthians 2:14)

Reason #5 –
The body of the believer belongs to God and it is holy.

"Do you not know that you are God's temple and that God's
Spirit dwells in you? If anyone destroys God's temple, God will
destroy him. For God's temple is holy and you are that temple."
(1 CORINTHIANS 3:16 AND 17 ESV)

Jesus paid a dear price to redeem each of us back to God and when he did, God accepted his payment in full for everything that separated us from God. When you and I accepted Jesus Christ as our Savior, God in the form of his Spirit took up residence inside of us. God is inside of you and me right now. Because of His residence inside of us, he calls our bodies his temple, and he declared the temple is holy. Physical, emotional, or spiritual abuse toward either spouse would be considered an attack on God's temple. God has no intention of standing around and allowing that attack to go unpunished. God knows His Son paid a high and painful price for the temple and to let that attack go unaddressed tarnishes the price Jesus paid.

It is the same for an owner who paid a hefty sum to acquire an original Van Gogh painting. If the painting was damaged by another person's neglect or mistreatment, the owner would seek reimbursement for the damage from the person who caused it. In the same way, God takes these attacks very seriously and has said his response would be to destroy such a person.

I heard a testimony of a wife whose husband had been physically abusive to her. One evening the husband got frustrated over a matter with his wife and retaliated as usual with a severe beating. By this time, the wife was fed up with getting beaten. She knelt beside her bed with her Bible open and poured her heart out before the Lord. Later that night, her husband woke up from a dream drenched in sweat. He shook his wife awake and immediately apologized for ever laying his hands on her. He swore never to beat her again. She asked him what prompted the change, and he replied he had a dream in which Jesus appeared and told him if he beat her again he would go to hell. According to the testimony, the man never again beat her again and treated her with the utmost respect and dignity until he went on to be with the Lord many years later.

When it comes to being abusive or sowing violence in a marriage, God is completely against it. The husband or wife with an abusive spouse does not have to be concerned God will require them to go back to the abuser. With all that said, if the abusive spouse were to make a true change of heart and completely seek repentance, God would engage in that situation. Understand at the moment the heart changed, whether through accepting Christ as Savior or allowing Him to be Lord, that person's old nature would have been crucified with Christ. This person would receive forgiveness from the Heavenly Father, and God would remember his sins no more.

What about the wife or husband who has been the recipient of the newly repentant person's abuse? God is not going to order them to go home. In fact, in none of the redemptive works of marriage does God order anyone to do anything. In earlier chapters we discussed the work God does in a marriage resurrection and He removes the deception. In this situation if there is any deception blinding the spouse who departed, God could cause that blindness to dissolve. With the deception eradicated, the opportunity for the couple to reconcile is possible. During the work of a marriage resurrection, both spouses face their faults, and God sets them on a course to reconcile with Himself first. As both spouses seek to reconcile with God, there is a possibility that with real work they may recover their lost love.

However, the point of this chapter is not to review all the possibilities but to bring hope and possibly relief to a spouse who has decided to depart from his or her abuser. The person does not have to worry with marriage resurrection they will be required to return to the abuse, be submissive, or they risk not pleasing God by leaving the abusive situation. As our study in this chapter shows, neither of these situations are correct, and the abused spouse can move forward with his or her life without fear that God would ever use any of His redemptive works to make him or her do something they have no desire to do. God's works always require a willing heart by both spouses.

Scripture:

> *"So ought men to love their wives as their own bodies. He that loveth his wife loveth himself.*
>
> *For no man ever yet hated his own flesh; but nourisheth and cherisheth it, even as the Lord the church.*
>
> *For we are members of his body, of his flesh, and of his bones."*
>
> (EPHESIANS 5: 28 – 30 KJV)

CHAPTER 11

DIVORCE AND THE MINISTRY

What should be done if a ministry leader divorces?

Nothing seems to put a church body on its heels more than a scandal with ministry leadership. Whether the church pastor has filed for divorce, is found in adultery with one of the church members, or has misappropriated funds, this news electrifies the congregation.

Unfortunately, individuals within the church feel as if the church leader betrayed them personally, and they usually publicly display their anger and frustration among the congregation. In my 42 years as a member of the Body of Christ in all sorts of churches (small, large, rural, urban, sub-urban, traditional, contemporary, spirit-filled, predominately white and some predominately black), I have come face to face with this topic more than a handful of times. In fact, I have been the top ministry leader and experienced the storm of scandal, and I resolved the matter by resigning from my post. At the time, I felt it was the right thing to do, and I maintained that stance up until recently when the Lord challenged my thinking through his Word.

The chapter you are about to read was a late edition to the book that received its merit for inclusion directly from the Lord. As I just mentioned, this is a subject I would have taken the other side on up until recently, but I always committed myself to allow the Word to speak for itself. I have also allowed the Word to be final authority in my thinking and ministry. What that means is when I find truth in the Word, I change my thinking to match the Word of God instead of changing the Word of God to match my thinking.

In this chapter we will examine what should happen when a ministry leader is found in sin, regardless of the sin. We will also examine why ministers are having a tough time keeping their marriages and families together.

The point of our review is to be obedient to the Lord's instruction to minister His Word to his Body. I will warn you right now the positions discussed in this chapter will not be popular. I have not seen public examples of the positions I will describe taken by church leaders who have had to deal with scandals that have rocked the entire Body of Christ on a national scale in the past 20 to 30 years. With that said, as I express these views, I humbly submit to the Holy Spirit's guidance to ensure I speak on behalf of our King with accuracy, recognizing everyone will not agree. This chapter is written for the benefit of those who truly want to hear from heaven on the subject rather than to be used as an accuser of the brethren to generate strife and division in the Body.

For clarity and simplicity, we will limit our study to a discussion of divorce and adultery, which by themselves have produced major scandals within the Body of Christ. Let us begin with a thought-provoking question. Who benefits when a ministry leader is found in adultery or divorce and they are asked to resign?

Does God receive any benefit?

Absolutely not. First, God needs to deal with a son or daughter who has ignored all of warnings from the Spirit, walked in disobedience, and made decisions which caused them to walk toward death instead of life.

Second, God now has to be concerned about losing the minister to condemnation, grief, unforgiveness and a host of other things. The gift and call on the minister's life may never be in operation again, and if it does continue, it will probably never operate at the level it did prior to the sin.

Third, God and His Kingdom are negatively impacted by the ill-witness the sin displays to other believers and the unbelieving world.

Does the congregation benefit?

Absolutely not. There are members of the congregation who attend the church because of the connection they felt with the leader. If the minister steps down, they will undoubtedly rethink their status within the Church Body. It is naïve to assume they will just go find another church because that doesn't happen 100 percent of the time. Whether or not people go or stay should not be the deciding factor. Asking the leader to resign does not teach the congregation how to walk in love and forgiveness or how to bear the burdens of others. One of the reasons I personally believe we are seeing families self-destruct rather than walk in love and forgiveness when their marriages and families hit rough patches is because they have not seen that exercised by its leaders.

If leaders are not able to demonstrate the love of God among their fallen brethren, how can we expect newborn Christians and the spiritually immature to do this? In this way, they are like children they are more apt to follow what they see us demonstrating rather than what we say to them.

Next, the congregation becomes divided because a diversity of opinions is allowed to fester. It is never good to teach believers to trust and rely on their human reasoning. Our task is to always point them to Christ. When a situation like this happens, it is much more beneficial for those who are spiritual in the congregation to put aside their personal feelings and submit their wills to what the Word has to say.

Does the minister benefit?

Absolutely not. One may argue with the resignation the minister can work to reconnect with the Lord, his family and his faith; that can be done effectively through a sabbatical. God's call on your life or the spiritual gifts you have do not go away because of sin (Romans 11:29). It will not be long after the dust settles the minister will reemerge wanting to fulfill the call of God and exercise the spiritual gifts in his or her life.

We should all understand once we are called, the Spirit constantly guides us to fulfill the will of God for our lives. The minister will most likely accept the conviction of the Holy Spirit and receive forgiveness from the Lord (Mark 2:10). It would be expected the minister would spend time with his or her family and reestablish connections, in addition to reconnecting with God. If the minister has lost his or her ministry, most likely he or she has also lost the financial resource for his or her family, and instead of spending this quality time with the family the minister will likely try to get reestablished as quickly as possible to feel that there is a solid ground to support his or her family.

Does the family benefit?

Absolutely not.

The reason just outlined for the minister applies to the family as well. One of the reasons the divorce or adultery occurred in the first place is the minister most likely did not feel completely fulfilled or at peace when he or she was at home before the sin was committed and before it was discovered. Thrusting the person back into that environment, now publicly brandished as a sinner and loser, will not make the minister more fulfilled or at peace with home.

Does the other person caught in the sin, benefit?

Absolutely not. That individual will have watched someone go through a public reprimand and stripped of what is a major driving force in his or her life. As the minister receives no mercy, grace, love or forgiveness, there will definitely not be any extended to the spouse or the other person caught in adultery.

Does anyone benefit from a minister's resignation after sin?

Yes. First, the non-believing community benefits. Viewing the scandal and resignation from the outside justifies the public's negative attitudes about the body of believers at church and solidifies whatever reasoning they have for not giving in to the Holy Spirit's conviction about becoming a part of that ministry. It further complements the attitude the entire Body of Christ is full of hypocrites who do not practice what they preach. We actually should not blame them because they are correct.

Another group who benefits are those who were seeking power, advancement and coveted things with which God had blessed that minister. The Bible lists Aaron and Miriam, Korah and his followers, Absalom, Gehazi and Judas to name a few. The thing all these individuals had in common was they were all very close to God's chosen leader. They were close enough to see and covet for themselves the very position given to the anointed person of God.

The spirit of these people exists today in every church and when the minister is asked to resign, position seekers want to be given the mantle. They are self-serving and prey upon the dissolution felt in the hearts of the congregation. Instead of being there to serve as God's administrator of grace and the restorer for the broken anointed person of God, they fan the flames looking for an opportunity to snatch the anointed mantle. These individuals work diligently to hide their true motives. The lesson learned in my own life and ministry is this: By the time the anointed one recognizes the true motive of the individual hungry for power, it's already too late. The person who wants to supplant the minister is ever ready with a trap to send the minister falling to a bad fate.

The last benefactor of the minister's resignation is Satan. With the minister gone, Satan wins on so many levels.

First, he benefits from the division and strife that occurred among the congregation. Second, he benefits from those in the church and in the community who lost hope and felt betrayed by the minister. Our enemy has hundreds of ways he can twist these feelings to cause those individuals to become offended at themselves, the Body of Christ and ultimately at God.

Third, Satan benefits because of the devastation to the ministry's finances and influence. Less resistance from the church only increases Satan's influence over the spiritually immature and the lost.

Fourth, he benefits because of the negative impact on the minister's family, the other party to the sin and the minister's supporters because he knows those ill feelings will put a wedge between people.

Fifth, as stated earlier, the minister may never take up the God's call again, and if he or she does, it likely will not make the same impact as before.

Sixth, the enemy's plans to steal, kill and destroy the work of God worked will be advanced.

Do we really want the Lord and the Body of Christ to take such a devastating blow and seriously sets back God's work? Hopefully you are feeling like I was when the Lord brought it to my attention. I thank the Lord there is a better way.

Principle #11:
The call of God and His gifts are irrevocable (Romans 11:29)

"For God's gifts and his call are irrevocable [He never withdraws them when once they are given, and He does not change

His mind about those to whom He gives His grace or to whom
He sends His call.]."

(ROMANS 11:29 AMP)

If God does not revoke His call and His gifts why should we? Marriages and families are a mirror image for what is occurring in the Church. If a pastor gets into sin or divorces, often the church requires the leader to step down, extending no mercy, grace, love or forgiveness. If it is not happening in the church, why should we expect it to happen at home? Revoking the call is not God's way. Here are some scriptures to support this:

- ❦ When Moses hit the rock instead of speaking to the rock did God ask him to resign from leadership? No (Numbers 20:11).

- ❦ When David was caught in adultery with Bathsheba was the kingdom taken away from him? No (2 Samuel 11).

- ❦ When Saul did not complete God's order to completely destroy everything that belonged to the Amalekites, was he immediately removed from being king? No. He ruled 38 more years (1 Samuel 15).

- ❦ When Peter denied knowing Jesus did he lose his role as an apostle? No (John 18:15-27).

In all of these cases and more throughout the Bible, we see God did not revoke the call or even the gifts given to these men. How did God deal with these situations?

"If your brother wrongs you, go and show him his fault, between you and him privately. If he listens to you, you have won back your brother. But if he does not listen, take along with you one or two others, so that every word may be confirmed and upheld by the testimony of two or three witnesses. If he pays no attention [refusing to listen and obey], tell it to the church; and if he refuses to listen even to the church, let him be to you as a pagan and a tax collector."

(MATTHEW 18: 15 -17 AMP)

"Brethren, if any person is overtaken in misconduct or sin of any sort, you who are spiritual [who are responsive to and controlled by the Spirit] should set him right and restore and rein-

state him, without any sense of superiority and with all gentleness, keeping an attentive eye on yourself, lest you should be tempted also. Bear (endure, carry) one another's burdens and troublesome moral faults, and in this way fulfill and observer perfectly the law of Christ (the Messiah) and complete what is lacking [in your obedience to it]."

(GALATIANS 6:1, 2 AMP)

"You have heard that it was said, you shall not commit adultery. But I say to you that everyone who so much as looks at a woman with evil desires for her has already committed adultery with her in his heart. If your right eye serves as a trap to ensnare you or is an occasion for you to stumble and sin, pluck it out and throw it away. It is better that you lose one of your members than that your whole body be cast into hell (Gehenna)."

(MATTHEW 5: 27 – 29 AMP)

"For where your treasure is, there will your heart also. The eye is the lamp of the body. So if your eye is sound, your entire body will be full of light. But if your eye is unsound, your whole body will be full of darkness. If then the very light in you [your conscience] is darkened, how dense is that darkness! No one can serve two masters; for either he will hate the one and love the other, or he will stand by and be devoted to the one and despise and be against the other. You cannot serve God and mammon (deceitful riches, money, possessions, or whatever is trusted in)."

(MATTHEW 6:21 – 24 AMP)

Here is how I believe these scriptures are to be interpreted and the actions to be taken when the ministry leader is discovered in sin.

Steps to Restoration

1. When the sin is first discovered, it should only be discussed with the minister in private, with a goal to gain a willingness for the minister to repent and open the door for restoration.

2. If the private conversation is not embraced by the minister, the discoverer must identify two or three people who have the minister's confidence and are willing to submit to the Holy Spirit's leading and not their own feelings and attitudes. They, too, should seek to gain a willingness to turn from the sin, repent and allow for restoration.

3. At no time in the steps above should the option of having the minister resign be considered; only restoration. If the minister does not embrace the conversation, then the matter is brought before the entire congregation to let the entire body encourage the minister in this direction. Once the minister embraces the conversation and repents, I suggest the next steps be taken to restore the minister. If the minister still is not willing to repent and accept restoration at that time, the church leadership should work to remove the minister from office.

4. The minister takes a sabbatical for a mutually agreed upon length of time to rekindle his or her relationship with the Lord after the broken fellowship occurred.

5. During the sabbatical the minister should not be allowed to minister the Word. Instead the minister should focus on receiving discernment from the Spirit regarding his or her disobedience and restoring his or her broken spiritual life.

6. The minister should work privately with the two or three brothers or sisters in the Lord who talked with him initially to help restore the minister. It is this group who should determine the length of the sabbatical and the path to reinstatement.

7. The matter should not be addressed in front of the church unless the minister refuses to listen to the two or three brothers or sisters in the Lord or if the minister refuses to submit to the sabbatical and restoration process.

8. If the matter is brought before the church, the purpose is not to focus on the sin or address the possibility of resignation. What should be addressed within the church is the minister's unwillingness to submit to the sabbatical and restoration process, and as a body the entire church should encourage the minister to submit to the process. They should show the minister they are not afraid and extend love to bear the burden of the sin. The sin is only to be addressed in front of the church if the minister refuses to turn away from the sin. At this point, with the congregation's knowledge of the sin, the congregation can more strongly encourage the minister to submit to the sabbatical and restoration process.

9. If the minister refuses to stop committing the sin or after all this refuses to submit to the restoration process, then the church is to treat him as a non-believer. A non-believer would not be able to minister the Word to the congregation nor hold the position as leader with the church.

Reasoning for a suspension from the ministry of the Word

> *"Once more Jesus addressed the crowd. He said, I am the Light of the world. He who follows Me will not be walking in the dark, but will have the Light which is Life."*
>
> (JOHN 8:12 AMP)

CHAPTER 11: DIVORCE AND THE MINISTRY

For a minister to sin, he or she would have had to make a decision to meditate on a desire that grew to lust and eventually yielded to the temptation of lust that gave birth to sin (James 1:15). It is important to understand the minister did not just turn the corner and fall into sin as so many times we have heard it described. Sin takes time to produce, and the minister had to follow a process to arrive at the place where the sin manifested. Jesus taught in the verses above if a man looks at a woman with evil desires he has committed adultery. Before the act of adultery or any other sin becomes apparent in the physical world, it first materialized in the heart of the man. This is why Matthew 6:21-24 AMP says, "But if your eye is unsound, your whole body is full of darkness."

> "Jesus told us He is the light of the World, and when we decide to fully commit ourselves, walk in His ways, and choose righteousness over sin, we are able to walk in the same light as Jesus."
>
> (JOHN 8:12 AMP)

Sin, lust and evil desires are all part of the darkness that continually tries to penetrate our lives. When the minister chose to embrace sin, the light Jesus put in him or her was replaced with darkness from Satan. This is why the Word tells us to give no place to the devil (Ephesians 4:27). When the minister allowed a small bit of darkness, the darkness filled the whole body (Matthew 6:21-24).

The principle of a little yeast having the ability to spoil the whole loaf can be found more than once in scripture (Galatians 5:9 and 1 Corinthians 5:6). The minister's actions violated this scripture, and as a result he or cannot bring a Word to bless the people. While it is true the minister can put together a sermon or dust off one from the past, the problem is the sermon will not be blessed. Without the light of the Spirit and blessing from God, the sermon may minister to the flesh of the congregation, but it will not feed its spiritual needs.

In this regard, the minister should be required to pass the ministry duties to someone else for a season so the minister can spend time reigniting the light in their lives. The minister needs time to be fed the Word. One cannot minister the Word if his or her life is empty of the life-giving Spirit of God.

This season of rest will give the minister an opportunity to reconnect with the Lord, to be cleansed by the Word and then reclaim the proclamation of the Word as if the sin was never committed (Ephesians 5:26). This is what the Word promises, and it is important we give our ministers the opportunity to have this period of refreshing for their sake and the for the sake of their congregations.

Why a sabbatical?

> "If your right eye serves as a trap to ensnare you or is an occasion for you to stumble and sin, pluck it out and throw it away. It is better that you lose one of your members than that your

whole body be cast into hell (Gehenna)."

(MATTHEW 5: 27–29 AMP)

The scriptural basis for the sabbatical can be found in the scripture above where Jesus warns us if a part of us serves as a stumbling block or causes us to sin then that body part needs to be removed. For example, if you went to your doctor and she told you that you needed to have surgery to remove your eye, what would happen? Would you continue to work immediately after the surgery? Absolutely not. Your doctor would require you to rest so your body could recoup. You would need time to become acclimated to living life without the eye that was removed.

Becoming acclimated to your environment and letting those around you become comfortable assisting you will take time. You will need appointments with your doctor so she can monitor your progress. At some point your doctor will clear you to return to work. When you do, your employer may be asked to make changes to accommodate your disability.

If we have to take these steps in the natural to accommodate surgery, what accommodations do you think should be taken to accommodate the surgery God intends to do in the Spirit? Through the sabbatical, God intends to remove the darkness that entered into the life of the minister. Just like in the natural world where the employee would be asked to be released from their work duties to allow their bodies and families to heal, God expects the same type of recovery process from spiritual surgery. In addition to the suspension of the ministry of the Word, the minister should be asked to take a sabbatical and released from all ministerial duties. During the sabbatical, the minister should be encouraged to accomplish the prescription that is laid out in Acts 3:19 NIV:

1) *Repent, then and*

2) *turn to God,*

3) *so that your sins may be wiped out,*

4) *that times of refreshing may come from the Lord.*

The times of refreshing will take place during the sabbatical, and the minister must be removed from the ministry for that occur. This will allow time for the minister to reconnect with God, him or herself and the family. It is an important time that should not be minimized in any way. When the minister initially begins the refreshing, there likely will be some anxiety to get back to the ministry. The team charged with restoring the minister has to allow the restoration process to become fully completed. What the minister is tasked with during the sabbatical is to wait on the Lord and let Him renew his strength (Isaiah 40:31).

The sabbatical should be treated just like a cake being baked in the oven with time, care and attention so the perfect cake emerge out from the oven. If the cake stays in too long, it will be burned. If removed to early, it will be under cooked. The minister needs to stay away on sabbatical until he or she becomes engulfed in the times of refreshing with the Lord. When those sessions with the Lord become so filling the minister longs to be in the presence of the Lord instead of returning to the ministry, then the time for the sabbatical has come to an end. The minister should have reconnected with his or her family in such a way they are ready to return to them. This is another indication the sabbatical should end.

The sabbatical is not about time, instead it is about refreshing and the restoration. The sabbatical should last for a specific time. As a doctor may give a post-op patient a certain period to recuperate, the patient needs to be prepared to take whatever time is necessary to heal adequately. Every few weeks the patient will meet with the doctor to see progress.

In the same manner, the restoration team should require a meeting with the minister at least once a month to determine the minister's progress. The team should be spiritually sensitive to the leading of the Spirit, and the only thing they need to address with the minister is whether he or she is ready for reinstatement.

The minister is not to be given updates about the ministry nor should anyone take advice from the minister during the sabbatical. Like Moses on Mount Sinai, the minister should be disconnected from the people and ministry to be with God. Some can even suggest 40 days or six weeks as an initial time for the sabbatical. There are a number of times in the scripture when holy men sought to be alone with God (Moses, Jesus and Elijah) and each spent 40 days with him. The number 40 seems to be a number God has chosen to emphasize times of trouble or hardship (Got Questions Ministries, 2016). The restoration team would, in my opinion, be making a wise decision to set the initial period at six weeks and then let the Spirit guide to any extensions after the initial period. Only the Holy Spirit and the minister knows how long the sabbatical needs to be.

With regards to rather or not the sabbatical needs to be paid or not, I believe if the goal is restoration and reinstatement for the minister, then he or she should not be concerned about meeting the needs of the family. Putting this kind of condition on the minister will be yokes and distractions, and the church along with the restoration team needs to be mindful God is holding them accountable for this task.

If they put undue hardships or conditions on the minister during the sabbatical that causes the minister to stumble further, then the church and members of the restoration team will have to give account to the Lord for their actions (Romans 14:13-23 ESV). When it comes to whether or not to continue to pay the minister during the sabbatical, I believe the answer can be found in the parable of the Good Samaritan in Luke 10:25-37. While supporting the minister during the sabbatical and the replacement minister who has taken over the duties is most likely going to be a hardship during the period, it is one which the church members, if they put their trust in God, will find He will make supernatural provisions during this period. The church can have faith as they show grace to their minister who has become poor in spirit (Matthew 5:3) and expect God to make provisions to cover the expenses (Proverbs 19:17).

In asking the minister to take a sabbatical, in addition to the suspension from the ministry of the Word, the church will allow God to do his work to refresh the minister and all those parties who were directly or indirectly impacted by the minister's failings. The minister's family and anyone else involved in the sin will also need to experience the refreshing times the Lord will provide. The restoration team should follow the same process with any individual involves as well. If they are workers or staff members within the ministry, they should be required to take sabbaticals as well. If they are not, the restoration team should take extra care to assign each person their restoration brother and sister in the Lord who will be responsible for extending Christ's love to that individual. All of those responsible for working with each of these individuals must be committed to seeing the person restored and reinstated into the congregation. This should be their ministry priority until all parties receive full restoration.

Why ministers have a tough time keeping their marriages and families together

Ministers' difficulties keeping their marriages and families together is another topic for this chapter. The answer is very simple: They are committing adultery with the Bride of Christ. This topic is just an extension of the previous topic and not a new chapter. I am calling it "adultery" because that is what it is called when a person is unfaithful to their spouse. Unfortunately, that can happen not only physically but also spiritually. Many times in scripture we see God compared the actions of the nation of Israel to that of an adulteress (Isaiah 57:3, 7; Ezekiel 16:23, Hosea 3:1) because they conducted what in the Greek is called "moichalis." It is used figuratively to indicate one who is unfaithful to God as an adulteress is unfaithful toward her husband.

Please remember here I am part of the ministry, so while I am writing about it in the third person here, I am part of the "they".

Pastors and other members of the fivefold ministry have to be mindful the congregations they minister to are in fact the Bride of Christ (Revelation 21:9-11). While they hold these offices and perform duties that minister to the Bride, they only do that because Christ called them to these offices. They get their authority and directives direct from Him.

What can happen when every counseling session, ministry opportunity or time to visit the sick is not appointed by God but instead are duties they put on their schedules because they think they are the things we are supposed to be doing so we do not "miss God."

Romans 10:15 tells us each member of the fivefold ministry is supposed to be the "sent ones." This means God is the one who appoints ministers, and He is the one who gives them specific assignments. Each day in the life of Jesus, we see him going from place to place only ministering to those whom God sent him to minister to that day. Jesus did not select his own route nor did he select his own schedule. Whatever God put on his schedule is what He addressed that day.

In ministry many members of the congregation tug on the ministers for time and they see many opportunities for ministry come across our desk. When this happens, they must start asking, "Is the Lord assigning me to this?"

When ministers are honest with themselves, they will acknowledge they assigned some of the things they did as ministries themselves. They accepted the ministry opportunity or scheduled a counseling session without seeking the Master's approval. It can happen so quickly and quietly nobody takes notice. Soon it will become second nature for them to respond without finding out what God wants on their agenda.

After a while they will fool themselves into thinking with each activity they are serving God because they are doing His work. In reality, they are not doing His work but rather they are serving themselves.

God has not assigned all those tasks to them but yet they are expecting Him to bless their efforts. What has happened is they have become too familiar with Christ's Bride and this has caused them to lose respect for who is sending them.

When they send themselves, they are no longer doing His will. If they are doing their own will and they are doing it with His Bride, then they have become unfaithful. Their faithfulness is not stable. Sometimes they do exactly as God commands and other times they direct themselves. When they are doing this with His Bride, they are doing it out of their flesh and there is no grace from Him to do that work.

This will result in the minister feeling excessively fatigued, burdened, and troubled because all the activities with the Bride of Christ far exceeds what the minister has been asked to do. The Bible tells us even God rested from his work (Genesis 2:3). However, the ministers keep going and going. The problem is they have not been given extra hours of the week to fulfill these added activities.

So where does these extra hours get taken from? Their family. Little by little they steal hours away from their spouse and children. Little by little the family has to go on with life without them. They justify this because they are doing the work of the Lord, but in fact they are not. They are doing the work of self. Their spouse and children are suffering without their presence, and their disobedience to being faithful with only the work God has given them to do tears their family apart.

A minister's marriage is his or her first ministry. You can find by reviewing the institution of marriage in Genesis chapter 2. Before anyone received a calling to do any work for the Lord, God created the institution of marriage. In fact, if you examine God's direction to, "Be fruitful, multiply and replenish the earth," in Genesis 1:28, notice it says that He spoke to them. The "them" was Adam and Eve. Though the creation of Eve happens in chapter 2, it sequentially took place before God spoke His purpose over Adam and Eve. This is extremely important because if ministers understand this, their ministry becomes a priority over their marriage and then the product of their marriage— their children.

Without this understanding, they will think they are pleasing God when in fact they are missing Him.

If you are called to the ministry and your spouse is talking about divorce, then you need to stop and see if you are committing spiritual adultery with the Bride of Christ. Take out your calendar from last week and spend some time with the Holy Spirit, asking him if each of the activities was assigned activity from Him or if you assigned them yourself. Ask yourself when you study for your next sermon or teaching assignment whether or not God gave it to you or if you are ministering the Word to yourself. It is time to stop and ask yourself if you have become too familiar with the Bride of Christ. Are you more excited about your ministry opportunities and activities than about being home with your spouse and children?

If in your time of reflection, you are convicted in your spirit to realize you have committed spiritual adultery, you need to go back and follow the "Steps of Restoration" outlined in this chapter. God is looking to bless you, not punish you. He knows your heart's desire and as you allow Him to minister to you during these times of refreshing, you will meet Him anew, and He will breathe new life into your marriage, too.

Scripture:

> "Therefore, if you have any encouragement from being united with Christ, if any comfort from his love, if any common sharing in the Spirit, if any tenderness and compassion, then make my joy complete by being like-minded, having the same love, being one inspirit and of one mind.

> Do nothing out of selfish ambition or vain conceit. Rather, in humility value others above yourselves, not looking to your own interests but each of you to the interests of the others.

> In your relationships with one another, have the same mindset as Christ Jesus:

> Who, being in very nature God, did not consider equality with God something to be used to his own advantage; rather, he made himself nothing by taking the very nature of a servant, being made in human likeness.

> And being found in appearance as a man, he humbled himself by becoming obedient to death – even death on a cross."

> (PHILIPPIANS 2: 1-8 NIV)

CHAPTER 12

THE IMPORTANCE OF MARRIAGE RESURRECTION

Understanding how God's work in marriage resurrection will make a difference.

Marriage resurrection is not a new work from God, instead its power and purpose has been hidden from the Church. God has chosen this day and hour to restore these lost truths in order to move His plan forward so a bride is ready to meet her groom.

In this chapter, we will examine the importance of the redemptive work of marriage resurrection and God's plans for it to make a difference in the lives of married couples today. There are five specific ways marriage resurrection will impact the Body of Christ and the world at large.

> **Impact #1 –**
> **Christ is coming back for an unblemished bride**
> **that does not have divorce on her mind.**

"Husbands, love your wives, as Christ loved the church and gave himself up for her, that he might sanctify her, having cleansed her by the washing of water with the word, so that he might present the church to himself in splendor, without spot or wrinkle or any such thing, that she might be holy and without blemish in the same way."

(EPHESIANS 5:25 -27 ESV)

Imagine a young man standing at the altar with his best man by his side and a church full of family members and friends who have come to wish him well on his wedding day. As the bride arrives at the altar to have her veil removed, she leans forward and whispers in her groom's ear, "About thirty-forty percent of me is ready for a divorce."

What future husband would want to marry her? None.

As the father of a grown son, I have had the proud opportunity to have a father and son conversation about marriage as he is contemplating this event in his future. During the conversation, it was clear he fully believes his impending bride is 100 percent prepared to give herself totally to him. Because he is sure of this, he is ready to ask for her hand in marriage. If he thought there was any doubt in her mind even in the smallest portion, he would postpone his proposal as no man wants to ask a woman for her hand and be rejected.

In that way, our Lord does not want to return for a bride who believes she is not ready to live forever with him or who believes she has an option to terminate the relationship with Him. It sounds preposterous to think any member of the Body of Christ would not want to spend eternity with Christ.

In earlier chapters, we studied over 30 percent of the Body of Christ has already experienced a divorce, and many divorcees have moved on to their second and third marriages. Divorce is so prevalent in our society that it no longer carries a stigma. It is now widely accepted as just another phase of life.

Acceptance of divorce is not a worldly concept; we studied in earlier chapters Christians are getting divorced at a higher percentage than atheists or agnostics. Realizing many believers have not closed the door on divorce as an option, it is not hard to understand from God's perspective, the Body of Christ does have divorce on her mind.

Christ cannot return for a bride who has not fully committed to conducting herself in the marriage to the King as God original intended it when he created Eve for Adam. After God created Eve, he presented her to Adam, and the institution of marriage was established. In its original and purest form, God designed it to be between a man and woman in a union that would last forever.

As Hosea redeemed and restored his wayward bride, God in his mercy and wisdom knew his Son's bride would also be wayward. Through his grace he offered two distinct redemptive works, the marriage reconciliation and marriage resurrection lifeboats. With marriage resurrection, God only needs one spouse and with one spouse he can turn an entire situation around.

Unfortunately, the church leans on marriage reconciliation as the only redemptive work God wants to do when love is lost in a Christian married couple. This leaves both the counselor and the spouse open to staying in fellowship with the marriage covenant without options when one spouse is determined to end the marriage. However, our ignorance of Christ's redemptive work on the cross has resulted in an untold number of marriages that possibly could have been saved had the work of marriage resurrection been known to us. Think of the carnage to families, communities and our nation could have been avoided if this truth had been discovered earlier. It always with us, we were blind.

That day is over because our God saw fit to remove the scales from our eyes and brought new meaning from the Bible. Today, God is restoring these truths to ensure His bride is fully persuaded to be married to the King of Kings in a commitment for eternity and she is ready to honor that covenant.

Impact #2 –
The Body of Christ will be separated from the world
in preparation for Christ's return.

As I travel through communities and different states, it always surprises me to see churches on every corner, and near the church is a lawyer's office that advertises family law, dissolution and divorce services. The Lord brought to my attention almost two decades ago this pattern of the enemy to surround his houses of worship with businesses that trip up believers to falling for the works of the flesh. When I first noticed, I would see churches and liquor stores in close proximity. Years later, the Lord brought to my attention the proximity between houses of worship and law offices. Unfortunately, there is a connection.

Christian married couples are not falling prey to lawyers who are pouncing on the troubles and ills in Christian couples. Instead, the lawyers are no different than the liquor store owners. They are business people who are going where the money is. The truth is Christians need to take a hard look in the mirror to find the financial resources supporting those in the legal profession to terminate their relationships.

According to a 2006 article on Forbes.com, divorce proceedings can range from a few hundred to many thousands of dollars, with the average cost of a contested divorce ranging from $15,000 to $30,000, mostly spent on legal fees (Magloff, 2010). The online website Nolo.com, which helps consumers find answers to everyday legal questions, shows most of their consumers reported paying around $15,500 for their divorces, which included $12,800 in attorney fees (Internet Brands, Inc, 2016). According to U.S. Congressional Life Surveys the average American worshipper contributes $1,500 a year to their churches (Religion Division of Lily Endowment, Inc., 2016). When you compare what couples are willing to spend to terminate their marriage compared to what they are willing to put in the offering plates, it shows how our priorities to the God's kingdom are lopsided.

It is unfortunate it will take 10 years of passing the offering plate to equal what a married couple will spend on their divorce. This is money a married couple is willing to part with on something God says He hates (Malachi 2:16). The millions of dollars spent by Christian married couples across the United States to terminate marriages in a single year could have been spent on supporting mission trips, building youth and children programs at churches, building new worship houses and a whole host of other programs for kingdom building.

The time has come for the Body of Christ to separate from the world, and marriage resurrection is one of God's tools that will be used. Imagine if Christians stopped hiring lawyers to handle their divorces because they turned to God's free mercy and grace offered through his redemptive work. Imagine pastors who would counsel married couple about the good news of God's alternative plans available to them when divorce enters their house. Jesus told us many stories in the four gospels that in these last days he would be separating his church from the world and His disciples from those who have not made him Lord (Matthew 13:24-30). Right after God says he hates divorce, a chapter later he said he does not change (Malachi 3:6).

Restoring marriage resurrection to the church will give the Body of Christ what God wants in the first place—people who have moved away from making decisions based on the values of this world. This is God's design for all marriages, and it is great to know when it seems our marriages have run their courses and hit what appears insurmountable walls, we no longer have to take what the world considers as the way out. Instead, we can choose God's redemptive work in a marriage resurrection to avoid the devastation a divorce causes. While doing this, we will get closer to God, rekindle our love relationship with our spouses, and save thousands of dollars. It literally pays to follow God and to separate ourselves unto Him by choosing His way in our marriages.

> ## Impact #3 –
> ## Christian married couples will learn how to
> ## appropriately respond to adversity.

"When you are in tribulation, and all these things come upon
you in the latter days, you will return to the Lord your God and
obey his voice. For the Lord your God is a merciful God. He will
not leave you or destroy you or forget the covenant with your
fathers that he swore to them."

(DEUTERONOMY 4:30-31 ESV)

Too often when a marriage hits a rough patch, which we discovered as the spirit of restlessness in chapter 2, the couple turns to friends, family, acquaintances and even their own feelings that have been grossly influenced by the media and the world instead of turning to God. While the tribulation should have caused them to seek God's ways, instead they are quick to hit the "I want out" button.

One of God's impact with marriage resurrection is to help the married couple learn to go deeper to seek His ways, hear His voice and obey His commands. Very few things in life are as emotionally, spiritually and physically tasking as a marital separation and divorce. It is through these tough times if they allow it, the Lord is able to get a couple's attention, encouraging them to choose His ways.

Learning to believe God for a marriage resurrection will show a couple they can believe him when there seems to be no way out. Statements we make in church such as, "He will cause water to appear in the desert" or "He will make a

way where to seems to be no way," are just sayings until we add faith to them.

When a couple feels they have done all they know how to do to save their marriage to no avail, marriage resurrection brings them hope in the middle of a dark situation. With this hope, they have an opportunity to put complete trust in the Lord, believing he can turn their situation around and do work in the life of the one we love.

Mothers almost always believe a child who has lost his or her way will one day meet Jesus on the road, repent and come home. These mothers do not lose heart as they believe God will perform this kind of miracles in the lives of their wayward children. Yet, these same women often fail to believe God is not only able but willing to restore their marriage. Current marriage and divorce statistics suggest, up until now, many have not been willing to believe in such a miracle. This is especially true since the church has not been able to show her in the Word this was a work God has promised he will do.

Believing in God for a marriage resurrection will cause both spouses to grow spiritually, which is the impact He wants to see in the Body of Christ; mature sons and daughters taking His word and overcoming the world. That is God's heart, and it is the same victory Jesus accomplished God now wants to it to be seen in us (1 John 5:4).

Growth is not going to happen to married couples who continue to choose to be carnally minded instead of led by the Spirit. A couple cannot arrive at having marital problems if the couple is walking by the Spirit because the Spirit would never lead them this way. The very fact that they are having marital problems indicates somewhere along the way they have relied on flesh instead of submitting to the Holy Spirit's guidance.

Unlike in a marriage reconciliation, where God gets involved as the couple submits, a marriage resurrection is a redemption. This means God seeks a lost one who is not seeking to be found. By its very nature, marriage resurrection will cause spiritual growth first for the spouse who seeks to stay connected in marital fellowship and then in the spouse who has departed. The couple will have seen salvation for their marriage can only be achieved by leaning on the Lord. Once the couple experiences this redemptive work, it brings a deep gratitude and desire to be closer to God and to each other.

Experiencing God in this way deepens your trust in Him and increases your confidence to turn to God in other times of adversity. At the first sign of trouble, seek God instead of responding to your flesh. In experiencing a marriage resurrection, the couple comes to realize while God is merciful, and His heart's desire is the couple seek His face daily and follow His commandments. Marriage resurrection is a crash course on growing up spiritually. God is trying to get your attention at the onset of the tribulation and looking for you to make a change that will result in being closer to him and his plans and purpose for your lives.

Impact #4 –
Marriage resurrection impacts the family unit,
the community and the nation.

Couples are fooled if they believe their divorce is just between them. The impact can be felt even down to the children and the children's children. Not only is the family unit impacted, but the community is impacted as it learns of the divorce occurring within it. As divorce splits up a family, and friendships the children developed can be torn apart.

As Christians we may be one of the few or only ones in our neighborhood or community who knows the Lord. God desires you and your kids to be a lighthouse to your neighbors. We do not always know the impact or influence we have on the person sitting right beside during that school recital. We are not always aware how the family nearby is watching us and seeing how the Lord blesses us. Watching you and your family every Sunday get up and go to church may be the only witness they have to make them interested in learning your beliefs.

Divorce destroys influence and says to the rest of the world we are no different than they are. However, when the world sees and hears your marriage was in trouble and saw how close to your family came to destruction but then they witnessed the salvation of God in your marriage, it becomes a great living witness of the Lord's goodness which can be shared with the community.

Divorce is public. More than any other time in your life, a divorce puts your life on display. We see it with celebrities when their divorce becomes headline news. In our communities, a divorce tells our neighbors God has no answer to either. This, of course, is not true. Where a divorce shatters hope, a marriage resurrection says to the community God is alive, cares and offers his children help only He can accomplish.

When a family unit stays whole as a result of a marriage resurrection, it makes in impact on the community. The impact God intended for the family to make when they moved into that house and into that community remains active. The work the enemy tried to bring against the family and for the community gets thwarted.

A family's impact on a community cannot be ignored. Think of Joshua's and his family's impact on the nation of Israel when he declared, "But as for me and my house, we will serve the Lord" (Joshua 24:15 ESV). The Bible records in the very next verse the people responded to Joshua's stance by declaring, "Far be it from us that we should forsake the Lord" (Joshua 24:16 ESV).

Later in the chapter it is recorded in verse 31, "Israel served the Lord all the days of Joshua, and all the days of the elders who outlived Joshua and had known all the work that the Lord did for Israel." Imagine the impact families will have on their community and the communities in their nation as they choose to serve the Lord through the redemptive work of a marriage resurrection. The more this option is chosen, the more of a marked difference there will be between the

world and the church. Like the impact Joshua had on the nation of Israel in his day, a married husband or wife can have a strong impact on their community and ultimately on their nation simply by choosing to believe God for new life into their dead marriage.

> ## Impact #5 –
> Marriage resurrection has always been available to the church, but God has chosen this hour in human history to restore the work.

Think of all the times in human history during the past 2,000 years God could have brought the work of a marriage resurrection back to the church, yet he has chosen our lifetime to make it happen. It causes one to wonder what it is about our time that makes the restoration of marriage resurrection so relevant. I believe the answer can be found in Acts 3:19-21 ESV, which reads as follows:

Repent therefore, and turn back, that your sins may be blotted out, that times of refreshing may come from the presence of the Lord, and that he may send the Christ appointed for you, Jesus, whom heaven must receive until the time for restoring all the things about which God spoke by the mouth of his holy prophets long ago.

Many prophets and ministers of the Gospel have declared we are the last of the last days. As you review scriptures like 2 Timothy 3:15, Luke 21:11, or Matthew 24:6, signs of famine, times of difficulty, and rumors of wars support the fact the last days are really upon us. Our Lord's return is quickly coming upon us.

With his return being so imminent, then what was promised in Acts 3:20 and 21 AMP must also be upon us, which is, "And that He may send [to you] the Christ (the Messiah), Who before was designated and appointed for you – even Jesus, whom heaven must receive [and retain] until the time for the complete restoration of all God spoke by the mouth of all his holy prophets for ages past [from the most time in the memory of man]."

Other than the earth and the creation of mankind, what is more ancient than the institution of marriage? Shortly after creating the earth and man, God recognized it was not good for Adam to be alone and he made a suitable, adaptable, and complementary companion for him (Genesis 2:18 AMP). With the creation of this suitable companion, God also created a union comprised Adam and Eve and called the union "one flesh." God's original design for Adam was for him "to become united and cleave to his wife and they shall become one flesh (Genesis 2:24 AMP).

Those seeking to be a marital unit God put together are far away from God's original design. God goes on to say what he put together let no man, which includes the man and woman in the marriage, separate (Mark 10:9). Since the time Moses first permitted the children of Israel to give their wives a certificate of divorce because of sexual immorality in Deuteronomy chapter 24, it seems with the passage of time permission has grown wider and wider. Through the ages, the governments of nations yielded to the desires of individuals to find even more permissible grounds for divorce.

Division has never been a path to wholeness, and God knew on the day he created Adam and Eve. He wanted them forever to enjoy the fruits of the union. Likewise, God wants us to enjoy the benefits of a marriage He ordains.

Just like wars and rumors of wars are signs point to the last day, the rediscovery of this revelation about marriage resurrection is now being restored to the church in this latter day, signals another sign the King is soon to return.

Scripture:

> "Repent therefore, and turn back, that your sins may be blotted out, that times of refreshing may come from the presence of the Lord, and that he may send the Christ appointed for you, Jesus, whom heaven must receive until the time for restoring all the things about which God spoke by the mouth of his holy prophets long ago."
>
> (ACTS 3: 19-21 ESV)

WIFE'S COMMENTARY

When you are deceived, you do not know you are being deceived. This definitely describes me before God intervened in my marriage. As I mentioned in the previous section, not too long after my 50th birthday, I had what I thought was a minor accident. Soon after I realized not only did it leave physical scars, the trauma of the event caused severe psychological damage that forced me to face my biggest fears and shook the foundation I had relied on most of my life to keep me grounded and balanced.

I became angry and full of fear. As I began to seek treatment for a number of issues, including post-traumatic stress disorder, an eating disorder, hypertension, and severe depression,. I didn't realize the impact of those mental illnesses I was struggling with and the toll they would take on my physical body as well.

I found myself questioning every relationship in my life, including my relationships with the Lord and my husband. Because I was having a hard time processing what was happening to me, I was unable to love myself and found my husband an easy scapegoat to help ease my pain. I used every negative word he said to me as proof I should not spend the rest of my life with him. I was angry with him for past sins. I was angry with him because he seemed disinterested or unable to help me heal. I was angry with him because he traveled too much for his job, and I was angry with him for leaving his job to become owner of several franchises. I took all of these actions personally. I saw them as his lack of concern about the issues I was facing.

Because my initial treatment for the eating disorder kept me away from home and work every weekday for several weeks, it became easy for me to justify my thoughts about him. I spent a lot of time thinking about things he said to me, playing them over and over in my head until I was convinced he did not have enough concern to be a part of my recovery. Because our times together on the weekends were often strained and stress-filled, I became more and more resolved in my decision to sever all ties.

Our relationship began to remind me of a time when we lived apart on weekdays for several years because of my job. As I thought back on those times, I believed then that rather than our hearts growing fonder, we had become more independent and more isolated from each other.

I moved out of the house about three months into my treatment and lived with my son for a while before getting my own place. I rented a house and moved all of my things, having no intention of living with my husband again. I felt as if we had grown apart, and I was convinced I could find happiness without him.

For a while this worked. I lived with my son for briefly, and when I rented a house he moved in with me for a couple of weeks as he prepared for an out-of-state move. Just a short time after that I had another roommate. In what seemed like a blink of an eye, I found myself engulfed in a relationship with someone I thought I would be with after I divorced my husband.

Even as I engaged in a relationship with another man and made plans with him for my life when I was free to marry again, I did not realize Satan was set-ting me up for complete and utter failure. Not only was the enemy looking to "sift me like wheat" (Luke 22:31), he was aimed at taking away my testimony and God-given purpose for my life.

The separation and divorce proceedings with my husband lasted six months. After five months of planning a life without him, in one night, I had an en-counter that removed the scales from my eyes and reset my course to regain my faith and dependency on God. I realized every single thing I did wrong. I felt sorry for my behavior and the way I felt about my husband. Though I had no idea how it would happen, I wanted to regain my dependency on God and reunite with my husband.

The details of that night are still fuzzy to me and because my experience de-fied logic and reason, it is difficult to explain.

Here is what I recall.

I was about to embark on a trip across the country to make a decision about a treatment option, and I intended to surprise the man I planned to be with as soon as my divorce was finalized. I struggled all day to get ready for the trip. I rescheduled my flight three times until I ran out of options and had to leave the next day. I had a sense of foreboding as the evening wore on. I felt as if someone was following me and, confused and uneasy, I decided to spend the night in a hotel rather than at my house.

I could not sleep no matter how hard I tried, and the night surrounded me in endless darkness. As I tossed and turned and tried to still my swirling emo-tions, the Lord began speaking to me, urging me to address every attitude, be-havior, and decision I had made in my marriage. After so many days of refusing to listen, He finally had my attention.

As it got later and later, something inside of me gave way, and I felt convic-tion so powerful I no longer wanted to continue down the path I had started. I was ashamed of myself and for the example I had set with my children. I real-ized that I no longer wanted to live contrary to what I really believed about my life, that I was a child of God and was created for reason. I wanted to find a way to use what Satan meant to destroy me and create a platform to inform others about the love and grace of God. I could no longer imagine a life with the man I had been seeing. I longed to return home, but panic struck as I thought of my husband. What would he think of me? Would he even want to see me again? How could I possibly explain all that had transpired since I had walked away from him for the third time? Would he forgive me? Would I still be desirable to him? What would be the best way to bridge a conversation about reconciliation? I had so many questions and no idea about the bridge that was under construction for my safe passage back to him.

If it wasn't for my husband forgiving me with an open heart and open arms and he and another attorney fighting for my patient rights while I was in the hospital and with the attorneys that had other ideas about how I should live my life, I honestly do not know where I would be today.

What happened to me is nothing short of a miracle. The Lord intervened on my behalf and because my husband was a willing vessel, he was able to be used for God's glory. I am in my right mind and in my rightful place beside my husband, not only because I repented but also because he prayed for me. His intercession on my behalf is what enabled the construction of the love bridge that made it possible for me to return to his side. I spent some time in a psychiatric hospital and while there, I terminated the divorce proceedings, cut off all communication with and connection to the person I had chosen over my husband, and started the process of beginning to repair the fissures that had developed in the relationships with my husband and children.

When my husband and I came together, it was like a miracle. The disagreements we had during the whole course of our marriage were suddenly gone, and we instantly found agreement. That was one of the outcomes from the Lord's visit with me.

A marriage resurrection is a miracle the moment it occurs. It's supernatural but that does not mean there is not any work involved. My husband prayed and believed earnestly in the sanctity and authority of God's Word to win me back.

You may be wondering what is different about this third time. I am different. Not only do I see myself differently, but for the first time I saw my husband in a new light. I was able to appreciate and be reassured by his gestures of love and concern where I had previously misinterpreted them as manipulating, controlling, and uncaring. Psalm 51:17 says the Lord desires the sacrifice of a broken and contrite spirit. Most importantly, I have begun to see myself as God sees me. I realized my sin and need for forgiveness. Because of my brokenness, God could finally get to me and pour His Spirit into me, showing me that His grace is sufficient for me and His strength is made perfect in my weakness (2 Corinthians 12:9).

God's Help in Marriage Resurrection

Exterior Components

What makes **Exterior** components unique?
- Can be observed by the human eye.
- Others don't have to be spiritual to properly recognize your character.
- You may receive encouragement from others as you positively display Christ's character.

Icon	Christian Character/ Belief	Bridge Component	Scripture
	Repentance	Parapet	Acts 3:19
	Intercession	Labor	Ezekiel 22:30
	Faith	Pillar	Hebrews 6:10–12
	Patience	Pillar	Galatians 5:22–23
	Love	Handrail	1 John 4:18
	Fellowship	Joints	Ephesians 4:16

Interior Components

What makes **Interior** components unique?
- Cannot be observed by the human eye.
- Others will have to be spiritual and seeking the Spirit's leading to properly understand your character and behavior.
- You may receive ridicule and discouragement from others as they question your motives and actions as you positively display Christ's character.

Icon	Christian Character/ Belief	Bridge Component	Scripture
	Forgiveness	Walkway	Colossians 3:19
	Obedience	Fasteners	Jeremiah 38:20
	Spiritual Warfare	Foundation	Ephesians 6:12
	Praise	Blueprints	2 Chronicles 20:22

SECTION THREE

RECONCILIATION, NOW WHAT?

Staying committed to the resurrection plan will definitely bring your spouse home. But now that they have come home does life go back to the way things were? Absolutely not. My wife and I have gone through the separation and reconciliation process three times in our marriage. The first two were similar. We reconciled because one of us was willing to look into the mirror, repent and ask for the other spouse's forgiveness. There was no gesture of repentance for their own actions by the spouse who was put in the position to judge and offer mercy to the repented spouse. During these types of reconciliations one spouse was allowed to hold their ground and this resulted in this spouse feeling as if she was right along. While it brought repentance for one spouse, to the other it felt like vindication.

All this does is kick the decision to divorce down the road. Nobody wants that because you are setting yourself up to go through this experience a second or in my case, a third time. You know how you feel right now. It seems like someone pulled your heart completely out of your chest, played with it for a while and shoved it back into your body. Not a pleasant experience you will want to repeat.

The beauty about the Lord's resurrection plan is it causes a heart change in both spouses. In the examination of their lives against the standards of God's Word, both spouses will learn they have fallen short. This puts both spouses on equal footing as they re-enter each other's lives.

One must realize because personal changes were made the spouse that left is no longer the same person coming home. You used the changes you have made during the resurrection plan as a tool to attract your spouse's attention and tantalize them to want to come home.

Dreaming about coming home and what happens when the spouse actually comes home are two different things especially when you are intending never to come this way again. From the moment your spouse contacts you to indicate their desire to come home, you better be ready with a vision on what this new marriage will look like or all your hard work during the resurrection process will be lost.

As your spouse takes a giant leap of faith to begin making their way home, rest assured they have many thoughts going through their head. Some thoughts are telling them they are doing the right thing. Others are suspect a reconciliation with you could actually work. For the moment, thoughts of moving ahead are taking the lead. It is important for you to realize the burden of laying out the plan for a new marriage is on you. You were the one bold enough to believe the marriage could continue when others thought it was completely dead. You are the one who interrupted your spouse's plans for divorce so know the decision to return home is the extent of any plans your spouse has.

Understand reconciliation was never an option in your spouse's mind and possibly never a consideration before this. Their decision to give reconciliation a chance is a response to your gestures and the changes you have made. A decision to give it a try is all they have made. Though your spouse has no specific plans there is one thought rising to the top of their thinking with each step towards home "We have reconciled, now what?"

CHAPTER 13

ENFORCE YOUR RIGHT TO BE FREE

With a successful marriage resurrection behind you, what happens next?

Very few married couples who go on to file for divorce escape the clutches of that monster and believing God can raise a dead marriage definitely defies the odds. It is a tremendous effort you are undertaking and the rewards of having the family divide mended and relationships made whole is a miracle unto itself. Despite where you are in the marriage resurrection effort, it is never too early to start planning for the day your spouse comes home. Having already experienced that day myself, I can tell you it will be one filled with all sorts of emotions, from sheer excitement at the return of your spouse to utter disbelief and anger when you learn about the things your spouse did during the separation. In this chapter, we will explore some very tough decisions you are going to have be ready to make if the victory you are striving hard for with the marriage resurrection is going to be maintained once your spouse comes home. You need to be aware once your spouse comes home, do not think for a moment that Satan is going to shrink in the corner, lick his wounds, and leave you alone because of the victory you gained. Unfortunately, that is wishful thinking. The victory you gained through the marriage resurrection needs to be cultivated and maintained or you will find all you worked hard for will be lost. In this chapter, I will share some of the tools you'll need to maintain your marriage resurrection victory.

One of the most profound parables is recorded by Jesus is of the prodigal son in Luke 15. If you are not familiar with the story, take some time to read the entire account. For our purposes, we will just look at some of the important points in the story. The parable tells of a wealthy father who has two adult sons. The younger son demands from his father immediately his share of the father's estate he would inherit. Upon receipt of his inheritance, the son takes off for a distant country and eventually loses everything in wild living. After the money is completely gone, a famine in that land causes the penniless son to seek employment among the local citizens. However, the only job he can find is one working on a farm feeding the pigs. His wages were so despicable that the Bible says he hungered after the pods the pigs were eating and no one gave to him anything to eat. Eventually, the Bible records the young man came to his senses and remembered the servants who worked for his father did not want for food and he decided to go back home. With a new commitment, the young man declared, "I will arise and go to my father, and I will say to him, "Father, I have sinned against heaven and before you. I am no longer worthy to be called your son. Treat me as one of your hired servants. (Luke 15:18, 19 NIV)." Upon arriving home, the father embraces the son and restores him fully, not as a hired servant, but as a son.

Many times I have pondered this parable looking at it from the father's perspective. Imagine having your son ask you for his share of your estate before you are done with it in death. The son shows a lack of respect and concern for the well-being of the father and his whole attention was just on what he believed the father owed him. How frustrated did the conversation between the father and the son get before the father gave into the young man's request? When the young man arrived back home, he did not have one penny worth of what the father had acquired. The parable does not show us this detail but imagine the father's reaction when he hears how the son wasted all he had worked so long and hard to obtain. Would he be angry? Disappointed, perhaps? Regardless of how these disclosures would make the father feel, if he intended on maintaining the victory he obtained through a lost son coming home, the father would have to deny his feelings of anger and/or disappointment and embrace the joy that comes when something precious is found. It would be impossible for the father to do both. If the father embraces the anger and/or disappointment, the joy would be short lived. The reason for this is because the father has decided what he values most. He can choose to continue valuing the amount of the family's wealth that was lost to wasteful living or he can value the return of his lost son.

When the younger son left, the father considered him as a dead man and treated him like he was forever lost. The father did not know if he would ever see his son again. During their separation, the father saw himself not as a father of two sons but instead the father of one living son. Given the end of the story, it is clear what the father chooses. He chose to value the return of his lost son and re-embraced being the father of two living sons than being the man with twice as much wealth as he currently had. Why would the father make such a choice? Does he not care about his wealth and possessions? Does he not care how the son left in the first place and the wounds he received as a result of his son's behavior? Of course, the father cared about these things. However, he valued his son more than the wealth, possessions and even his own feelings. Riches, possessions, and feelings can be replaced but a son cannot. This is what the father recognized and this is what he embraced the day his son came home. When his son walked out the door, the father counted all of that wealth as nothing to himself but he valued the son returned. As the days continued and he learned about all the wrongs his son committed during the separation, when the anger or disappointment inside him would start to rise the father would have to remind himself he was the father of two living sons.

The lessons learned from observing the father in the parable of the prodigal son is going to be critical to maintaining the victory God gave you when He breathed new life into your dead marriage. Like the prodigal son, when your spouse comes home you will be faced with two major emotional issues. First, you will have to deal with the things your spouse said and did that hurt you as they left. Second, you will have to deal with the things your spouse said and did while they were separated from you. These are very heavy emotional areas to tackle because if you choose not to deal with these situations, Satan will consider them as opportunities to try to unravel the victory that God has given you.

Too often as Christians we focus on believing God for a miracle in our lives but negate to realize once the miracle manifests, the victory must be maintained. A great biblical example of this can be found in the book of Esther. Even after obtaining the crown and being set into the office of queen she continued to keep her Jewish identity and faith a secret until the time came when all the lives of the Jewish people in the kingdom were at stake. Realizing as queen she could choose to risk her position and possibly her life to go make her petition before the King on behalf of herself and all her people but to not do that she would risk something far worst, losing the favor of God. In that situation, Esther chose to reveal her secret and risk offending the king rather than risk offending God. The end result for Esther is she maintained the favor of the king despite disclosing she was Jewish. God allowed the king's favor to be extended even after he learned she was a foreigner. Her actions to continue yielding herself to God instead of acquainting herself to the fear of the king's response netted her being able to remain as queen and save her people.

Your successful completion of a marriage resurrection is nothing short of a miracle in your life. Now, in order to maintain the miracle, you need to know about two important biblical truths—freedom and blessing. With Jesus' death at Calvary and resurrection three days later, His work delivered us from the law of sin and death (Romans 8:2). The law held us in bondage under a curse because of our failure to obey it perfectly (Galatians 3:10). With Christ's redemption, we were set free to be released from the law but married to Christ and we should bring forth fruit to God (Romans 7:4).

Your marriage is a part of the fruit God is looking for you to develop and bring to Him as a result of the freedom given to you through Christ. It is difficult for us to think of our marriages as fruit for God but they are. Take time to think of it and you will see what can be produced from your marriage is the very fruit God sought from Adam and Eve at the beginning when He declared to them, "Be fruitful, and multiply, and replenish the earth, and subdue it... (Genesis 1:28)" God was looking for Adam and Eve to multiply themselves in the form of other humans who would spring forth as a result of their union and offspring would bring forth fruit to God in the very same way. In addition, the offspring would enjoy the benefits of all God had given to Adam and Eve and as a result would be become benefactors of God's providence and provision. Finally, as God had given to Adam the authority and governing of everything in the earth, this too would pass from Adam to his offspring. In this simple act from God, Adam and his seed received the right to be free and walk in His blessings.

CHAPTER 13: ENFORCE YOUR RIGHT TO BE FREE

When Adam and Eve ate the forbidden fruit in Genesis 3 and the curse was pronounced upon them (Genesis 3:14-19), their life status transitioned from freedom to bondage and from walking in the blessing to walking in the curse. With Jesus we are redeemed from the law and once again given the right to be free and walk in the blessing. What was the difference from all of those who lived during the times of the Old Testament and you and I who live post resurrection? The difference is the blood of Jesus. Before Christ's death and resurrection, if someone sinned, they had to wait until the one time a year they could go to the priest to sacrifice animals for the remission of their sins. Today, we can walk in the always and forever cleansing of the blood of Jesus, no longer needing the blood of animals for the remission of sin. Instead of the law, we are under grace.

> For sin shall not have dominion over you: for you are not under
> the law, but under grace.
>
> (ROMANS 7:14 KJV)

You are probably wondering how this is important your marriage resurrection. It is vitally important because if you are not aware Christ has made you free and through freedom you have been given the right to walk in all the blessings God bestowed upon you as in the beginning, then you are subject to be fooled by the enemy and having these blessings stolen from you. Satan planned to entangle you and your spouse in strife, sin, and unbelief causing the two of you to fall out of love with each another and ultimately, become willing to abandon what the blessings of God on your lives. However, you thwarted Satan's plans when you learned about God's marriage resurrection lifeboat and because you chose to believe Him. What will keep you from returning to a place of bondage? What will keep you from allowing you and your spouse to walk in a new deception? Just because you reconciled does not mean the enemy is going to stop his plans to try and break the two of you. Remember, his plan is to keep you bound and walking in the curse. As long as you are in bondage, he is free to enjoy all of the bounty of this earth as his own even though it really is God's gift to you as a seed of Adam and Abraham. The answer to maintain the victory you gained through the marriage resurrection is by learning how to enforce your right to remain free.

Freedom and blessings are two spiritual states with a dependency relationship. If you understand and receive the freedom Jesus paid for then you have the opportunity to walk in the blessing. If you desire to walk in the blessing from God, you must first recognize it only comes after one understands and receive the freedom that comes from the redemption Jesus paid. God's response to our request is often limited by how much we truly believe in the freedom he gives us. (Hebrews 11:6, John 8:36 and 1 John 5:15). When it comes to being free or walking in the blessing of God, every Christian, based on what they truly believe, is somewhere in one of four positions.

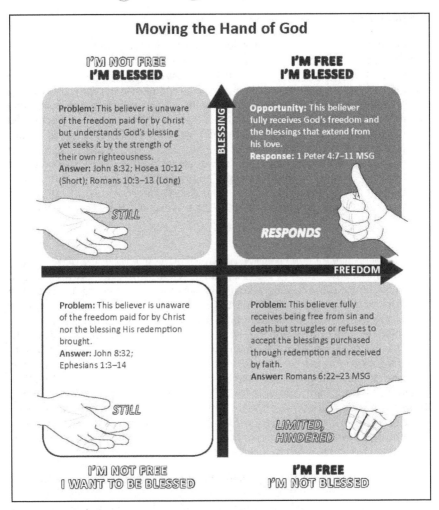

I'm Not Free, I Want to be Blessed

Whether it is ignorance or unbelief, this believer lacks understanding of the freedom and the blessing have been given to them. As a result, they do not have the faith it takes to believe God has made them free despite having desires to receive the blessings of God. Unfortunately, Christians who believe like this have their hope in trying to do good works or by "living right" so they can please God and become worthy of righteousness. Righteousness is a free gift. It can be accepted or rejected but it cannot be earned. Without faith for accepting the free gift of salvation, it is impossible to have faith to believe God has blessed you (Ephesians 1:3). Instead, they are hoping with their prayers and through their good works God will answer one of those prayers and decide to bless. Both are not in agreement with the Word of God. As a result of what this Christian believes, God is not able to move on behalf of this believer.

CHAPTER 13: ENFORCE YOUR RIGHT TO BE FREE

I'm Not Free, I'm Blessed

Like the story of the rich young ruler, which can be found in Mark 10:17 – 22, this Christian has led a good life and through their obedience to the laws of God they have seen things go well in their lives. However, they have not walked in the gift of freedom God has made available to them. Instead, they are working to "live right" to make themselves free. Living right in your own eyes makes you puffed with a false pride instead of humble realizing the freedom was not earned (Romans 11:21-31). Another faulty belief is when one believes because we are working towards perfection as the scripture indicates (Hebrews 6:1), if someone sins is a proof we are not fully free. Individuals taking this stance may be trying to bless their lives through the strength and power of their own hands instead of receiving the blessing that comes from God (Deuteronomy 8:17, 18). None of these beliefs are in agreement with God's Word and they hinder God from working in a person's life.

I'm Free, I'm Not Blessed

Some Christians respond to God like those from Jesus' own town responded to Him when He came around teaching in synagogues and laying hands on the sick. The scripture says in Mark 6:5-6 KJV, "And He could there do no mighty work, save that He laid His hands upon a few sick folks, and healed them. And He marveled become of their unbelief. And He went round about the villages teaching." Many Christians believe through the redemptive work Jesus did at Calvary they have been made free. This belief is in agreement with the Bible teachings yet when it comes down to believing they can walk in the blessings of God; they struggle at embracing things paid for by Christ. There were plenty who suffered from some sort of sickness or disease when Jesus came through his hometown. They even acknowledged mighty works were being done by the hands of Jesus. Yet, because it was Jesus the son of Mary who grew up to be a man of God, they grew offended and refused to receive their healing.

Another example is in Mark 7, where the Pharisees and scribes came to Jesus and asked him why His disciples eat bread with unwashed hands instead of honoring the tradition of the elders. Jesus' ultimate response was, "Full well you reject the commandment of God, that you may keep your own tradition (verse 9)...making the word of God of none effect through your tradition, which you have delivered: and many such like things do you." The Bible teaches us in 3 John 2, "Beloved, I wish above all things you may prosper and be in health, even as your soul prospers." Prosperity, blessing, and good health are all blessings God would have all of us as his children receive. Yet there are many who believe these blessings are not available to us today or they are rewarded conditionally. These beliefs from Christians stem from a multitude of traditional beliefs the Body of Christ held for many years until God gave deeper revelation of his Word. Some refuse to let go of their traditional view to let God speak to them new and afresh today. As a result, they are like those sick in the hometown of Jesus, though he comes to heal all their unbelief, they limit what the Master can do for them.

I'm Free, I'm Blessed

This is the position in which the Father wants all of us, who are his children, to respond to Him in this manner. Doing so removes any restraint and allows God to freely respond to the faith we release. Multiple times in the Gospels, we see Jesus respond to someone who has reached out to Him by faith with the following saying, "Your faith has made you well" or "Your faith has saved you (Mark 5:34, Luke 17:19 and Luke 8:48)." In each of these cases, we see the sick, blind or the troubled able to put aside which takes away from their life and be made well because of their faith in the Lord. The Lord is looking for us to do the same and when we do He can respond by granting the petitions we ask of Him (1 John 5:15).

Enforcing the Rights of Others to be Free and Blessed

By now you see if you want God to move on your behalf, you must accept his freedom and choose to walk in His blessing. This is not a new concept for you because in order to conduct the marriage resurrection, one of the first things you had to do was repent for your responsibility in your marriage relationship. In doing so, you had to realize though your actions were wrong, once you confessed those mistakes, you were to avoid walking in condemnation whether self-imposed or brought to you by others who refused to accept your change of heart. The bottom-line for a believer is we are not supposed to walk in condemnation (Romans 8:1).

This will be important to remember as your spouse comes home. Regardless of what your spouse may have done, you must remember just as Christ has set you free, he set them free also.

> # Lesson Learned #15 –
> ## Your spouse is God's son and daughter;
> ## this takes precedent.

My wife is God's daughter. Your spouse is God's son or daughter. Keeping this in mind is critical to the success of marriage reconciliation and foundational to marriage restoration. You must be just as willing to fight to exercise your spouse's right to be free from condemnation of their past sins and walk in the blessing as you would expect for yourself. You may have feelings of concern. This is how Satan brings fear. He is trying to slink back inside of you to generate distrust in the commitment made by your spouse. Remember commitment was not just made from your spouse to you, it was also made to God.

We have to be careful our human attachments to our spouses do not negate, even in our own minds, the attachment God has toward them. God's attachment is greater and always takes precedent. Why? Because you never died for your spouse and used your own blood to redeem him or her from an eternity in the lake of fire (1 Corinthians 6:20). Our Lord and Savior Jesus Christ did the very thing for your spouse.

At best, your marriage and the time you are going to spend with your spouse will only last while the two of you are here on earth (Matthew 22:30). Having this as your frame of reference makes it easier to put things in the proper perspective when it comes to your spouse and their relationship to God as His son or daughter forever. God's plan, purpose, and perspective of your spouse's life is far above the attachment you may feel or have experienced with your spouse. Knowing God's attachment to your spouse is forever, if you are ever going to have another chance to experience being in real attachment with your spouse, your only opportunity is to become an integral part of fulfilling God's plans, purpose, and perspective for their life.

> **Principle #12:**
> **God is committed to finishing**
> **the work started in your spouse.**

> *"And I am convinced and sure of this very thing, that He Who*
> *began a good work in you will continue until the day of Jesus*
> *Christ [right up to the time of His return], developing [that good*
> *work] and perfecting and bringing it to full completion in you."*
> (PHILIPPIANS 1:6 AMP)

Before you met your spouse, God was doing a work to bring them to himself. At one point, he used you as an instrument to bring love, happiness, and joy to your marriage. God is not about to sit around and let Satan's deception destroy the beautiful work He started in your spouse. Instead, His plan is always to redeem His child back to Himself. God entrusted you initially with the work of carrying out His plan in their life. With the marriage resurrection behind you, He is entrusting you again with that duty. Your decision to participate in the marriage resurrection gave God the commitment you would be his extension of love in your spouse's life and you would do all necessary to work towards the restoration of your spouse to all God had originally planned for his or her life.

Restoring your spouse to himself is the work God wants to do and it is incredibly important you understand. Now your spouse has walked across the love bridge, it is time for you to get busy helping to complete the restoration.

Take note of the areas of restoration needed in life by asking the Holy Spirit through prayer to give you spiritual insight as to your part in the work. Remember, there is your spouse has ever done wrong that Jesus has not already forgiven when they came across the love bridge. It would be wrong for you to even for a moment remind them of what Jesus and God have both forgotten or to use information to bring condemnation. Remember the words of Jesus in Matthew 6:15 that says, "But if you forgive not men their trespasses, neither will your Father forgive your trespasses to be free."

The answer on how to prevent a future separation or divorce in your marriage can be found in you and your spouse's continuous work to enforce the freedom

and right to walk in the blessings of the other spouse. Dealing with the needs of our lives is the natural thing most feel comfortable fighting. We set no limits to fighting on our own behalf but when it comes to others, we set limits. For your marriage reconciliation to last and solidly return your marriage back onto the road of restoration you are going to need to take off the limitations when it comes to you and your spouse. Continually remind yourself your spouse is God's child first and your brother or sister in Christ and then finally your spouse. Keeping focused on this hierarchy will ensure you put proper focus on the relationship you have with your spouse. Though you have intimacy with your spouse, you know the intimacy they share with God always takes precedent. Never look to take God's place in their life and vice versa, nor treat them in a way contrary to how God treats them. As the extension of God's love, that is what you learned through the marriage resurrection. When you thought you had lost your spouse forever, God's love for them returned them back to you. Never forget to be the extension of His love to them and they will forever be by your side.

Scripture:

> *"It is for freedom that Christ has set us free. Stand firm, then, and*
> *do not let yourselves be burdened again by a yoke of slavery."*
> (GALATIANS 5:1 NIV)

CHAPTER 14

OVERCOMING INFIDELITY

If infidelity is an issue, your marriage resurrection cannot be maintained unless you overcome your hurt feelings.

Betrayal of any kind hurts. Whether it is your best friend who reveals all of your deepest secrets or the one person on the planet you trust with your life is trying to kill you, discovery of betrayal breaks your heart far worse than whatever evil the person has planned for you. In marriage, learning your spouse has had sexual intercourse with another can be the straw that would break any marriage. Once you know, you have to decide what to do with that knowledge, and you may feel like someone has stabbed you in the heart or stolen what is most precious to you. Some people may be okay with believing for new life in their marriage, but once they hear infidelity has taken place they lose their desire to continue believing God for a miracle.

If you are a person who is having to come to grips with your spouse's infidelity, let me say I can relate. During our separation, my wife became emotionally and sexually involved with another man. Now we have reconciled, she will be the first to tell you those were not her finest hours. Daily she has to fight off feeling of condemnation for her choices in this area. Likewise, I have to fight off feelings of anger and betrayal that try to enter into my consciousness to freshly remind me what was done. In this chapter, we will explore why it hurts so bad when we learn about a spouse's infidelity, understand what adultery really is and how to let the hurt go.

WHY IT HURTS SO BAD

It does not matter whether you learn about your spouse's infidelity before you separate, during the separation or after you reconcile as a result of the marriage resurrection. In the end, you will still have to deal with the feelings you have about the infidelity and with all the parties involved. You feel the way you feel, but it is more important to understand the reason why you feel the way you feel. If you can understand why you feel the way you do, then you can find a way to lessen the impact on your life.

VIOLATING THE HOLY OF HOLIES

After learning about my wife's relationship with the other man, I was devastated beyond words. I felt as if someone had literally ripped my heart right out of my chest without anesthesia. I felt horrible all the way to the core of my being. With time, though, I began to examine why I felt the way I did. I was hurting because my holy of holies was violated. The Bible describes an inner chamber of the sanctuary in the Jewish Temple was separated by a veil from the outer chamber as the "Holy of Holies" (Hebrews 9:3-4). This place was reserved for the presence of the Lord and the place could only be entered into by the High Priest on the Day of Atonement (Exodus 26:33). In marriage, our spouse's sexuality is for us our holy of holies.

Like the High Priest, when it comes down to my spouse's sexuality, I expect the same exclusivity. What else can have those same kind of expectations? Not our money because over the course of a life there will be many (taxes, bills, charity, etc...) who will try and make a case to cause us to part with our money. Not our children. While they are very young, we might be the holders of their attention and affection. As they grow older, the same attention and affection gets shared with potential mates. The bottom-line is the love, affection and sexuality of our spouses is for many of us the only exclusivity we will have over the course of our lives. It is what makes us different than the person next door. When our spouse's infidelity is discovered, that exclusivity is ripped away from us. Suddenly, feeling special in the world, if in no one's eyes but your spouse's, is taken away. It is for this reason discovering your spouse has been unfaithful hurts so much. It feels like betrayal because it is betrayal. A betrayal of our love, affection and confidence.

UNDERSTANDING INFIDELITY

> "Adultery is a brainless act, soul-destroying, self-destructive; Expect a bloody nose, a black eye and a reputation ruined for good."
>
> (PROVERBS 6:34 MSG)

There is nothing you can do about your feelings after discovery of your spouse's infidelity. It is going to hurt. You are going to feel as if the entire world around you has imploded. At that moment, you may feel like you died because inside, a massive event has occurred. It was the tearing of the veil. Even though the act of intercourse with another outside the bounds of marriage could have happened many times before and even over a period of years. However, when the infidelity becomes known to you, that is when the veil is torn in two and you realize the most precious and secret of all that was yours has been violated. You may feel powerless and like all the decisions about your future have been stripped away. The truth is, this is a moment of your finest hour as a Christian. This is an opportunity to prove to the world you do walk with Jesus and your love for Him reigns supreme. What we fail to realize is, at that moment, it is much more a test of your walk with Christ than it is a test of your spouse's character.

Your spouse's character has already been tested in the temptation and it came up lacking. That is one problem but the other and more devastating problem may occur based on how you respond to the moral failings of the one you love. Before we go any further let me say without reservation I very much understand how you feel. Yes, I had all of the emotions I described above and many more I do not discuss. I understand what the pain and anger of betrayal feels like. In those hours I realized something I am trying to communicate to you. You and I are not the only ones who experienced betrayal, had to deal with an adulterer and see the one we love being embraced by another. Who else experienced this same situation not once or twice but too many times to count? God and Jesus.

Read the books of Chronicles, Isaiah or any of the Minor Prophets and you will start to have an understanding of the depth of betrayal our heavenly Father has endured over centuries with his bride, Israel, who had numerous adulterous relationships with other gods. Our God has a lot of in-depth experience when it comes to dealing with an unfaithful lover. Despite delivering Israel out of Egypt, rescuing them from enemies a multitude of times and then giving them a land flowing with milk and honey our Lord had to see them throw aside their marriage with Him as they chose other kings or gods over Him. Jesus also is very adept on this subject. Think about the woman caught in adultery that was brought before him in John 8 or the fact he was betrayed by one of his own disciples. Peter, one of the three disciples in Jesus' inner circle, denies Him three times during His darkest hour. None of us have experienced the depth of being betrayed to the point we have to suffer a gruesome death as a result of the betrayal. So, yes, our Savior and Lord understands greatly the feelings and experiences you may be going through in dealing with the knowledge of your spouse's betrayal.

I soon realized it wasn't my wife's character being tested at that moment but mine. What our enemy wants you and I to do at those moments is bask in the horror of our feelings. He would like to see us let our imaginations run wild and internally play tapes in our heads of the act(s) of adultery and with each playback our disgust, anger and impassionate pleas for justice grows. Our society wants you to do the same thing as you pick up the telephone and call all of your closest friends and family telling them how you have become a victim as a result of your spouse's indiscretion. This bodes well in the entertainment-first culture in which we live. When you pick up the telephone to discuss this with friends and family what you think you are doing is getting solace from those who love you but in reality you are feeding the monster that fuels our Christ-less society. These actions feed your fleshy feelings of anger, despair, disgust and cries for justice and you may feel better after you do it. What these things will not do is allow God to take control of the situation.

There was a country song a few years back that called on Jesus to take the wheel. Well, when you are faced with the one you love sinning against you, that is the time when you really need to let Him take the wheel. You must park your emotions and let the King of Kings take over. If you do not do this and you let your emotions run wild, you have allowed Satan to take the wheel and you are not going to enjoy where the ride is going to take you.

Here is what I pondered when I needed understating in my heart so I could heal: I simply asked myself the question, "What would Jesus do?" Now that may sound cliché but what it did for me is freeze my emotions long enough for me to consider the experience of the Lord in this area. The Bible is very clear there is coming a time for all of us when we will need to give account to God for everything we have done on earth (Romans 14:12). In that moment, the decisions may have played well among our friends and families, maybe gotten us 15 minutes of fame on some reality television show or launched us on a campaign where we received sympathy from those around us but that is not going to be the standard before God. Earlier we talked about how God and His Son have extensive experience in this area so we are not going to be able to say with any real substance, "Well, Lord you just don't know how I feel." If you take that faithless stance you will find how grossly incorrect you are. For me, I thought it more prudent to stop my crying and find out what the Lord knows on the subject.

> **Lesson Learned # 16 –**
> **Understand that adultery is not about sex,**
> **romance or love, instead it is about deception.**

The Lord took me to the book of Hosea in the Old Testament and he had me study the story of Hosea and Gomer. In this story Hosea's wife, Gomer, would not remain faithful. For a period of time, she kept seeking pleasure and satisfaction outside of her marriage to Hosea. At first, she would have sexual relationships and thought she was getting away with her conduct because Hosea would not separate from her. Despite his knowledge about her behavior, he continued to love her even when he questioned if he was the father of the child being born to them. Over time, she became flagrant with her conduct by having more lovers on the side and the next child she bore Hosea clearly knew it was not his. Despite her conduct, because of what God told him, Hosea would not depart from her. Instead he loved her and remained faithful. Eventually, Gomer could not continue living with Hosea. She found it more pleasing to be with her lovers than to be wife and mother at home. She departed and thought she was free to follow her heart's desire and be unrestrained with her lovers. The story unfolds and Gomer learns the treatment she experienced with her lovers was not the love she had become accustomed to experience with Hosea. Unfortunately, she did not realize this until she had lost everything. Her lovers threw her into slavery when they were completely finished with their wild fantasies. Destitute and enslaved, Gomer was without hope until she saw Hosea had come and paid the 15 pieces of silver to buy her freedom. Not only did he pay for her to be released from slavery but through his love, he restored her to the position of his wife.

In this story, the Lord revealed adultery and infidelity come as a result of our spouses falling for the deception the grass is greener on the other side. Our enemy is working night and day to destroy us and any of us can become victims of deception. In our case, my wife embraced the enemy's lies about us and about this new relationship she had entered into. We had been married for quite a while and over the course of those years, as we really got to know each other intimately, we discovered things about each other that were not as pleasing to

our eyes as during the days when we courted each other. What God wanted us to do was not use those things against each other or get offended because our humanity finally showed up in the relationship, but He wanted us to be like Moses and be the deliverer for our spouse. God expects us to cover them in love, prayer, forgiveness, and understanding until through God's power, mercy and grace, their weaknesses would be covered by the blood of Jesus. Each time we find our spouses become more and more like the image of Christ and become the man or woman our hearts desire. Instead, we too quickly get repulsed by these defects in our spouses and quickly run for the exit. In my wife's new relationship, enough time had not expired for her to learn the defects this new man was bringing to the table. In the meantime, like Gomer, my wife allowed herself to be enticed by the freshness of this new relationship and the differences this man brought to it.

> ## Lesson Learned #17 –
> ## Adultery is no different
> ## than any other sin.

Adultery is not the unpardonable sin. When the Word tells us if we confess our sins he is faithful and just to forgive us and to cleanse from all unrighteousness, that includes adultery (1 John 1:9). Despite the way we feel, God does not count adultery in any greater weight a sin than gossiping, gluttony or telling a lie. It is only in man's eyes we put these different weights on sin and decide what we can and cannot live with.

Thank God our Heavenly Father did not do that to us or we all would be toast. Sin is sin and there is no such thing as big sin or little sin. All sin separates us from God (Isaiah 59:2), the wages of sin still remain death (Romans 6:23) and if it was not for the love and grace offered through Jesus, we would all be lost in our sin. Thankfully, the redemptive work through Jesus allows us the opportunity to repent and be restored back to God.

Repentance and restoration is God's work for the adulterer and the betrayer. Remember how Jesus dealt with the woman caught in adultery:

> *"Jesus went across to Mount Olives, but he was soon back in the Temple again. Swarms of people came to him. He sat down and taught them.*
>
> *The religion scholars and Pharisees led in a woman who had been caught in an act of adultery. They stood her in plain sight of everyone and said, "Teacher, this woman was caught red-handed in the act of adultery. Moses in the Law, gives orders to stone such persons. What do you say?" They were trying to trap him into saying something incriminating so they could bring charges against him.*

Jesus bent down and wrote with his finger in the dirt. They kept at him, badgering him. He straightened up and said, "The sinless one among you, go first: Throw the stone." Bending down again, he wrote some more in the dirt.

Hearing that, they walked away one after another, beginning with the oldest. The woman was left alone. Jesus stood up and spoke to her, "Woman, where are they? Does no one condemn you?"

"No one Master." "Neither do I," said Jesus. "Go on your way. From now on, don't sin."

(JOHN 8: 1 – 11 MSG)

Jesus responded with forgiveness. If that stance was good enough for the Master, then should not we be following His example? Some might say that Jesus did not have any emotional stake in the woman or the adultery she was caught doing. That is not the case with Judas, Peter and even the crowd which cried for Him to be crucified. Every whip he bore, the piercing of his side, the thorns in his head from the crown he wore and the holes in his hands and feet were all the direct result of the actions of Judas and the crowd. Yet, Jesus' response was to pray to the Father and ask for them to be forgiven (Luke 23:34). When Peter denied him in his darkest hour, very few of us would be willing to stay friends with someone who abandoned us when we needed them the most. For many of us, it would be the unpardonable sin, but not for our Lord. He forgave Peter and restored him as His disciple (John 21:15-17).

We have to be very careful about getting our moral standards from the world and going back in forth with our Christian walk between the world's standards and God accepting what fits us for the moment. That is why when our spouse sins, it is not their character at stake, it is ours. How we respond will tell the world either we are true followers of Christ or a pretender; a believer who follows the Lord only when it is convenient or costs them nothing.

Lesson Learned #18 – We have all committed adultery at some point.

Let me be clear, I am not talking about sexual intercourse only. In the eyes of God, we have all lusted after the things of this world and chosen them over following God. Whether that is choosing to walk in unforgiveness instead of choosing to forgive or taking a drink or a pill to deal with the stress of this life instead of choosing to walk in the peace of God. It could be we have chosen to attend an event or engage in a worldly activity instead of attending church and fellowshipping with other believers. Just as Israel was in a marriage with God, we as the Body of Christ are in an active marriage with Jesus. There is not one of us who has been consistently faithful to marriage, and we have to be very careful about condemning others and pardoning our own wrongdoings. This is not right in the sight of God and the adultery caused by sexual intercourse or by not being faithful to the Lord is all the same before Him. The standard for adultery in the New Testament is much more stringent than in the Old Testament in that the Lord says anyone who looks at someone with lust has committed adultery (Matthew 5:28). We have to be careful how we judge our spouses because the Bible is very clear the measure we judge we will be judged with the same measure (Matthew 7:2).

In the end, you need to understand the tempter, which is Satan, tempted your spouse and instead of leaning on the arm of the Lord for strength, your spouse fell for the temptation. Stop feeling like a victim and open your eyes to who the real victim is. Your spouse. Satan is a very dangerous tempter. He is very aware of what excites us and leads us astray and there are no boundaries he will not cross. Your spouse has been deceived and until the scales of deception fall from their eyes, they cannot perceive they are being led down a road to destruction by their enemy. While being deceived, they think the grass is greener on the other side and they believe they are going to find love that you cannot give them. It is sad to be deceived. I have been deceived and I personally know how horrible it is to be on the end of one of Satan's schemes. Just when he gets you in the crosshairs, he leaves you in the middle of a compromising situation. He enjoys seeing you get punished.

This is what opened my eyes and understanding about infidelity and adultery. Satan had deceived my spouse away from her covenant relationship with me and doing so ripped the veil on the holy place meant for my experience only. There Satan left my spouse ready to receive her punishment when I discovered her infidelity. In our case, the joke was on the devil because no punishment would ever come. Instead, thanks to God, He showed me a better way and to show unconditional love to my wife and her friend. It was to sow forgiveness instead of bitterness; to show love instead of hate. That is what I chose to do. That is why my wife and I enjoyed our 30th year of marriage instead of our first year of divorce. It was a decision to trust in Jesus rather than to let my emotions take control.

It all begins with understanding adultery is about deception and to put your focus on the real betrayer, which is the devil. Your spouse, while not innocent, is a victim. No different than the sins any one of us have made over the course of our lives. That is how Jesus saw that woman caught in adultery. He saw her as a victim who gave into one of Satan's wiles. He did not see her as a criminal, which is how the Pharisees and the rest of the crowd saw her. They did not care about her. They were more interested in the law and their opportunity to punish someone for breaking the law. When Jesus turned the mirror on them and gave them the opportunity to do what was in their heart as long as they had no sin in their lives, they were unable to follow through on their threats. Jesus was the only one in the crowd without sin. He was qualified to stone her, yet He choose not to. I experienced the same thing with my wife.

I, too, have sinned many times in my life and God showed me mercy and grace. How could I now do less than what God bestowed on me? There is a parable from Jesus which drives this point home for all of us.

CHAPTER 14: OVERCOMING INFIDELITY

"At that point Peter got the nerve to ask, "Master, how many times do I forgive a brother or sister who hurts me? Seven?

Jesus replied, "Seven! Hardly. Try seventy times seven.

"The kingdom of God is like a king who decided to square accounts with his servants. As he got underway, one servant was brought before him who had a run up a debt of a hundred thousand dollars. He couldn't pay up, so the king ordered the man, along with his wife, children, and goods, to be auctioned off at the slave market.

"The poor wretch threw himself at the king's feet and begged, 'Give me a chance and I'll pay it all back.' Touched by his plea, the king let him off, erasing the debt.

"The servant was no sooner out of the room when he came upon one of his fellow servants who owed him ten dollars. He seized him by the throat and demanded, 'Pay up. Now!'

"The poor wretch threw himself down and begged. 'Give me a chance and I'll pay it all back.' But he wouldn't do it. He had him arrested and put in jail until the debt was paid. When the other servants saw this going on, they were outraged and brought a detailed report to the king.

"The king summoned the man and said, 'You evil servant! I forgave your entire debt when you begged me for mercy. Shouldn't you be compelled to be merciful to your fellow servant who asked for mercy?' The king was furious and put the screws to the man until he paid back his entire debt. And that's what my Father in heaven is going to do to each one of you who doesn't forgive unconditionally anyone who asks for mercy."

(MATTHEW 18:21-35 MSG)

I did not want to be in a situation having my eternity impacted because I did not know how to show unconditional love to two individuals when they gave into temptation. Instead, mercifully I was not like this wicked servant. I never want the mercy windows of heaven to close on me, so I decided to pour on others what heaven has so liberally poured on me.

GETTING OVER THE HURT

Knowing adultery is no different than any other sin, that it is really deception and your loved one is really of victim, is a great first step to releasing the hurt and anger stored in your heart. A second step is studying for yourself the various accounts God and Jesus experienced themselves dealing with spiritual adultery, betrayal and the hurt that comes as a result. No one has more experience than them on the subject. Read the accounts I outlined earlier for you in the chapter to put a huge damper on your feelings as you realize your Heavenly Father and Lord truly understand what you are feeling. As you pray, you will begin to experience and welcome their loving arms around you and you will have the reassurance in your heart they are arms of experience. The comfort will be real as you experience their love. Next, you will have to come to grips with whether or not you are going to be like that wicked servant who was not willing to forgive or to be like Jesus who did not condemn a woman who was clearly guilty of what she was accused. Once you make the decision to forgive, your broken heart will be on the road to becoming whole.

There are few other things that will help you overcome the hurt:

- ❦ Now that you see your spouse as a victim, help with their restoration.

- ❦ Help with the restoration of all parties who were victims of Satan's temptation.

- ❦ Remember, it is your walk with Christ being tested.

No test or temptation comes your way is beyond the course of what others have had to face. All you need to remember is God will never let you down; he will never let you be pushed past your limit; he will always be there to help you come through it. (1 Corinthians 10:13)

Scripture:

> *"Now is the time to forgive this man and help him back on his feet. If all you do is pour on the guilt, you could very well drown him in it. My counsel now is to pour on the love."*
> (2 CORINTHIANS 2:7-8 MSG)

CHAPTER 15

GOD IS A RESTORER

No matter what was lost or destroyed during your divorce or separation, you can look to God for restoration.

The need to have new life back into your once dead marriage indicates for a period of time, regardless of how long, you and your spouse relinquished the foundation of your relationship together to be influenced by Satan. This is important because many wonderful and needful things sprout from the foundation of your relationship together. Children may have come as a result of that relationship. Your home, neighborhood, and friendships also came as a result of that relationship. The jobs, employment, and businesses that support your family also came into being or at least became attached to you as a result of the marriage. I could go on and on adding to this list, all of the things have their attachment to you and your spouse's lives as a result of the relationship between you. When the two of you relinquished control and influence over to Satan, he does what is in his nature to do – steal, kill, and destroy (John 10:10). Now through the power of God's mercy and grace of which He showered through marriage resurrection, you and your spouse have reconciled. As the smoke clears from the divorce and separation, your eyes will become open to all Satan stole, destroyed, and killed while you were oblivious to his work.

While you are reconciling you might discover jobs have been lost, savings have been depleted, credit scores have been tarnished, or valuable property destroyed or sold for less than its value. You may experience bodies suffering from sickness or disease and severely broken relationships. All of the work Satan can and does during a separation or divorce is mind boggling. Though you have reconciled, looking around at all the destruction that has taken place is enough to make your heart sink and your blood boil. That was exactly Satan's intention. Even if you fought off his attack to cause a divorce, the amount of damage he caused would still have him come out the victor.

To embrace your feelings and thoughts, you need to be aware of God's plan to restore. Just as God did not leave you and your spouse without a lifeboat during the divorce or separation, he surely did not leave you to face the destruction alone. In fact, if you truly trust him in this area, not only will he restore what was lost, he will also strip away from Satan more than what he took away from you. God's intervention will get you a win for reconciliation of your marriage and a bounty of blessings that erases the memories of anything you may have previously lost. In this chapter, we will explore God's plan of restoration and give you the tools to access that work to bring wholeness back into your life and in the life of your spouse.

GOD IS A RESTORER

Let's begin by establishing in the scripture God is a restorer. When can begin by looking at Deuteronomy 30:

> "While you're out among the nations where God has dispersed you and the blessings and curses come in the just the way I have set them before you, and you and your children take them seriously and come back to God, your God, and obey him with your whole heart and soul according to everything that I command you today, God, your God, will restore everything you lost; he'll come back and pick up the pieces from all the places where you were scattered. No matter how far away you end up, God, your God, will get out of there and bring you back to the land your ancestors once possessed. It will be yours again. He will give you a good life and make you more numerous than your ancestors."

(DEUTERONOMY 30: 1-3 MSG)

Even before the children of Israel arrived into the Promised Land, God gave Moses His plan for restoration. God anticipated there would come a day after his people entered into the Promised Land when they would allow their hearts and minds to get carried away from reliance on Him. Despite the warnings of blessings and curses God outlined in Deuteronomy 28, He did not leave the children of Israel without a way back to Him. God's intention was for the blessings Israel enjoyed to be permanent. Unless God put in a restoration plan, all the blessings would be lost forever. Here are a couple of important points of God's restoration plan outlined in Deuteronomy 30:

1. Restoration took place once their hearts and minds returned to God and their lives began to reflect all God had commanded them to do.

2. God took the responsibility for captaining the restoration, thus leaving nothing for Israel to do but enjoy the return of all that was lost.

3. God takes inventory of everything lost and takes responsibility for its complete return.

4. When the restoration is complete, your life will be better than it was before.

If we look more closely in Deuteronomy 30 at what God restored to Israel, you will realize that He restored more than their relationship with Him:

- He restored them to the land – vs. 5

- He restored them to work (employment) – vs. 9

- He restored them with children – vs. 9

- He restored them with cattle (wealth) – vs .9

- He restored them with crops (nutrition and riches) - vs. 9

It is important to realize God is not only interested in your spiritual life. He is very much interested in you living a good life and part of his promise of restoration is to give you a good life. What we have learned from this is restoration is not an afterthought with God or a response to the needful prayers of the saints for deliverance. Instead, restoration is very much a part of God's initial plan. Even before Israel entered the Promised Land, he provided a plan for their restoration.

The plan of restoration for Israel is inspiring but let us continue investigating the scriptures to determine if there are other instances where we see God bringing restoration to His people. Examining the Book of Job, we can read another account starting in Chapter 1:

Sometime later, while Job's children were having one of their parties at the home of the oldest son, a messenger came to Job and said, "The oxen were plowing and the donkeys grazing in the field next to us when Sabeans attacked. They stole the animals and killed the field hands. I'm the only one to get out alive and tell you what happened."

While he was still talking, another messenger arrived and said, "Bolts of lightning stuck the sheep and the shepherds and fried them – burning them to a crisp. I'm the only one to get out alive and tell you what happened."

While he was still talking, another messenger arrived and said, "Chaldeans coming from three directions raided the camels and massacred the camel drivers. I'm the only one to get out alive and tell you what happened."

While he was still talking, another messenger arrived and said, "Your children were having a party at the home of the oldest brother when a tornado swept in off the desert and struck the house it collapsed on the young people and they died. I'm the only one to get out alive and tell you what happened."

*"Job got to his feet, ripped his robe, shaved his head, then fell
to the ground and worshipped."*

(JOB 1: 13-20 MSG)

We can all agree we have had some bad days but I suspect none of us have ever had a day like the one Job faced. In a single day, he received four messengers with four messages of gloom and doom. With four swift actions occurring roughly around the same time, Job's oxen, donkeys and camels were stolen, his hired hands were killed, his sheep were burned alive, and all of his children were killed when the house they were in collapsed as a result of tornado. The destruction Job experienced was ghastly and complete. Examining verse 12 of the same chapter, you will recognize all of the calamity Job experienced came at the hands of Satan. Satan is a thief, a destroyer, and a killer just the way the Bible says he is (John 10:10). Reviewing the destruction Job endured compared to what you and I saw during our divorces and/or separations makes ours pale in comparison. How does someone bounce back from this type of experience? Satan took everything Job had and believe it or not he was not satisfied with these calamities on Job by themselves. Because we read in verse 7 of chapter 2 Satan returned with a second round of surprises for Job.

"Satan left God and struck Job with terrible sores. Job was ulcers and scabs from head to foot. They itched and oozed so badly that he took a piece of broken pottery to scrape himself, then went and sat on a trash heap, among the ashes."

(JOB 2:7 MSG)

Not even giving Job time to grieve for the loss of his children, wealth or employees, Satan strikes his body. Talk about kicking a man when he is down. Now we understand Satan does not play fair. He is pure evil. Job was now poor, childless, and sick. How did Job endure all of these calamities? The scripture says he, "fell down upon the ground and worshipped (Job 1:20 KJV)." This response shows the depth of his commitment to God. Despite his hurt, pain, and losses, Job kept his eyes on God. This resulted in God restoring everything back to him Satan stole.

"After Job had interceded for his friends, God restored his fortune — and then doubled it! All his brothers and sisters and friends came to his house and celebrated. They told him how sorry they were, and consoled him for all the trouble God had brought him. Each of them brought generous housewarming gifts.

God blessed Job's life even more than his earlier life. He ended up with fourteen thousand sheep, six thousand camels, one thousand teams of oxen, and on thousand donkeys. He also had seven sons and three daughters. He named the first daughter Dove, the second, Cinnamon, and the third, Dark-eyes. There was not a woman in that country as beautiful as Job's daughters. Their father treated them as equals with their brothers providing the same inheritance.

Job lived on another 140 years, living to see his children and grandchildren – four generations of them! Then he died – an old man, a full life."

(JOB 42:10-17 MSG)

"Just like we saw with the children of Israel, with Job we see God intervening in the midst of the destruction Satan brought and with his presence, he brings restoration. Another similarity with the restoration plan that unfolded with the children of Israel is God's restoration with Job included his livestock, his children, his wealth and additional years on his life.

Already we have found two scriptural accounts confirm God's role as a restorer. In case you think because these accounts occurred in the Old Testament, you wonder if restoration is for today, I would encourage you to examine the story of the woman with the issue of blood found in Luke chapter 8.

In the crowd that day there was a woman who for twelve years had been afflicted with hemorrhages. She spent every penny she had on doctors but no one had been able to help her. She slipped in from behind and touched the edge of Jesus' robe. At the very moment her hemorrhaging stopped. Jesus said, "Who touched me?"

When no one stepped forward, Peter said, "But Master, we've got crowds of people on our hands. Dozens have touched you." Jesus insisted, "Someone touched me I felt power discharging from me."

When the woman realized that she couldn't remain hidden, she knelt trembling before him. In front of all the people, she blurt-ed out her story – why she touched him and how at that same *moment she was healed.*

Jesus said, "Daughter, you took a risk trusting me, and now you're healed and whole. Live well, live blessed!"

(LUKE 8: 43-48 MSG)

This New Testament story further demonstrates what we learned in the restoration accounts with the children of Israel and Job. As a result of sickness, this woman had lost all of her money after spending it on physicians who could not make her well. Bravely, she put her faith in Jesus and was willing to expose herself to ridicule for breaking the law of being in public with a flow of blood. She put her fears aside and knew in her heart Jesus would heal her. In fact, healing was not all she received that day. If you examine further, you will see she received more than what she sought. Jesus said to her in verse 48 (MSG), "Now you are healed and whole. Live well, live blessed!"

Initially, the story tells us the woman received her healing when the flow of blood stopped. But with Jesus' response, we see other gifts given to the woman. First, the gift of wholeness. The Greek word for whole is sozo, which can be translated into English as meaning to save, deliver, preserve safe from danger, loss, and destruction. With the issue of blood stopped, the woman had already been saved from the sickness she had carried so long. What else could Jesus be extending to her? Is there anything else the woman needed deliverance from? Absolutely. Upon re-examining the story, you will see the woman had spent all she had. In addition to being saved from sickness, she also needed to be saved from poverty. If she were married, having an issue of blood for 12 years would have had a significant impact on her marriage. in looking at the customs of the day, you will see this sickness impacted every aspect of her life.

"When a woman has a discharge of blood, the impurity of her menstrual period lasts seven days. Anyone who touches her is unclean until evening. Everything on which she lies or sits during her period is unclean. Anyone who touches her bed or anything on which she sits mush wash his clothes and bathe in water; he remains unclean until evening.

If a man sleeps with her and her menstrual blood gets on him, he is unclean for seven days and every bed on which he lies becomes unclean.

If a woman has a discharge of blood for many days, but not at the time of her monthly period, or has a discharge that continues beyond the time of her period, she is unclean the same as during the time of her period. Every bed on which she lies during the time of the discharge and everything on which she

sits becomes unclean the same as in her monthly period.

Anyone who touches these things becomes unclean and must wash his clothes and bathe in water, he remains unclean until evening."

You are responsible for keeping the People of Israel separate from that which makes them ritually unclean, lest they die in their unclean condition by defiling my Dwelling which is among them."

(LEVITICUS 15: 19-27, 31)

It is very important to realize the woman did not just suffer from the physical outcomes of the sickness but her sickness caused social problems for her as well. Here is a possible list of issues that the sickness caused her:

- The inability to touch or be touched by her husband or children.

- The need to refrain from touching anything her family would end up touching; ultimately she would have had to leave home.

- Unable to work, pick crops, work with livestock, or go into the marketplace.

- Unable to go to Temple.

- The need to warn people she was "unclean," stigmatizing her as someone to avoid.

For 12 years, she lived a miserable and lonely life. So when Jesus told her to be whole, He was pronouncing a blessing which meant she would no longer be in poverty, she would no longer be a social outcast, her relationship with her husband and children would be restored and life would go well for her. When he said "You are healed and whole. Live well, live blessed," some translations have the word "peace" instead of "Live well, live blessed." The first blessing came with the word "whole" and the second blessing is "peace." The Greek word for peace is eirene, which can be translated to mean health, welfare, prosperity, or every kind of good. This blessing of peace can only come from God and it is a blessing that fills every aspect of your life. After her encounter with Jesus, this woman walked away with a truck load of blessings she had no idea would come her way.

Imagine this woman going home after being healed from her infirmity. The blessing of wholeness restored her money, husband, children and even her place in the community. The restoration did not stop there. Remember, Jesus blessed her with "peace." When she returned home, if there was anything not well in her life, it turned to good. In today's terms that would mean if the car was having maintenance issues, it was repaired; if the children were having trouble in school, the trouble stopped; if bills were outstanding, they were paid; if the husband was out of work then good employment came his way; if she had been experiencing infertility issues, her body was now fertile.

In all three accounts outlined above, we have seen that God does not want you to have merely what you had before. He wants to give you well beyond. While I do not know all you may have lost as the result of the devil involving himself in your marriage, the great news is God knows and He is a restorer. If through the devil's effort you found his destructive ways left you with debt (Acts 13:8), infertility (Psalm 113:9), issues with your children (Proverbs 22:6), lost savings, jobs, businesses (Jeremiah 29: 11-14) or whatever he has stolen, God has a plan to get you paid back.

RESTITUTION IS PART OF GOD'S RESTORATION PLAN

"People do not despise a thief if he steals to satisfy his hunger

when he is starving. Yet if he is caught, he must pay sevenfold,

though it costs him all the wealth of his house."

(PROVERBS 6:30, 31 NIV)

God is aware Satan is a thief and one whose intention is to rob you of everything he has bestowed upon you. God does not want you to be afraid of the thief. You do not have any circumstances that cannot be leveled against him. In Job's story, we read God restored Job to twice what he had before. God's plan for you is restoration; his plan for the thief is restitution.

The first instance in the Bible about restitution can been in the life of Jacob in Genesis 31:39. Restitution can be defined as the act of returning something lost or stolen back to its owner or the payment(s) made to someone to compensate them for damage, trouble, or loss (Merriam-Webster, Inc, 2016). While we may think of restitution as a legal concept, its origins can be traced to the Bible.

In the Books of the Law (Exodus, Leviticus, Numbers and Deuteronomy), the concept and acts of restitution are laid out for each of the wrongs that would be committed. It is very clear if someone steals, restitution must be made.

"Anyone who steals must certainly make restitution, but if they

have nothing, they must be sold to pay for their theft. If the

stolen animal is found alive in their possession, whether ox or

donkey or sheep – they must pay back double."

(EXODUS 22: 3B AND 4 NIV)

There are two elements of restitution. The first element is the payment to compensate the individual who was wronged. The second is the compulsory payment required of the transgressor to punish them for theft or loss in the first

place. This compulsory payment is required on top of the value or return of the original item and could amount to several times the value of the original item was stolen.

Restitution is not just a concept of the law of the Old Testament. This concept is also found in the New Testament. Restitution takes a different form in the New Testament. Whereas in the Old Testament it was meant solely as a concept to punish, in the New Testament it becomes an avenue for blessing from God and from believer to believer. Here are three examples of restitution in the New Testament:

> "But Zacchaeus stood up and said to the Lord, "Look, Lord! Here and now I give half of my possession to the poor and if I have cheated anybody out of anything, I will pay back four times the amount."
>
> (LUKE 19:8-9 NIV)

> "Truly I tell you," Jesus replied, "no one who has left home or brothers or sisters or mother or father or children or fields for me and the gospel will fail to receive a hundred times as much in this present age: homes, brothers, sisters, mothers, children and fields – along with persecutions – and in the age to come eternal life."
>
> (MARK 10:29, 30 NIV)

> "Bear with each other and forgive one another if any of you has a grievance against someone. Forgive as the Lord forgave you."
>
> (COLOSSIANS 3:13 NIV)

> "If God instituted restitution as part of the law among the children of Israel and it stills applies today from believer to believer or from God to believer, then how does restitution impact Satan, the thief of all thieves? Here is the Lord's plan of restitution for Satan:

> So Jesus called them over to him and began to speak to them in parables: "How can Satan drive out Satan? If a kingdom is divided against itself, that kingdom cannot stand. If a house is divided against itself, that house cannot stand. And if Satan opposes himself and is divided, he cannot stand; his end has come. In fact, no one can enter

a strong man's house without first tying him up. Then he
can plunder the strong man's house."

(MARK 3: 23-27 NIV)

God's plan of restitution for Satan is to have his house (this world and the world system) plundered by the children of God. God's intention is to strip Satan of the very goods (wealth, land, riches, power and influence) that currently lie in his house and give them to you. As we have seen many times with the children of Israel, in Job and with the woman who had the issue of blood, God will make Satan compensate you for the original value plus a compulsory payment that is on top of the original value of what was stolen.

"God is just: He will pay back trouble to those who trouble you."

(2 THESSALONIANS 1:6 NIV)

"Do not take revenge, my dear friends, but leave room for
God's wrath, for it is written: "It is mine to avenge; I will repay,"
says the Lord."

(ROMANS 12:19 NIV)

"People do not despise a thief if he steals to satisfy his hunger
when he is starving. Yet if he is caught, he must pay sevenfold,
though it costs him all the wealth of his house."

(PROVERBS 6:30, 31 NIV)

We have already identified Satan as the thief. Just as you did with the marriage resurrection, you have the right to go before God in prayer and ask him to require restitution from Satan on all he has stolen from you and your spouse for at least two-fold as with Job and as much as sevenfold as listed in Proverbs 6:30, 31. What you actually receive is not a condition of what God is willing to give you but what you are willing and ready to believe Him and receive. The key is realizing God's restoration plan is alive and well. He is waiting on you to go into the enemy's camp and take back what has been stolen from you.

KEYS TO RECEIVE YOUR RESTORATION

1. ***"Seek the Kingdom of God first"*** (MATTHEW 6:33).

    From all the accounts we discussed, it is clear each of our subjects sought the Lord and not the blessing. With the children of Israel, God's command was for them to return to Him and keep his commandments. With Job, despite all the bad news he received, the scripture says he worshipped him. The woman who had the issue of blood fell down before Jesus and confessed all that was in her heart. For you, your restoration begins when you do what it says in 1 Peter 5:6, which is to "Humble yourselves therefore under the mighty hand of

God, that He may exalt you in due time."

2. ***Have faith in God and believe in His reward for steadily seeking Him*** (HEBREWS 11:6).

You had to have faith to receive your marriage resurrection and you will need to continue believing if you are going to see your restoration come to pass. Everything with God requires you to believe Him and to put aside your human reasoning. Believing him is not an event, it is a lifestyle decision. Your belief needs to be like clothes; something you will never leave home without. Every morning and throughout the day you will need to choose to continuing believing God. With each thought that enters your consciousness you will need to take it into captivity and decide if it aligns with what you believing from God and His Word. If it lines up, then meditate on that Word but if it does not, the Bible tells to cast that thought down (2 Corinthians 10:5). Engaging in this activity every day is the work of believing Him. The other thing you have to do is to look for God's reward consistently. Have an expectation every day God will show up to bring you want you are believing Him for. Be willing to have your expectation set on "receive" no matter how many days transpire because that is what it is going to take if you are truly going to believe God to bring restoration to your married life.

3. ***Identify the thief and seek God for restitution*** (PROVERBS 6:31).

It is up to you to open your mouth before God and declare what you want Him to restore. It is up to you to call out the thief and stand before God seeking His help to make Satan repay. This is the work each of us need to do. What is not a part of this work is to use your mouth to identify your spouse as the thief while seeking God help's to get restitution from the devil. It may be a fact it was by you or your spouse's hand the savings are depleted or the job loss. They may have totaled the car or maxed out the credit card but you are going to have to make a decision right now who you are going to make as the source of your restoration. Every time you open your mouth or do anything to remind your spouse of his or her participation in the loss, you are trying to bring condemnation on them. As we already learned in Chapter 13, this is the same as walking in unforgiveness. Condemning your spouse may make you feel better but you are killing your restoration effort. The Bible says in Romans 8:1, "There is therefore now no condemnation to them which are in Christ Jesus, who walk not after the flesh, but after the Spirit." This means if your spouse has already been forgiven by the Lord you do not have the right to lay any guilt or condemnation of them for something they have already received forgiveness for from God. When we do this, what we are really attempting to do is lay on our spouse punishment for the loss and extract some form of payment from them. In effect, we are laying on them the expectation of restitution. We have been commanded to love them not extract restitution. That is why God says, "Vengeance is mine says the Lord. I will repay (Romans 12:19)." God knows we don't have the means to make things right ourselves, which is why he says he will repay. Only God has the means to extract a restitution from Satan. This is why God wants us to believe him to make everything right. God is not going to give you things from heaven. The things you seek are earth bound and they can only be transferred here on the earth. Since the devil acts as the god of this world, God forces him to repay from his house. When you condemn your spouse, you let Satan off the hook and that is not God's plan. Trust God to make this right for you. Start by enforcing you and your spouse's right to be free and seek your blessing only from the Lord.

4. **Be patient and do not get ahead of God** (PSALM 37:7).

When your life is on fire it seems impossible to wait on God. But if you do not wait on God you will miss what He has for you and you will end up settling for something far less. There are two key scriptures you need to keep in mind at all times.

"Every good and perfect gift is from above, coming down from the Father of the heavenly lights, who does not change like shifting shadows."

(JAMES 1:17 NIV)

The blessing of the Lord brings wealth, without painful toil for it.
PROVERBS 10:22 NIV

What I have learned over time is many Christians start out believing God but over time their commitment wanes. Their desire for the things they are believing God for overshadows their love for God and his promises. Frustration comes and, as they focus on the frustration, it begins to grow. Soon they will begin to examine ways they can bring to pass in their own strength a different version of what God has for them. Mentally, they justify this as a possible interpretation of what God meant in his promise. Though they started off believing God for all their bills to be paid off, to go full-time into ministry or receive healing without the need for surgery, because the days on the calendar start to pass, soon they are willing to settle for something less. The Bible tells us in 2 Corinthians 2:11 AMP, "To keep Satan from getting the advantage over us; for we are not ignorant of his wiles and intentions." Unfortunately, the truth is because many Christians are not studying to present themselves to be approved by God as a workman that need not be ashamed, through their ignorance, the devil is bringing shame on them (2 Timothy 2:15 NIV). One of the tactics I have identified from Satan is to play the time game. If you have watched any professional football or basketball game, you will notice as the final minutes of the game are drawing closer each of the teams start to play a variety of time-related games. The winning team tries to maintain their point advantage while running the clock out as quickly as possible. The team behind plays a different game. Their tactic is to stall the clock and do whatever they can to keep the game from running out in hopes that in those extra moments they will find a way to claim victory. Satan operates the same way. He knows your restoration plan, like your marriage resurrection, is captained by the Lord and while he cannot defeat the Lord in a person-to-person match up, his tactic is to go against you in a waiting game. Just like in the professional sports game when you see the team call time-outs, cause intentional fouls or penalties to lengthen the clock, the devil uses some of the same tactics. In my own life, the first tactic is to not respond at all to any of the prayers I have laid before the Lord. With that he is hoping you and I will believe the silence means either our prayers where not answered or our request was denied. Both are a lie. If you stay steadfast, soon the clock will run out on this tactic and the devil will have to submit to trick. The next tactic I have noticed is to be tested on your commitment to what you asked of God. In my life, I have noticed he will initially present some options in the vicinity of what I am expecting but not what you have asked for from God. For example, you may be currently unemployed and believing God for a great paying job with a great company near your home. What Satan will offer you is a low paying job with a known company but in order to take the job, you will have to relocate to another city. If you are not fully committed to what you have asked of God, you might let the fact no other offers have been presented and it has been a few weeks since any employer responded to one of your inquiries frighten you into thinking this is your only option. It will take courage and trust in God to stay committed to what you have asked of God and say "No" to this opportunity. When you say, "No" he will try to punish by allowing time to transpire to when your next offer comes in. This too is part of his tactic. He is hoping during this period you will sweat and become uncommitted even to the decision you made. Should you allow his pressure tactic to work on you, then it will put you in a positon to be more inclined to accept his next offer. It will not be long and the clock will run out on him and he will be required by the Lord to present you with another offer. Going with the same unemployed situation, he might raise the salary, making it a company with a great benefits package, even a company that you have heard of but again the opportunity means you have to relocate. Now you have gotten two of the three things you have asked of God this becomes a real temptation. If you are not careful you will start having conversations with your spouse trying to determine if a relocation is something you can accept despite it will take you from the church where you have grown spiritually, the friends who supported you through your marriage resurrection and the network of support took you years to build. Once the devil knows he has you thinking about the situation, he will introduce thoughts into your minds about how wonderful it would be to start over and possibilities can be earned if you move.

The problem is you have forgotten the two verses above. Remember, every good and perfect gift comes from God and his gifts do not come with sorrow. As you examine the opportunity, you realize it is good for you but it will mean your spouse will have to look for new employment. Your children will have to be in a new school and perhaps it will be difficult to find a new church home that suits your spiritual needs and those of your family. If you are not careful, you will end up with something that is not what you asked of God. It will take a strong commitment and trust in God to say, "No" when the temptation is so tantalizing. You may have to go through several rounds with the devil presenting different solutions. Each may be a little closer to what you have asked of God but not exact until you indicate you will accept nothing short of what you have asked of God. When you get this committed, the clock will run out on Satan and all of what you have asked for will manifest.

Earlier in the book, I used the example of my wife's blood pressure. After we reconciled, because of several health problems, my wife's blood pressure was high. Together, we were believing God for her blood pressure to hit a target that we set. For weeks we did not see any movement but yet each day we stood firm on what we prayed. After a while, we started seeing a change. One of her blood pressure readings would be at or below the set target but the other number would be way above the target. Day after day for weeks we saw the numbers jumping around waiting to see if we would accept them. Daily we would reject the number and reclaim the target. Rejecting the reading and reclaiming our target became normal for us when the fight for our target finally ended it actually seemed anti-climactic. It just so happened one day my wife took her evening

blood pressure reading and for the first time in months, both numbers were below the target. In fact, it has been a couple of months and they have stayed that way. We have noticed the same kind of restoration in other areas.

When we first reconciled, neither of us were working, our savings were depleted and the disability payments my wife was receiving were placed on hold. There were two months when we did not have a dime of income coming into our home. Of course, we were believing God for restoration of our finances and just as with the blood pressure, we saw Satan play many of the same games. We made a commitment to live debt free and when no income is coming in, the enemy wants to see how committed you are. Thanks to God we held fast to our commitment. After that quiet period transpired, we started to see things surrounding our finances change. At first they were not great breakthroughs but we have to be thankful for every little thing as well as the big things. In time, we went from no income to about eighty percent of our household income being restored. We went from no savings to having more savings than what we had prior to our separation. Where we are today is really the most dangerous because comfortability has re-entered our lives. The question is will we settle for what we have or continue to believe God for what we have asked of Him? This book should give you a huge clue to our stance on the matter!

5. ***Give God thanks for everything*** (1 THESSALONIANS 5:18).

"At all times and for everything giving thanks in the name of our Lord Jesus Christ to God the Father."
(EPHESIANS 5:20 AMP)

Giving God praise and thanking Him for everything and at all times says to the devil you trust God at this moment, all day, tomorrow, and always. Praising God shows Him you are unmovable in your faith. The message to Satan is loud and clear, "Give me my stuff back." Your thanksgiving also tells Satan none of his tactics are getting to you. To God this is the sound of victory and to Satan it is the heralding of his impending defeat. Satan will continue bringing you disappointing situations, hurtful and completely opposite of what you want. Giving God thanksgiving in those times will be the death nail to the enemy's tactics. The more you thank God, the sooner your restoration will manifest.

Restoration is God's gift to you and your spouse. You now understand it is yours. You understand the enemy's tactics to prevent you from getting it. You even understand the five things you need to do to see the manifestation of your restoration. Start putting your faith in God today and know restoration is yours for the taking!

Scripture:

"Here's what will happen. While you're out among the nations where God has dispersed you and the blessings and curses come in just the way I have set them before you, and you and your children take them seriously and come back to God, your God, and obey him with your whole heart and soul according to everything that I command you today, God, your God, will restore everything you lost; he'll have compassion on you; he'll come back and pick up the pieces from all the places where you were scattered. No matter how far away you end up, God, your God will get you out of there and bring you back to the land of your ancestors once possessed. It will be yours again. He will give you a good life and make you more numerous than your ancestors.

God, your God, will cut away the thick calluses of your heart and your children's hearts, freeing you to love God, your God, with your whole heart and soul and live, really live. God, your God, will put all these curses on your enemies who hated you and were out to get you.

And you will make a new start, listening obediently to God, keeping all his commandments that I'm commanding you today. God, your God, will outdo himself in making things go well for you; you'll have babies, get calves, grow crops, and enjoy an all-around good life. Yes, God will start enjoying you again, making things go well for you just as he enjoyed doing it for your ancestors.

But only if you listen obediently to God, your God, and keep the commandments and regulations written in this Book of Revelation. Nothing halfhearted here; you must return to God, your

God, totally, heart and soul, holding nothing back.

This commandment that I'm commanding you today isn't too much for you, it's not out of your reach. It's not on a high mountain – you don't have to get mountaineers to climb the peak and bring it down to your level and explain it before you can live it. And it's not across the ocean – you don't have to send sailors out to get it, bring it back, and then explain it before you can live it. No. The word is right here and now – as near as the tongue in your mouth, as near as the heart in your chest. Just do it!"

(DEUTERONOMY 30: 1-14 MSG)

CHAPTER 16

ON THE ROAD TO MARRIAGE RESTORATION

With the marital crisis behind you, it is important you know how to live married.

Before you sought to gain information from this book to bring new life to your dead marriage, you were living in marital crisis. It is a living hell to wake up next to someone who has lost their affection for you and to realize you are losing your best friend and confidant. With the knowledge of God's redemptive works in marriage reconciliation and marriage resurrection, you can achieve new life for your marriage. Once reconciliation takes place, you quickly realize you have another fight on your hands as a result of the damage you may receive to your finances, reputation, relationships, and other areas of life due to Satan's destructive efforts during the separation. It will take time, but you will gain the victory as you continue with the same tools you deployed to bring your spouse home to rebuild your home. It may seem like a dream now, but there is going to come a time when all of the negativity surrounding your marriage will be placed in your rear view mirror. Weeks or months will have passed since the day your spouse returned home, your financial life will be on the road to recovery and broken relationships will start to mend. It will seem like spring to you yet it will be your most vulnerable time. As your married life transitions from crisis to normal again, it is important you take with you the lessons you have learned during those crisis periods to squarely put your life with your spouse solidly on the road to marriage restoration.

In chapter 1, we identified the root of martial problems is spiritual immaturity and you are quite aware of what it looks like in your life. Soon the crisis will be over and you will need to know how to live married or you risk generating another marital crisis. People assume because they start to have marital problems again it is proof that they and their spouse are not meant to be together. The reality is when peace and tranquility enter into our lives there is a tendency to lower our spiritual defenses, seek pleasure and slowly walk away from our relationship with the Lord. It was the Lord who brought new life into your dead marriage. It was the Lord who brought restoration to your life and removed the devastation. Time and time again we see scriptures like the one below where the people of Israel had forgotten the God who delivered from their enemies:

> "As soon as Gideon died, the people of Israel turned again and whored after the Baals and made Baal-berith their god. And the people of Israel did not remember the Lord their God, who had delivered them from the hand of all their enemies on every side, and they did now show steadfast love to the family of Jerubbaal (that is, Gideon) in return for all the good that he had done to Israel."
>
> (JUDGES 8:33-34 ESV)

Despite all God has done for you, you, too, will slowly drift away from the awakened state of spirituality it took to bring your spouse home unless you keep the Lord as the head of your marriage. Continuing to recognize Christ is the leader of your marriage will keep it fresh and healthy. Instead of just hoping and praying you will do this, the sure fire way to ensure this happens is to understand spiritual immaturity was the root cause and by continuing to let the Lord lead you, He will help you avoid the ditches and potholes come from being drawn away. Where will the Lord lead and what does that look like? That is what we will study in this chapter in order the new love you have found can be maintained.

Do you remember the plans you and your spouse set for yourselves when you were first married? Many people have forgotten how excited they were to learn there was another person interested in living the rest of their life together with them. Many times couples get so wrapped up into planning the wedding they fail to plan on how to live together after the wedding. In chapter 5, we defined that as marriage restoration. Just to refresh, we said marriage restoration is the work of each married couple that fellowships with God through the covenant to conduct restorative work in their marriage and bring it in alignment with God's original plan and purpose he established with Adam and Eve.

It has been thousands of years since Adam and Eve walked on the earth when the institution of marriage was created by God. In all that time, the institution of marriage has undergone a lot of transformation at the hands of men and women. It is not good enough for us take on the bounds of matrimony and observe other married couples to get our understanding of what marriage is meant to be. Too many people are doing this and look at the results. It would be very foolish after having the experiences with God we have had and take our marriages back to those dry examples. There is only one example to draw life and understanding from and it comes from looking at God original design. The good news is through the Bible we can understand God's original design and draw insight to be added to our marriages today.

THE BEGINNING OF MARRIAGE

> "When no bush of the field was yet in the land and no small

plant of the field had yet sprung up – for the Lord God had not caused it to rain on the land, and there was no man to work the ground, and a mist was going up from the land and was watering the whole face of the ground.

Then the Lord God formed the man of dust from the ground and breathed into his nostrils the breath of life, and the man became a living creature.

And the Lord God planted a garden in Eden, in the east, and there he put the man whom he had formed. And out of the ground the Lord God made to spring up every tree that is pleasant to the sight and good for food. The tree of life was in the midst of the garden, and the tree of the knowledge of good and evil.

A river flowed out of Eden to water the garden, and there it divided and became four rivers. The name of the first is the Pishon. It is the one that flowed around the whole land of Havilah, were there is gold. And the gold of that land is good; bdellium and onyx stone are there. The name of the second river is the Gihon. It is the one that flowed around the whole land of Cush. And the name of the third river is Tigris, which flows east of Assyria. And the fourth river is the Euphrates.

The Lord God took the man and put him in the Garden of Eden to work it and keep it. And the Lord commanded the man, saying, "You may surely eat of every tree of the garden, but of the tree of the knowledge of good and evil you shall not eat, for in the day that you eat of it you shall surely die."

Then the Lord God said, "It is not good that the man shall be alone; I will make him a helper fit for him." Now out of the ground the Lord God had formed every beast of the field and every bird of the heavens and brought them to the man to see what he would call them. And whatever the man called every living creature, that was its name. The man gave names to all livestock and the birds of the heavens and to every beast of the field. But for Adam there was not found a helper fit for him.

So the Lord God caused a deep sleep to fall upon the man, and while he slept took one of his ribs and closed up its place with flesh. And the rib that the Lord God had taken from the man he made into a woman and brought her to the man.

Then the man said, "This at last is bone of my bones and flesh of my flesh; she shall be called Woman, because she was taken out of Man."

Therefore, a man shall leave his father and his mother and hold fast to his wife, and they shall become one flesh. And the man and his wife were both naked and were not ashamed."

(GENESIS 2: 5-25 ESV)

From the biblical account we can see when God created the man he gave him more than life. God could have easily created man and then let him go into the world to see how he would respond. He did not. Instead he had a purpose in mind for the man and with that he provided everything man would ever need. There were trees in the garden that bore fruit good for consumption. The rivers were laden with land that had gold, bdellium and onyx stone, which gave the man the materials to build whatever his heart desired. These precious raw materials are still greatly sought after even today. The first thing God did for man was ensure he had **provision**. Provisions are a supply of food and other things needed, which are available in advance to prepare for something else (Merriam-Webster, Inc., 2016).

We see God put the man in the garden he made and give him a **purpose.** Man's function was to work and keep the garden. Purpose can be defined as the reason something exists (Merriam-Webster, Inc., 2016). There was never any doubt in Adam's mind why he was on the planet. He knew he was supposed to tend the garden. He had been responsible for naming all of the creatures God made and he was there to ensure the well-being of all of creation. Today, men struggle at understanding their purpose. As men are growing up they cannot wait until the day when they can get out of their parents' house and live on their own. Once they are on their own and have gained all of the freedom their hearts desire, they still may lack is purpose and direction.

Without direction, many men drift around aimless. One day they meet a woman and decide to get married. In order to take care of his family, he goes out into the working world to find a job. Initially, the man is thrilled about the job he has found because it allows him to do some wonderful things for his bride and new family. He may be able to move to a better neighborhood, from an apartment to a house, and buy other material things to make life more comfortable. It will not be long after accomplishing some level of comfort the man feels an empty space in his heart because though he has a good job, it does not mean he has found his purpose for being alive on the earth and this time in history. With emptiness in

his heart, the man begins to grow restless.

Finally, we see God give the man one last gift; the gift of providence. In Genesis chapter 2 and verse 18, we have a clear example of the level of care God intends to involve himself in the man's life when he declared, "It is not good that the man should be alone; I will make him a helper fit for him." What makes God care for Adam so much is he realizes his need and of his own accord creates the perfect response to that need. It is called **providence**. Providence can be defined as the protective or spiritual care of God. Even before Adam knew he had a need, God identified it and provided a solution. Notice Adam never had to ask God for a helper, let alone have the intelligence to ask for a woman. The creation of woman was entirely God's idea. With all the animals He had made, God felt Adam still needed someone else. It is possible for all of the world to be around us and yet still feel a sense of loneliness inside. It was this "aloneness" God did not want man to experience. When Adam's duties of a caretaker were done for the day, God wanted someone in which Adam could share his life.

We can see God's gifts to man were provision, purpose and providence but with all these gifts, God did not want him to partake of these gifts by himself. Instead, He wanted man to have a companion. **Companionship** for the woman is what purpose is for the man. Man's purpose would always be to complete a work in the earth and for the woman to be a companion in life and in the work with man. The Bible specifically called her as his "helper," which means that Eve's purpose was to support and accompany Adam on all of the assignments that would come to him from God. Eve would be more than an extra pair of eyes and hands to Adam. As part of God's declaration about Eve God said she was "a helper fit for him." The Greek word for helper is **neged,** which can be translated partly into English as counterpart. For the purpose of counterpart, it would be the following: 1) someone that has the same job or purpose as another, 2) a thing that perfectly fits another, or 3) remarkably similar to another as having similar characteristics (Merriam-Webster, Inc., 2016). However, the English definition of counterpart does not fully convey the depth of the Greek word because neged also means opposite. So taking into consideration, the woman will have the same purpose as man but not same job. She will perfectly fit with man but her talents will be different than his and though remarkably similar in characteristics, the woman will not be identical to him. The woman will bring a set of talents, insights, and abilities to the work God gave to the man the man does not possess. With the woman involved in the work, she completes the man.

Completeness is the second possession the woman has been given by God. Completeness can be defined as having all the necessary parts, not lacking anything and not limited in any way (Merriam-Webster, Inc., 2016). We have all seen movies or heard songs where the artists describe their love for one another by saying, "You complete me." While it may sound cliché, the reality is it was always God's plan for a man not to be able to reach his best self until he united in matrimony with a woman. The key is she would not be his identical but in many ways be his opposite. Like fasteners, they would be fitted together though their grooves flow in the opposite direction. With fasteners, one is male and the other female. A woman by her different views, talents, and insights brings out of the man the best of himself as she challenges him in ways that no one else ever could. Like Adam in the garden, without Eve, the outside world would just respond for better or for worst to the dominance God gave man. If man were ten-derhearted and loving, the rest of creation would fare well. If man were coarse and brutal, the rest of creation would not do well. Thus, the woman's role was to give to man all the help he would need to complete God's assignment. Without a woman, the man is still able to complete God's assignment but he would never reach the same height and depth of his assignment without the woman willing or allowed to fully engage all that God gave her. There are elements of God's assignment which can only be completed as a results of the talents, insights and abilities possessed by the woman. Without her, God's work would be a shell of its true ability.

If you read carefully, verse 9 of Genesis chapter 2, you will see the writer spent considerable care pointing out while God made almost all of creation by form-ing them from dust of the ground, with the woman He did an entirely different creative work was never repeated. This in itself should speak volumes to women and men about the uniqueness God has bestowed on the female side of the hu-man race. When He formed Eve, He did it by removing a rib from Adam's rib cage. Out of all of the parts of the body, God chose a rib. Obviously, there is some sig-nificance to the selection of this bone. The rib cage, according to the Medical Art Library, gives protection to the vital organs in the upper body (Medical Arts Stu-dio, Inc., 2016). The rib cage has three important functions: protection, support and respiration (Medical Arts Studio, Inc., 2016). It is a strong framework onto which the muscles of the shoulders, girdle, chest, upper abdomen, and back can attach (Medical Arts Studio, Inc., 2016). The rib cage is flexible and expandable and contracts by action of the muscles of respiration. Even with all of these vital organs such as the heart, lungs and the rest in proper working order, without the rib cage they could not operate properly and the man would die or be extremely limited in functionality. A single touch on your chest without the rib cage could rupture a lung or slice a hole into a vital artery of your heart. So when God took a rib from Adam, He was making a very strong statement by selecting this bone. God's gift of woman was actual a gift of charity meant to protect the man's heart and all that sustains his life.

This brings us to the third possession a woman brings to the relationship, which is **charity**. God will invest in the woman an ability to touch the man's heart and provide such a flexible framework around the man's life whatever he faced in life she would be able to expand, contract, or flex into exactly whatever the situ-ation required. With all God had created for Adam, without someone to share it with he would have become self-centered and all of the other creation would not have fared well under a self-centered Adam. When God created Eve, God did not double Adam's provision, purpose or providence. He did not give Eve her own provision. Instead, it was expected Adam would voluntarily give of all he had and share it with Eve. Thus, charity was added to the institution of marriage. Charity can be defined as the voluntary act of giving help (money, food or other type of assistance) to one in need.

Without Adam sharing what he had with her, Eve would have died of hunger, thirst, or exposure. When he did share, Adam did not experience a reduction in what he had but, I believe, he experienced an increase. How? When Eve added her talents, insights, and abilities to the work that Adam was assigned, he experienced an increase in the amount was completed, which produced a greater yield and new discoveries that were previously unseen by Adam. It only became visible when Eve appeared. With Eve on the scene, Adam learned to love, give, and share, all of which are attributes like His Father God. God is a giver and there are many verses in the Bible which tell us that when we give, multiplication is the result of giving, not reduction.

Give to everyone who begs from you, and from one who takes away your good do not   demand them back. And as you wish that others would do to you do so to them. If you love those who love you, what benefit is that to you? For even sinners love those who love them. And if you do good to those who do good to you, what benefit is that to you? For even sinners do the same. And if you lend to those from whom you expect to receive, what credit is that to you? Even sinners lend to sinners, to get back the same amount.

"But love your enemies, and do good, and lend, expecting nothing in return and your reward will be great, and you will be sons of the Most High, for he is kind to the ungrateful and the evil."
(LUKE 6: 30–35 ESV)

INSTITUTION OF MARRIAGE DEFINED

Now we have the possession or gifts from God to the man and the woman we are ready to define the institution of marriage. The description can be found in Genesis chapter 2 and verse 24.

"Therefore, a man shall leave his father and his mother and shall become united and cleave to his wife, and they shall become one flesh."
(GENESIS 2:24 AMP)

Institution of Marriage: Therefore, shall a man (possessor of God's purpose, provision and providence) leave his parental authority and shall fasten himself to his wife (a certain possessor of companionship, completeness and charity) and the two shall grow together and be one spiritual unit.

The institution of marriage can be defined as when a man leaves behind his father and mother's authority in pursuit of the purpose, provision, and providence God has promised for him. Along the way he encounters a certain woman whom he desires to make his wife. She possesses a companionship that makes him thirst for her presence, a charity that makes him willing to give to her freely, and with a set of unique talents, insights, and abilities to complete the man in a way only she can. The man and his wife, forsaking all others, will become one heart, one mind, one voice, and one set of hands to be used by God.

Most married couples seem as part of entering into a marriage they have to let go of being under their father and mother's authority. For those who struggle with this, it is because they have not yet really grasped it is time to grow up and stand on their own two feet. If either of the parents are too involved or one of the spouses will not cut the umbilical cord with the parents, this needs to be addressed directly and quickly with the spouse. That spouse has to make a choice between being married or having a dependent adult under their parents' care but they cannot have it both ways. The spouse is trying to avoid letting their spouse and parents down but in marriage, the first priority is to honor God. I remember when I had this issue with my mother when I was newly married to my wife. Right after my wife and I married, my relationship with my mother changed. My mother wanted to be involved in the day-to-day affairs of my marriage. For a few weeks, I pretended not to recognize the friction this was having between my mother and my wife until one day I read Genesis 2:24. That night I had a direct and honest conversation with my mother that put our relationship in its proper place. In another personal example, I have a sister who never addressed this head on with her husband and her mother-in-law. Unlike me, she thought she was taking a more diplomatic approach in trying to accommodate her husband and her mother-in-law's involvement in their marriage. All that did was keep her husband from truly growing up as a man and every time my sister did something he did not like; he would run to his mother. Unfortunately, those seeds of discord have come to full maturity and now the couple is in divorce court with a couple of teenagers in tow.

> Principle #13 –
> For whatever one sows, that will he also will reap
> (Galatians 6:7 ESV).

The root of this principle can be found in Genesis 8:22, and it is called "seed-time and harvest." The principle is very simple in whatever you decide to sow into your life it will return to you in a greater measure than what you originally sowed. If you take a seed and put it in the ground, over time you will reap a crop. It is the same thing in life. Every day you sow seeds. They can be seeds of love, mercy, and grace or seeds of blame, strife, and anger. In the example I shared above, my sister and her husband sowed seeds of avoidance. She was uncomfortable early on in their marriage holding herself, her husband and her mother-in-law to the principle of Genesis 2:24 and eventually it generated a crop of strife that led them towards divorce. The Bible is clear t as long as the earth remains, this principle will continue. With that in mind, it is important you pay attention to the seeds you plant in your marriage daily.

Going back to Genesis 2:24, there is another lesson to be learned regarding "leaving father and mother" that is more figurative than literal. Our parents also represent guardians who made our decisions for us when we were young and were our first tutors who taught us how to walk, talk and read. There is

an important lesson God is trying to teach to every married couple in Galatians chapter 4:

> *"What I am saying is that as long as an heir is underage, he is no different from a slave, although he owns the whole estate.*
>
> *The heir is subject to guardians and trustees until the time set by his father.*
>
> *So also, when we were underage, we were in slavery under the elemental spiritual forces of the world. But when the set time had fully come, God sent his Son, born of a woman, born under the law, to redeem those under the law, that we might receive adoption to sonship.*
>
> *Because you are his sons, God sent the Spirit of his Son into our hearts, the Spirit who calls out, "Abba, Father." So you are no longer a slave, but God's child; and since you are his child, God has made you also an heir."*
>
> (GALATIANS 4: 1-7 NIV)

THE MARITAL BLESSING

What God is trying to get every married couple to understand is he has set aside an inheritance for them. He did for Adam and Eve. Think about all that came into Adam's hands. There was land, gold, animals, the fruit bearing trees and everything else he ultimately shared with Eve. God did not stop there. He gave them an inheritance in the form of the blessing found starting in Genesis 1:28:

> *"He created them male and female. God blessed them: "Prosper! Reproduce! Fill Earth! Take charge! Be responsible for fish in the seas and birds in the air, for every living thing that moves on the face of Earth." Then God said, "I've given you every sort of seed-bearing plant on Earth and every kind of fruit bearing tree, given them to you for food. To all animals and all birds, everything that moves and breathes, I give whatever grows out of the ground for food."*
>
> (GENESIS 1:28-35 MSG)

God has never backed down from the blessing he gave to Adam and Eve. Today, as part of marriage restoration, he is looking for more Adam and Eves to come and believe him in areas where Adam and Eve did not, so he can fulfill the promise of his blessing. Jesus said he came to fulfill the law (Matthew 5:17), which includes what God promised to us in Genesis 1:28-35. God did not make Earth and all of its wonderful bounty to be the property of Satan or those who refuse to be in relationship with him. Absolutely not. Instead, he is looking for those who love, accept his Son, and believe His Word to take up the mantle and watch God fulfill His Word through them. God is looking for every married couple in covenant with him to commit to restoring their marriage through marriage restoration, taking the place Adam and Eve abdicated. Adam and Eve may have abdicated all of these blessings but God is waiting for you to take their place and walk in His blessing. Hopefully, you have an understanding why it was so important for Satan to stir up strife in your marriage. Adam and Eve abdicated these blessings when they ate of the fruit from the Tree of Good and Evil; they released their claim over the earth and all God made over to Satan. God wants it back, which is why He sent Jesus. Not only to redeem us back to God but to redeem all of creation back to Him as well.

> *"For the creation waits with eager longing for the revealing of the sons of God. For the creation was subjected to futility, not willingly, but because of him who subjected it, in hope that the creation itself will be set free from its bondage to corruption and obtain the freedom of the glory of the children of God."*
>
> (ROMANS 8:19 – 21 ESV)

There is a lot more at stake than just the wellbeing of you and your spouse. God is looking for us to be the replacements for Adam and Eve and with his blessing, take up where the first couple left off. With the redemptive work at Calvary, we are no longer subject to the curse but have been given our freedom. Satan wanted to break the union with your spouse because he was afraid you would eventually come to the knowledge of the truth, recognize you are no longer subject to the curse of the law or his bondage, and begin to reclaim the inheritance (blessing) he stole from Adam and Eve. With you and your spouse reclaiming what was stolen, Satan will be booted out from the inheritance. This is God's plan for you and your spouse and even His plan for Satan. Satan tried to keep you from it by taking advantage of your spiritual immaturity.

What God is looking for you and your spouse to do is not just leave father and mother but leave behind spiritual immaturity like a child who develops into adulthood. Each of us should understand and apply the Word of God to our lives like we are adults able to handle the meat of the Word (Hebrews 5:12). Unfortunately, far too many of us settle for being children and as a result, the inheritance (blessing) that God has for us is still under the care of guardians and tutors waiting for us to grow up.

The time has come for you and your spouse put aside childish things in your lives and get serious about restoring the marriage you have been given

by the Lord until it aligns with God's original design. When you do, you will receive what He has always had in store for you, which is the inheritance of his blessing.

Scripture:

> *"So Jesus said to those Jews who had believed in Him, if you abide in My word [hold fast to My teachings and live in accordance with them], you are truly My disciples. And you will know the Truth, and the Truth will set you free."*
>
> (JOHN 8:31, 32 AMP)

CHAPTER 17

RESTORING ADAM AND EVE

Putting it all together to make a
marriage restoration relevant to you.

In the previous chapter, we provided you with a basic understanding of what God's original plan for marriage entailed and what he put aside for both Adam and Eve. It is time to go deeper with our understanding of the story of Adam and Eve, in order for you to see how it relates to you today. We have talked about the marriage restoration and it is the work every married couple in covenant with the Lord should choose to follow. Why, you might ask? There is an Adam or an Eve in all of us today in need of restoration. If you are ever going to be all you are called to be in Christ, it is going to come through a marriage relationship. Whether that marriage relationship is with another person or you choose to not physically marry and instead stay solely married to the Lord. (1 Corinthians 7:8) In the end, as a member of the Bride of Christ, marriage is a part of all of future. There is no denying the importance of being married or more importantly, being a part of a biblical marriage is to each of us fulfilling our life's purpose and ultimate plan God has for our life.

There is more to the story of Adam and Eve for us to explore. After Adam and Eve ate of the Tree of Knowledge of Good and Evil, everything changed in their lives. Their relationship with God was no longer intimate. Their relationship to each other changed. Their relationship to the very creation they were supposed to possess and taking domain over changed. It was not until the redemptive work done by Christ at Calvary, a pathway was restored to all God had originally designed and planned is made available to all of the current and future descendants of Adam and Eve willing to forgo all other paths and embrace what Christ freely offers. With Christ, what was lost by the first Adam and Eve has now been restored. In this chapter, we go deeper in looking what was specifically restore to Adam and likewise to Eve and how it applies to you and me today.

RESTORING ADAM

Far too often when the story of Adam and Eve is examined it is presented the first disobedient act towards God came when they ate of the forbidden fruit.

When with closer examination of the story it becomes clear that on two specific occasions, Adam failed to follow what God had commanded. Adam initially did not follow God's commanded when he failed to eat of the tree of life.

> *"And the Lord God commanded the man, saying, "Of every tree*
> *of the garden you may freely eat: But of the tree of the knowl-*
> *edge of good and evil, you shall not eat of it: for in the day that*
> *you eat thereof you shall surely die."*
>
> (GENESIS 2:16, 17 KJV)

Adam was fully aware of the Tree of the Knowledge of Good and Evil, but he was also aware of the Tree of Life. They were both in the midst of the garden which made them both distinctive from the rest. Surely, Adam saw both of these trees as he walked from one side of the garden to the other side of the garden. Of all of the trees in the garden, these trees received prominence from God in his naming of them, placement and even the instructions he gave to Adam about them. Adam could eat of The Tree of Life but the Tree of Knowledge of God and Evil he was commanded not to eat of it. So why did Adam not take a bite of the fruit from the Tree of Life. He was told it was good for food and it stood out right in front of him? Adam got caught up in the work and missed the subtle meaning and presence of the beautiful and delicious tree that stood in the garden. Adam was too busy doing the job he was created to do. He became so engrossed in giving names to the animals and cultivating the garden he failed to take time to enjoy and explore the garden.

Adam had become work focus instead of being life focused. That is why the Tree of Life did not have much appeal to him. I am sure he meant to explore the tree but he kept his focus on the work at hand. The scripture tells us in Genesis 2:19 and 20 God would make a creation and then Adam would give a name to the creation. This became his focus and you can tell from the scripture about his tenacious attitude towards doing the work because it goes on to tell us he gave names to all the cattle, all the birds and every beast in the field. That is a lot of naming. I am sure in the naming he got hungry and needed to rest. Adam lost sight of working to live. Instead he was focused on living to work. When he ate of the fruit the garden produced he did it to get back to work. When he rested, he did so to get back to work. Adam lost himself in the work and so his intention of exploring life slipped further and further from his list of priorities with each passing day. God recognized this and hear what his response to the situation was:

> *"And the Lord God said, "It is not good that the man should be*
> *alone; I will make him a help meet for him."*
>
> (GENESIS 2:18 KJV)

God recognized unless he did something Adam would continue being work focused instead of being life focused. Imagine if just for one day, Adam had been life focused instead of work focused. He would he realized the garden was basically taking care of itself. He would have spent time interacting with the animals instead of just doing the work. He would have also taken time to explore the Tree of Life and remembered God said it was good for food. He would have eaten. With just a single bite from the fruit of that tree, Adam could have avoided, for all of us, this life we now know as our reality. We would have never known sickness, war, death, poverty, toil or any of the things mankind suffers through as a result of sin. Instead he stayed work focused. God tried to intervene and break up his work focused attitude by giving him a help mate in Eve. What was Eve created to help Adam with? Surely, it was not work. If that was the case, he would have created her to be strong like Adam. Instead, Eve in her composition was very different from Adam. Where Adam was strong and firm, Eve was mild and tender. She was pleasing to the eye. God intended Eve would help Adam take his focus off of work and shift it to life. She was designed to help Adam realize there was more to this life God had given him than work. Prior to Eve's creation, Adam was just existing to work but now God was trying to get Adam to embrace living. God had intended with Eve's creation for Adam attention to shift from working to living and, with this shift, Eve would lead Adam to the Tree of Life. Eve would help Adam recognize what he had previously ignored when he was work focused. She would help Adam to recognize the subtle things in life and how to enjoy them. Enthralled by the beauty and splendor of Eve, Adam was to start building a life not just work.

The Bible goes on tell us there was some immediate excitement from Adam when God presented him with Eve. Look at Adam response as he turns and sees this creation that God made specifically for him.

> "The Man said, "Finally! Bone of my bone, flesh of my flesh!
> Name her Woman for she was made from Man."
> (GENESIS 2:23 MSG)

There is some passion in Adam's response. It was as if someone hit his excitement button and he was very happy with the creation God made for him. As you read the rest of the story, Adam and Eve enter into marriage. (Genesis 2:24, 25). God responded to the marriage by announcing the blessing of which he said, "Be fruitful, and multiply, and replenish the earth, and subdue it, and have dominion over the fish of the sea, and over the fowl of the air; and over every living thing that moves upon the earth." With God creating this beautiful creature who was to help Adam shift from being work-focused to life-focus and the blessing God pronounced over them it should have been a fairy tale ending that says "...and they lived happily ever after."

Unfortunately, there would be no happily ever after with Adam and Eve. Why? Shortly, after the wedding and blessing ceremony Adam returned to being work focused. He never made the shift to being life focused as God had intended. This is the second time now Adam was missing God. How do we know he returned to being work-focused? It can be deduced from two scriptures. The first is the fact despite God giving them the blessing to be fruitful and multiply, the Bible does not record Adam actually having intercourse with Eve until after the fall. (Genesis 4:1). Adam's initial excitement about Eve and her being with him got lost not long after the ceremony. Adam did not do what God told him to do which was be "fruitful and multiply". Implied in God's blessing to Adam and Eve was a blessing of life. If Adam had immediately focused on pursing this life as God intended, he would have found several things. He would have found how to have a relationship. Something up to that point Adam did not know how to do. Adam knew God as creator but God wanted him to see him for much more. If Adam had been obedient and had sexual intercourse with Eve, she would have conceived. Adam would have now seen Eve in a whole new light as not only wife but mother. He, as the father, would have been open to seeing life to a whole new perspective and out of this new perspective he would see God as Father and not just Creator. This would never happen because Adam chose not to immediately know his wife.

In addition, Adam progress in developing a relationship with Eve was still very much at the beginning stage at the time of the fall. He had not grown to see her life as critical to his own. He did not feel it was necessary to be her protector and guider. A responsibility which surely came on Adam when Eve was created. God took of his own personal time to spend with Adam and show him how he was doing the creation (Genesis 2:19, 20). This eventually became Adam's work but when it came down to Eve he did not show the same care.

When God discovered Adam had eaten of the forbidden fruit Adam did not take direct responsibility instead he blamed Eve for giving him the fruit and God for creating Eve. Adam was so easily able to put the blame on Eve and God because he did not view Eve as precious to him. Somewhere in his reasoning he had hoped because Eve had given him the fruit that God would take responsibility for what he had happened. God did not take responsibility because that responsibility lands squarely on Adam. As the first to be created, he should have made sure Eve was properly taught God's commandment. He did not follow God's pattern of how he taught Adam after his creation and he made sure Adam wanted nothing. When Eve went to respond to the inquiry of the serpent, she was fully aware of what God had said. In her response back to the serpent she said, "We may eat of the fruit of the trees of the garden; but the fruit of the tree which is in the midst of the garden, 'God has said, you shall not eat of it, neither shall you touch it, lest you die.'"

She was incorrect in her response. There were two trees in the midst of the garden one could be eaten and one could not be eaten. God never said anything about not touching the tree. How could Eve so grossly misunderstand what God had said? Because Adam had failed to give the proper care necessary when passing the instruction on to her. It was clear Adam had not taken the time to make sure that Eve accurately knew what God had said to him. Eve did not have the benefit of hearing from God on the subject instead she had to receive it second hand. It was Adam's responsibility to dispense this knowledge. While we can credit Adam for at least informing her about the general details of the tree, he did not take the same protective care God had extended to him toward Eve.

When the serpent arrived to have this talk with Eve it is clear in the scripture Adam was nowhere to be found. Where was he? Adam had returned to the

work and he left Eve to busy herself. Adam was not around because developing a relationship with Eve was not his top priority. Instead, he was off interacting and working with other the creations of God. Even though Eve was also a creation of God, Adam somehow felt his presence with the others were more of a priority and one he didn't feel it necessary to bring Eve with him in doing. The serpent was able to have this very long and crafty discussion with Eve because Adam was not present. The serpent was able to win Eve over to his manner of thinking because Adam had not fully prepared Eve with the truth. Adam had only equipped her with a limited vail of knowledge about the tree, its fruit and what God had said about it. The first time Eve had even laid eyes on the fruit from the tree was a result of the serpent's discussion and it was then she saw that it was good for food and pleasant to the eyes. (Genesis 3:6) If Adam had been taken her with him to do whatever he was doing in the garden, Eve would have seen this fruit before. She would have known there were two trees in the midst of the garden, not one. She would have already known the fruit was good for food and pleasant to the eye. When the serpent presented the fruit to Eve these would have not be much of a temptation to her but due to Adam's neglect she had very little information. Adam did not properly prepare her nor include Eve in the life and work he was enjoying. It seems clear Adam did his thing and Eve was left to figure out a work for herself. In this environment, there was room for the serpent to enter in and steal the life God had so richly left them.

Eve may have not known what the fruit looked like but Adam should have definitely known its distinctive qualities. According to the Bible in Genesis 3:6, the fruit is described as "pleasant to the eyes" which means its physical description was vastly superior to all of the other fruits. Adam and Eve were surrounded by fruit bearing trees. To describe this fruit as being "pleasant to the eyes" means of all of the other fruit form the other tree this one stood among the rest. You would be hard to ignore what this fruit looked like, which was God's very purpose of creating it this way. It was supposed to be distinctive as to not be mistaken for another fruit. It was not the only distinctive fruit in the midst of the garden. The fruit of the Tree of Life was also distinctive. Their distinctiveness was an indicator of their importance and as the fruit of the Tree of Knowledge of Good and Evil was "pleasant to the eyes" as it was considered important enough for God to especially name and provide a commandment for it, likewise, one could argue the fruit of the Tree of Life was equally as beautiful. We know both trees were "good" because the Bible tells us when God saw all he had made in Genesis 1:31 he declared them as good. God intended for man to eat of the Tree of Life, so it is equally understanding God would not have put in any condition secondary to the Tree of Knowledge. Also, he would have not made the Tree of Knowledge with rotten or ugly fruit because everything God made was good. It is not in God's nature to create bad, spoiled or rotten because these are elements of death. In God, there is only life not death. Again, because the tree was important its fruit was beautiful. Adam who was put into the garden by God himself, surely knew what the forbidden fruit look like. So why did Eve offer Adam the fruit when she ate it?

Adam knew it was the forbidden fruit, yet he ate it. The Bible does not clearly indicate Adam's reasons for eating the fruit; there are a few possibilities which can be drawn from the text. We have already seen Adam did not cultivate a relationship with Eve and he still saw God as creator not father. By this time, Adam had already shown he was not making following God's commands as a top priority instead his priority were being work focused. If he had made following God's commands his top priority, even before Eve was created, he would have taken measures to ensure fruit from the Tree of Knowledge was never eaten. Because destruction or death was not yet something he had experience with, it would not be a first thought for him to cut the tree down or set it on fire. It was not out of the realm of possibility because he had to have some understanding of death when God told him in Genesis 2:17 he would "surely die", otherwise it would not have been a valid communication. If a living thing could die by eating the fruit of the tree, then Adam could have inquired of God for understanding on what to do to properly respond to his command. Adam did not inquire of God because his relationship with him was limited to God being creator not father. Therefore, Adam either did not want to or felt he could discuss that with God.

Adam could have also built a structure around it making virtual impossible for any of the animals or himself to so easily get to the tree. This would have been in keep with his duties of dressing and keeping the garden. The Bible does not record Adam building any structure around the Tree of Knowledge. In the end, Adam was not as motivated to comply with God's commandments. Maybe all along he meant to after completing with his work of naming the animals. He clearly had no plan on how to address his response should he ever been presented with the forbidden fruit. Some have argued Adam ate the fruit because of his trust of Eve. However, even if he trusted Eve, his own knowledge about the physical characteristics of the fruit and knowing he would die should have kicked in his desire to obey God which would have caused him to overlook whatever trust he had with Eve. It did not because his response to eating the fruit was in keeping with his response to everything beyond doing the work God had done or said to him. Adam had not been quick to obey or thorough in his care. It became evident in his partaking of the forbidden fruit because he eats it without a comment.

There is another possibility. Adam could have been so engrossed in his work he failed to notice the fruit was being served to him. Adam had already shown he missed the subtle things. Though Adam knew exactly what the fruit looked he was focused on his work. He ate in order so he can get back to work. He slept so he could rest in order for him to get back to work. It seems Adam and Eve's relationship may have deteriorated to the point Adam was showing up just eat and sleep. We know from the scripture that they were not having sex. We also know Eve had not spent much time in the garden otherwise should would have already had a clear visual experience with the forbidden fruit. The Bible says in Genesis 3:6 "Eve took of the fruit thereof, and did eat and gave also to her husband with her; and he did eat." There are a couple of things you need to notice. The serpent is not mentioned as being with Eve and Adam when she partook of the fruit of the Tree of Knowledge. The serpent had already done his part when he planted in Eve's thinking the seeds of doubt about what God had said. The serpent was not present because it was a time when Adam and Eve were out picking fruit for them to eat. We know Eve had never seen the Tree of Knowledge before and somehow on this fruit gather trip they end up in the midst of the garden. Obviously, this is Eve's first trip to the midst of the garden. Imagine them going from one tree to another tree picking fruit. Eve is enjoying the trip and the experience while Adam is focused on gathering food. From time to time, she shares with Adam a piece of fruit and he takes a bite out of what she is presented. While the experience is new for Eve, it is routine for Adam. For Eve, the trip is a life changing experience and she is taking full vantage of it and everything she experiences she shares with Adam. Adam ate of that fruit because he was not focused on what he was doing. How many other pieces of fruit did Eve give to Adam to eat and he would partake would giving it his attention. When Eve gave of him the fruit, he ate it without even asking a question because it was a habit of doing and his focus was somewhere else. I am sure Adam had every intention of obeying God's command and he thought he had plenty of time to do something about it.

In his own heart, his desire was to follow God's commandment so he felt like he had nothing to be concerned about. He felt like he had informed Eve about the tree so in his mind that door was closed. The Bible tells us the serpent was more subtle and crafty than any living creature of the field which the Lord God had made. (Genesis 3:1 AMP) The Bible does not tell us is if the conversation between the serpent and Eve was the only conversation between the serpent and mankind. If there was another conversation, it would have occurred between Adam and the serpent. If there was another conversation, we know its outcome. Adam did not give in to the deceiving words of the serpent and he did not tell Eve about that conversation. Regardless of whether there was or was not a conversation with Adam, when Eve gave of Adam to eat of the fruit his attention was elsewhere. He ate the fruit and the Bible says immediately the eyes of them both were opened. (Genesis 3:7) I believe there is sufficient biblical evidence to support Adam's attention was elsewhere when he explained what happened to God this is what he said, "And the man said, 'The Woman whom You gave to be with me, she gave me of the tree, and I did eat." (Genesis 3:12 KJV) Adam did not take responsibility for what he ate because he felt he was innocent, He did not pick it and choose it to eat. He blamed Eve. His argument was all on Eve and he eat it because she gave it to him to eat. What is missing is he ate it because he was focused on other things. He ate it because instead of enjoying the life experience moment with Eve and deepen his relationship with her, his attention again was on other things and as a result he was not paying attention to what was happening in the moment. The very thing God was trying to get Adam's attention on and avoid from happening is exactly what happened because Adam failed to shift his attention from being work-focused to life-focused.

Adam lost everything his home in the garden, the work that he so valued, the wealth of the gold and onyx stones that was by the river, work without toil and having dominion over the Earth because he failed to be life focused.. Being work-focused caused him to miss out on the very thing he needed in his life to enjoy all benefits from God forever because he failed to eat of the Tree of Life.

More importantly, being work-focused caused Adam to lose the blessing that God had given to him.

You and I have do not have to end up like Adam but far too many of us are not learning from his lesson but instead continue making the same mistakes he made. Adam never saw the garden restored to him while on Earth. Adam never saw the blessing restored to him either. All he lost remained lost to him. That is not our condition. Jesus' death and resurrection secured us another path. That path is a marriage restoration. Every husband that is in a covenant relationship with Christ can be the Adam who has everything lost restored. He can have his own Garden of Eden here on Earth. All we lost, Jesus restored to us. It will mean we have to operate differently in our lives than how Adam did. Where Adam saw God as only as creator we will need to see and relate to him as Father. Where Adam was slow to recognize what God valued, we will need to be quick to value those things and to take the necessary steps to cherish them. Adam did not put a boundary around the things God said not to have in his life. We have to take time to learn what God has said about what is good and what is evil for our lives. The good we are to embrace and the evil we are to build a barrier around that prevents giving any access for those things to take a place in our lives. We are not to ignore the Eve God has given us but to realize through her we will learn how to have proper relationships. She will help lead us to the Tree of Life and is the only fruit we are to enjoy. We have to help her develop because we do not want the enemy to destroy what we have. There is only one path for husband and wife not multiple paths to God's blessing, and we have to arrive there together. As the husband, we have to realize there are responsibilities that are own our shoulders God did not put on our wives. We cannot just zone out of the life experiencing moments because when we do we open ourselves to losing it all. Being a restored Adam means you are going to be quick and focused on obeying God. God has called you to live His quality of life. We are not our definition of life from this world or from to others. It is time as men and as husbands we embrace being a restored Adam.

RESTORING EVE

Adam is the not the only one needing a restoration. If you continue to take a deeper look at the story of Adam and Eve you will see in many ways Eve was placed in a bad situation. Adam failed to give her proper instruction and guidance with regards to the Tree of Knowledge. She failed to develop a deep and meaningful relationship with Adam, and this opened her up to listening and being deceived by the serpent instead of hearing and staying true to what her husband had told her. It was not until after the fall Adam and Eve became sexually intimate prior to that there seems to be biblical evidence there was gaps in their relationship. There are four specific areas of which every wife in a covenant relationship with God will need to find restoration as a result of what occurred in the garden. She will need restoration in helping her husband connect with the blessing of God, helping him to be life-focused, helping him to develop and appreciate meaningful relationships and not allowing herself to feel inferior to man. These are the four lessons for every Eve that come out of the biblical account between

Adam and Eve in Genesis 1-3. When a wife goes on the road of marriage restoration, these will be the areas she will pay particular attention to as these will avenues God will use her in to bring their union towards God's original design for their marriage.

It is clear Adam did not properly prepare Eve and in this Eve was a ripe target for the deception that came to her from the serpent. This does not absolve her from responsibility, but it does show that if Eve is going to fulfill the call of God on her life she is going to have to do so by having her own direct relationship with God. It would be wonderful if her God-fearing husband is already connected with the Lord and squarely on the road to marriage restoration. If the Bible is true, then God will use the wife to reach the heart of the husband. Which means right from the moment the two say "I do" there are going to be things revealed in the man that are going to cause some problem down the road. In Adam's case, it was him being "work focused", him not taking time to develop a meaningful relationship with Eve and his slow response to do all that God commanded. Eve was the recipient of Adam's actions and it is clear even with him being directly created by God, Adam made some decisions on his own that ultimately caused them to lose everything. Eve had a hand in them losing everything because she was not aware of what her role in Adam's life was supposed to be. Adam had the benefit of God directly telling him his role and placing him in the garden. Adam benefited from God coming and bringing him the things he had made and giving Adam the opportunity to name the animals. Yet Eve did not have God show her role directly. Instead, those instructions were supposed to come as a result of the time they both spent with God and from the things God shared with Adam. Eve was in the presence of God for the blessing and when God entered into the garden at the cool of the day in Genesis 3:8, Eve was present. Eve's relationship with God was not as advanced as Adam and, though she had been in God's presence, it was clear the order of things when from God to Adam and from Adam to Eve (Genesis 3:9-13).

When Eve was created one of the things God wanted as an outcome of her creation is she would help Adam eat from the Tree of Life. Eating from the Tree of Life would have eternalized them living in the blessing of God. However, after Eve was created Adam did not take her to the midst of the tree of the Garden. In fact, from her own words she only talked about one tree in the midst of the Garden when God said there was two. Ultimately, Eve had fulfilled part of her purpose of creation. She got Adam to take to the midst of the garden and she got Adam to eat of the fruit from the tree that was there. However, it was the wrong tree. She did not lead Adam to the Tree of Life but instead to the Tree of the Knowledge of Good and Evil. That is why when Eve ate the fruit her eyes did not immediately open. They only opened after Adam ate of the fruit. (Genesis 3:7) Because the commandment to not eat the tree rested with Adam and not with Eve. Adam's work-focused attitude caused Eve to not being properly equipped to fulfill her role to lead him to the Tree of Life. If he had spent time with her, properly educated and protector her from the craftiness of the serpent then they could have avoided the problem in the first place. Adam failed to recognize that his inactions were causing opening a huge doorway for Satan to take advantage of them. God provision of salvation which he bestowed in Eve was neglected by Adam. The good news is through Jesus every Eve (wife) has been set free from having to depend on learning about what God has said through her husband. God has made it so she can have a direct relationship with him herself. In fact, God is still looking for every Eve to help Him win over the heart of their husband.

> *"In like manner, you married women, be submissive to your husbands [subordinate yourselves as being secondary to and dependent on them, and adapt yourselves to them]. So that even if any do not obey the Word [of God], they may be won over not by discussion but by the [godly] lives of their wives."*
>
> (1 PETER 3: 1 AMP)

As a wife, it is imperative you realize God led you to your imperfect husband because God wants to partner with you to win over your husband's heart. Do not be hurt because your husband does not go to church or is not on fire for the Lord like you are. Do not be hurt because what started off as a loving and passionate relationship with your husband has since cooled. If you really take Eve's account to heart, you will realize God is not surprised and knows your Adam is screwing up. God is not putting his confidence in Adam it is in you, Eve. You keep on going to church and let your godly character speak for you. God will honor your commitment to leading your husband to the Tree of Life (Jesus); he will answer your prayers and now you know about all the various life boats God has bestowed to resurrect and reconcile your marriage just be ready to put your faith in Him. In Adam's day, God wanted Eve to lead Adam to the Tree of Life but today he is looking to you to help lead your husband to Jesus.

Beyond helping the husband with his relationship to Jesus, every woman will need to help to their man develop a life. Men, by nature, are task driven and this is why it is very easy for them to struggle at the things that come to building a life.

From the biblical account, here is a classic example. Adam saw God created Eve. He saw how beautiful she was. He had heard God given unto them both the command to be fruitful and multiply. However, it was not until after the fall Adam did two things. First, he has sexual intercourse with his wife. Before he did that, the scripture records in Genesis 3:20 Adam finally give her a name. Eve was just called "Woman" before the fall. Now during that time Adam was not called man because he had been given a name. In fact, in Genesis 3:9, God does not call to the man it says he called out to Adam. So Adam had a name. Why did not Adam give Eve a name? He knew how to name the animals, but when it came down to Eve he was not quick to give her a personalized name even though it was a task he was very familiar at accomplishing. It was not an issue of ability but an issue of relatability. Only after he lost everything, did Adam learn how to relate to his wife. Building a life did not come easy to Adam and do not expect it to come easy to your Adam. Adam missed the subtle things of life and missed every life experiencing moment and it was because of that God said the boy needed help. Even after God created Eve and presented him this wonderful gift, Adam did not immediately start understanding he needed to build a life. He did not let Eve help him with building a life. Instead, he left her to her own business which resulted in his downfall. If your Adam is ever going to build a life it is because you Eve are there. Don't be surprised that your Adam is doing all he should be doing in this life with you. You need to think about Eve. Your Adam may not be fully engaged with you. He may not be giving you his full attention when you talk. Spending time with his buddies may seem more important than you at the moment. Regardless of what is causing difficulty in the relationship you have to know God has you there. He knew in advance your husband would not fully realize all he has in you and that is why at times husbands will have to experience losing it all or what seems valuable to them before they eyes toward you are finally open. Like Adam, they will come through the experience realizing how much of a fool they had been. Can you imagine how many nights after the fall Adam hit himself thinking about all the mistakes he had made? What if he had valued Eve more properly and taught her everything he knew about the Tree of Knowledge then they could have avoided the nightmare they were in.

No matter how much of a home Adam tried to build for Eve, nothing would compare to what they had in the garden. For Eve, she had to lose the garden and the blessing from God which came with it. However, that is not the case with you, Eve. Jesus restored the garden and a life with blessing for you and your Adam. All you have to be willing to do is trust him and get on the road of marriage restoration. Know it does not matter how your Adam is presently acting. If you believe God, you will have the Eve experience. Your Adam will experience a losing of what is precious and there his eyes will be open. In the meantime, keep trying to engage your Adam and building a life. Whether it is raising the children or just taking a meaningful vacation. It will not come natural to him and you are going to have understand that part. If it did come natural, God would have never created you as his help mate. Helping him understand, build and enjoy life is your part of what you bring to the relationship. Understand your role and do it as unto the Lord and there He will honor you by bringing Adam's affection back to you.

> "During the entire time Adam and Eve where in the Garden of Eden, Adam saw God as creator. It was until Genesis 3:20 do we see change. And Adam called his wife's name Eve: because she was the mother of all living."
>
> (GENESIS 3:20 KJV)

If Adam was able to see Eve for more than being his wife, he could see God for being more than just the creator. It was God who gave Adam life. It was God who had given Adam the garden. It was God who gave everything to Adam. It was because he failed to recognize who Eve was to him he lost it all. That is why the first thing he said or did after God had pronounced judgment on Adam, Eve and the serpent was to call Eve the mother of all living. Another way to say it is mother of all life. Adam wanted to make sure that he did not make the same mistake again. Eve was created to help him recognize and enjoy life. If he had embraced her relationship to him, it would have ultimately lead him to the Tree of Life. Instead, he failed in building a meaningful relationship with her and it cost him everything. The same thing with God. If Eve was the mother of all living, then surely God was the Father of all living because time after time Adam witnessed the creations God had made come to life. If Adam had recognized him as father and not as just creator, he would have valued more the things God had set aside and done for him. Even after the pronouncement of judgment, God does another act of providence by shedding of blood of an animal and making coats of skin and clothing for them. Wives have to realize building meaningful relationships for men is another thing which does not come naturally. Women are naturally built for birthing and bearing relationships from the numerous words they produce to their ability to quickly empathize with others. These are qualities every man has to work on. God produced Eve as the mother of life for Adam to cause him to pursue life building. Learning how to build and nature relationships, if the man did not learn it from his mother, he will need his wife to help him significantly in this area. He will be like Adam and, after the woman becomes his wife, he will return to his work and other focuses. This is where God is looking for the wife to not get frustrated but to learn from the Lord on how to help the man to learn to build and nature relationships. God's very own relationship with the man is at stake and he is looking to every Eve to help him with this. Eve do not get angry at your Adam, the promise of the Word is with the Lord's help you will learn to help him build and nurture relationships and the two of you will experience what God had always intended which he called "becoming one flesh".

This last work the wife will undertake has more to do with herself then it has to do with Adam. One of the reasons I believe Eve pursued the forbidden fruit is because of how Adam had been treating Eve. Whether his treatment of her was intentional or not, the end result for Eve was the same. She felt inferior or she lacked something and when she was presented with the forbidden fruit in it she found her salvation. She was not pursuing it because she was interested in being disobedient or even in need of food. Let us return to Genesis 6:3 and discover what Eve was pursuing:

> "And when the woman saw that the tree was good for food,
> and that it was pleasant to the eyes, and a tree to be desired to
> make one wise, she took of the fruit thereof, and did eat, and
> gave also to her husband with her and he did eat."
>
> (GENESIS 6:3 KJV)

What is very interesting is Eve saw the fruit was not only good for food and pleasant to the eye but what really got her to take the fruit was it would make her wise. Why was it so important that Eve wanted to become wise? Because she was tired of being made to feel like she was not smart, stupid or her husband was smarter than her. Somehow Adam had used the knowledge he obtained by being created before Eve and the knowledge he obtained during his times with God and when he presented that information to Eve it resulted in her feeling

bad about herself. This should have never been the case. Adam had experience nothing but grace, understanding and patience with from God in his creation and subsequent times with God. It is apparent how God dealt with Adam when you read from Genesis:

> *"And He said, "Who told you that you were naked? Have you*
> *eaten of the tree, whereof I commanded you that you should*
> *not eat?"*
>
> (GENESIS 3:11 KJV)

God was not asking these questions of Adam because he lacked knowledge. God, who can see the end from the beginning, was not asking these questions for his sake but to educate Adam (Isaiah 46:10). Before God asked, He already knew they had eaten of the tree and how events actually planned out yet when he asks Adam for his answer he does so with the intent of sharing knowledge to him. Adam did not pick up on God's character, methods or heart in his dealings with God because, if he did, he should have shared what little knowledge he had to Eve in the same way. Instead, Eve gained the impression she was less than and she needed some outside help to be all she should be. Eve was not created feeling it came as a result of Adam's treatment of her. If Adam had treated her in the same way God had treated him than Eve would have not been seeing the fruit from the Tree of Knowledge in that way.

Remember, there were two trees in the midst of the garden. The Tree of Life and Tree of Knowledge. Both had fruit that was pleasant to the eye. Both had fruit that would was good for food. But only one according to the serpent had the ability to make her wise. Her need to gain wisdom was so great she was willing to risk death and even disappoint Adam to get it. In her mind, the only way to remove the shame of being unwise and gain acceptance from Adam in this area was to gain wisdom. Adam was not properly teaching and guiding her so she could not see him as a source. Earlier, we that the order of knowledge flowed from God to Adam and then from Adam to Eve. Eve did not see going directly to God as an option. Here the serpent offered to her what seem like a way out of shame and feelings of inferiority that Adam had placed on her. So she risked it all. Because of Adam's bad teaching she believed by touching it she could die. This didn't come from the serpent it came from Adam himself. Risking everything, she had learned from Adam about what God had commanded she reached out to take hold of the fruit. Adam was there with her and he did nothing to stop her. Either he was paying attention or was not interested in her actions, his actions bolstered her need to get ahold of that fruit. In her desperation for a better relationship with Adam, she took hold of the fruit and was surprised she did not die.

The key to that story is while Adam should have never made Eve feel inferior to himself or below what God had created her to be, Eve's value should not have come from how she thought Adam saw her or how he related to her. Her value is why God created her in the first place and gave to her in the creation. Every woman needs to remember their value and self-worth should never be linked to how their fathers, lovers or husbands think or say they are. Their worth and value was set by God and he values every woman greatly. It is time every Eve ignores the way their husbands try to make them feel inferior. Listen to these words from God and burn them into your heart and mind forever.

> *"And God saw everything that He had made, and behold, it was*
> *very good."*
>
> (GENESIS 1:31)

Every woman is a product of God's creation and when God sees every woman he sees nothing but good. It is only after the Adams of the world gets involved do our Eves start to gain the impression that somehow God made them as inferior or they are less than good. Both are absolutely untrue in God's eyes and these untruths need to stop!

Eve you are the key to Adam becoming who he was created to be. God's plan for you is far greater than being a mother to the children. It has taken Jesus to free you to have a direct relationship with the Father and to restore you to being a possessor of the blessing right alongside Adam. That is why the woman's movement was so critical and God inspired because it reintroduced to the world all God put in Eve and caused the world to stop limiting her role to being the mother of the children. God is trying to restore you to being the mother of life which is a far greater role. God will use whatever he needs to use to accomplish his purpose and he used the woman movements to start the process of restoring Eve to her rightful place. Eve has her own special place and through Jesus, God is working to restore Eve.

Don't get discouraged Eve at the cruelty, lack of respect and abuse coming from Adam. God sees it and he is working to restore all things. It is already restored in heaven but God's promise to you right now is before Jesus returns he will restore your place here on Earth. Acts 3:21. Take the time to learn in the Spirit who you really are. Understand not all you are hearing about a woman's right to be free is coming from God and it is Satan's attempt to use human reasoning to separate you from Adam and with unrighteousness pump you up higher than you ought to think of yourself. Satan's whole intention is to exploit Adam's cruelty and abuse to cause you (Eve) to travel a course will have you forgo the restored place God has for you. That is the trick he played on the first Eve and he is still playing that same trick today. Remember Eve, Adam needs you to become who he was created to be and you need Adam to be who you were created to be. It is important Eve you also know this, Satan knows God is working to restore you and Adam to your rightful places. When that occurs you and Adam will receive what was promised "the blessing of dominion of the Earth." Right now the Earth is still in Satan's possession. The power and authority was restored back to Adam and Eve as redeemed children of the Most High God and joint heirs with Jesus. What is missing is Adam and Eve have not come back to reclaim possession of the Earth. Adam cannot achieve the promised blessing without Eve and Eve can't achieve the promised blessing with Adam. The promised blessing can only be achieved when Adam and Eve become one flesh.

BECOMING ONE FLESH

With the deeper understanding of Adam and Eve's relationship in the Garden of Eden and what you must do on the road of marriage restoration if you're going to receive God's blessing it is now time to unveil how you become one flesh. Becoming one flesh doesn't just automatically happen because you get married. It happens because of conscience decisions made by Adam to love his wife and give to her the role in his life that God created for her. One flesh can be achieved because of Adams love for Eve and Eve's respect for Adam. It can also be lost because of Adam neglect of Eve (lack of love) or Eve's disrespect of Adam. Becoming one flesh occurs when Eve finds that openness, honesty and love from Adam to be who she is meant to be to him. When she is able to point him to the tree of life, help him become life focus and she is able to enjoy the deep and meaningful relationship he has built for her there they will find have become one flesh and there they will discover the blessing that God has promised. With that blessing they will find everything was bestowed upon mankind in the Garden and subsequently stolen by Satan restored to them (purpose, provision providence companionship charity and completeness). Adam or Eve can be blessed of God for fellowship with Him. An example of that can be found in the examination of Noah's life in Genesis chapter 6. There the scripture says, "But Noah found grace in the eyes of the Lord." (Genesis 6:8 KJV). The Amplified Bible of that verse reads it this way, "But Noah found grace (favor) in the eyes of the Lord." (Genesis 6:8 AMP). When an Adam or Eve walks in fellowship with God and obeys his commands what they find is favor. Here are a few scriptures to help you better understand having the favor of God.

> *"But the Lord was with Joseph and showed him steadfast love and gave him favor in the sight of the keeper of the prison. And the keeper of the prison put Joseph in charge of all the prisoners who were in the prison."*
>
> (GENESIS 39:21, 22 ESV)

> *"Now the boy Samuel continued to grow both in stature and in favor with the Lord and also with man."*
>
> (1 SAMUEL 2:26 ESV)

> *"And Jesus increased in wisdom and in stature and in favor with God and man."*
>
> (LUKE 2:52 ESV)

In all three biblical accounts, we saw these three men because of the favor that they had with God and men go on to accomplish amazing things during their time on Earth. Joseph ascended from the jail house to second in command of Egypt saving the people of his day from starvation. Samuel grew up to become the greatest judge over the people of Israel before the time of kings. Jesus, as we all know, went on to fulfill the will of his father and now sits on the right hand of God as the "King of Kings". The Hebrew word for favor is "chen" it means to be well-favor, accepted, approved and pleasure. (Bible Hub, Inc, 2016) It is defined as an absolute free expression of the loving kindness of God toward men to exercise to men the idea of every kind of favor, blessing and good. (Bible Hub, Inc, 2016). Having the favor of God is great and in Noah's case having that favor allowed him and his family to miss perishing in the flood. Once the flood was over, Noah and his family enjoyed the bounty of the Earth by themselves and the condition of the Earth was in a renewed state because the temporary elimination of the curse to the ground.

But with all that said about favor it is not the same as the blessing offered when a couple unites to become one flesh. When a couple makes the decision to enter that state of their relationship and obedience to God's original command what they receive is the promised blessing offered in Genesis 1:28 and in particular they receive the right to take dominion over the Earth. While Noah was one biblical example of obtaining favor with God, Abraham and Sarah are our biblical examples for becoming one flesh. If you recall the stories of Abraham and Sarai which beginning in Genesis chapter 12 here is the promise that God made to Abraham:

> "Now the Lord had said to Abram, "Get you out of your country, and from your kindred, and from your father's house, to a land that I will show you and I will make of you a great nation, and I will bless you, and make your name great: and you shall be a blessing and I will bless them that bless you, and curse him that curses you and in you shall all families of the earth be blessed."
>
> (GENESIS 12:1-3 KJV)

Does that promise sound very familiar? Of course it does, it has its basis in the promise that God made to Adam in Genesis 1:28. But that was not the only promise God made to Abraham.

> "And the Lord said to Abram, after that Lot was separated from him, "Lift up now your eyes and look from the place where you are northward and southward and eastward and westward. For all the land which you see to you will I give it and to your seed forever. And I will make your seed as the dust of the earth so that if a man can number the dust of the earth, then shall your seed also be numbered. Arise, walk through the land in length of it and in the breadth of it: for I will give it to you."
>
> (GENESIS 13:14 -17 KJV)

Again, does this promise sound familiar to you? Just as the promise in Genesis

12 had its foundation in Genesis 1:28 this promise also founded in God's original promise to Adam and Eve. When the promised blessing comes upon you it like favor makes you achieve great things but it extends well beyond that you make you rule, reign and gives you everything in abundance. Because of God's mandate for this book, I can only give you a glimpse into what happens when a couple receives the promised blessing. For that glimpse we will take a quick look at the life of Abraham when he started out on the journey with God.

> *"And Abram went up out of Egypt, he and his wife, and all that he had and Lot with him into the South. And Abram was very rich in cattle, in silver and in gold. And he went on his journeys from the south even to Bethel to the place where his tent had been at the beginning, between Bethel and Hai.*
>
> *To the place of the altar, which he had made there at the first; and there Abram called on the name of the Lord.*
>
> *And Lot also, which went with Abram, had flocks, and herds, and tents.*
>
> *And the land was not able to bear them, that they might dwell together: for their substance was great, so they could not dwell together."*
>
> (GENESIS 13:1-7 KJV)

Abraham's wealth and prosperity grew so much more than at his beginning that his nephew grew wealth just because he went with him. But the story for Abraham doesn't end here. In fact, it is just the beginning. For you, the question is having wealth, prosperity and dominion that comes from having the promise blessing. If that is interesting to you, then that is what awaits you and your spouse on the road of marriage restoration.

Scripture:

> *You know the story of how Adam landed us in the dilemma we're in – first sin, then death, and no one exempt from either sin or death. That sin disturbed relations with God in everything and everyone, but the extent of the disturbance was not clear until God spelled it out in detail to Moses. So death, this huge abyss separating us from God, dominated the landscape from Adam to Moses. Even those who didn't sin precisely as Adam did by disobeying a specific command of God still had to experience this termination of life, this separation from God.*

But Adam, who got us into this, also points ahead to the One who will get us out of it.

Yet the rescuing gift is not exactly parallel to the death-dealing sin. If one man's sin put crowds of people at the dead-end abyss of separation from God, just think what God's gift poured through one man, Jesus Christ, will do! There is no comparison between that death-dealing sin and this generous, life-giving gift.

The verdict on that one sin was the death sentence; the verdict on the many sins that followed was this wonderful life sentence. If death got the upper hand through one man's wrongdoing, can you imagine the breathtaking recovery life makes, sovereign life, in those who grasp with both hands this wildly extravagant life-gift, this grand setting – everything-right, that the one man Jesus Christ provides?

Here it is in a nutshell: Just as one person did it wrong and got us in all this trouble with sin and death, another person did it right and got us out of it. But more than just getting us out of trouble, he got us into life! One man said not to God and put many people in the wrong: one man said yes to God and many in the right.

All that passing laws against sin did was produce more lawbreakers. But sin didn't, and doesn't, have a chance in competition with the aggressive forgiveness we call grace. When it's sin versus grace, grace wins, hands down. All sin can do is threaten us with death, and that's the end of it. Grace, because God is putting everything together again through the Messiah, invites us into life, a life that goes on and on and on, world without end."

(ROMANS 5:12 -21 MSG)

CHAPTER 19

TURN ON THE LIGHT

The time has come for a restoration of love
to take place in the Body of Christ.

When I first sat down to write this book, it was unclear to me what it would turn out to be. Would it be a testimonial about the various separations and near divorce of a single couple or would it become more than that? Without a clue, I embarked on quest to fulfill a heavenly command to release His message into the Earth. What that message would be was not revealed in its entirety until the keys were punched on the laptop. Together as author and reader, we have experienced heaven unloading a critical message that strips away the blanket of deception that surrounds the church. It is a message that has the capacity to usher the Body of Christ into becoming the glorious bride we've been called to be. Why? Because we will be finally addressing the problem outlined for us as a body of believers in Revelations 2:1-7 NIV.

> *"To the angel of the church in Ephesus write: These are the words of him who holds the seven stars in his right hand and walks among the seven golden lampstands. I know your deeds, your hard work and your perseverance. I know that you cannot tolerate wicked people, that you have tested those who claim to be apostles but are not, and have found them false. You have persevered and have endured hardships for my name, and have not grown weary. Yet I hold this against you: You have forsaken the love you had at first. Consider how far you have fallen! Repent and do the things you did at first. If you do not repent, I will to come to you and remove your lampstand from its place. But you have this in your favor: You hate the practices of the Nicolaitans, which I also hate. Whoever has ears, let them hear what the Spirit says to the churches. To the one*

CHAPTER 19: TURN ON THE LIGHT

who is victorious, I will give the right to eat from the tree of life,

which is in the paradise of God."

(REVELATIONS 2:1-7 NIV)

We need to stop thinking of Jesus as "coming soon" but instead think "Jesus is at the door." Imagine you have invited a special guest over for dinner. Your preparation and your commitment to that preparation is very different two to three hours before the guest's arrival as opposed to when they are coming up the driveway. With the lateness of the hour, our soon coming King's return is so near it is nearly at hand. It is time for us to take our preparations and push them into overdrive. Our enemy wants us to sleep at our posts and believe that our King is not coming back. The truth is, though, is our King is returning and his return will be upon us soon. What preparations are needed at this time?

Restoration of love in the Body of Christ is the underlying message of this book. As a body of believers, the time has come for us to address the love issue. There is a lack of genuine love in our churches and in our homes. There are acts of kindness, friendship and even consideration but what we are missing is God's kind of love. We have discovered the nature of God's kind of faith but His love escapes us. God is looking for us to express the type of love that would send His Son and be the epitome of His love to the world for a world that wouldn't love Him back. This type of love is in short supply in our churches. The reason it is in short supply in our churches is because it is in short supply in our homes. This restoration of love must start in our homes. You cannot have love in the church if there is no love at home. As a body, we have been duped. In marriage, we look at each other as husbands and wives before we see each other as brothers and sisters in the Lord. We have to change this because it is one thing that separates us from the world.

If we truly believed the bible, we would realize how ridiculous it is to think we can divorce one another and believe it is somehow going to be okay with the Lord. We are going to spend eternity with one another. Do you think the Lord wants the petty squabbles that separate us on earth to follow us in heaven? Do you really believe we are going to be allowed to keep our distances from one another or pretend as if we don't need to deal with one another in heaven? When you start to see things from heaven's perspective and through the eyes of the eternity, you realize how narrow-minded we have become and how deceived we really are.

In Genesis chapter 4, God asked Cain a question about the whereabouts of his brother Abel. Cain responded in verse nine of that chapter by saying, "I don't know...Am I my brother's keeper?" For far too long with have allowed Cain's question be our motive for how we treat one another as brothers and sisters. Christ paid the price for us to answer Cain's question by saying, "Absolutely, we are our brother's keeper!"

In Mark 16:17 NIV, it says, "And these signs shall accompany them that believe: in my name they drive out demons; they will speak in new tongues; they will pick up snakes with their hands; and when they drink deadly poison, it will not hurt them at all; they will place their hands on sick people and they will get well." If this is true (and it is), then why do we not see more of these signs in our churches in America as every day occurrences? In the opinion of the author, it is the same wall is keeping the unbelieving world from embracing Jesus. The answer lies in the fact instead of being adorned in the apparel of Christ's love, we are wrapped in the clothing of fleshly works. Without the love of Christ, we cannot wear the clothes of His power. The world does not see more of a difference between the Body of Christ and their own efforts in the world. We have many of the same problems and for the most part we are using the world's solutions to solve them. If we solved our problems using solely the answers that Christ paid for and were getting the results that the bible promises, there would not be an empty chair at any church in the world. We do not and so seats remain empty in many churches.

What is keeping us, those who bear his name and clothed in his righteousness, from accessing the power comes with the authority He entrusted to us (Luke 10:19)? The power of God can only be accessed by faith and the faith it takes can only be operated by love. The scriptures say "faith works by love" (Galatians 5:6). Our faith is not working because the love in the church is too limited to work the faith we are attempting to yield and for the miracles we seek.

Satan has always had an incredible plan to stop the Church. When he realized he lost the battle with Jesus in hell and was stripped of the keys to death, hell and the grave, it was clear he dusted off an old plan that had worked before. He put a wedge between Adam and Eve. As a result of the deception, the committed treason when they sold out God's plan for the forbidden fruit. His plan divided Adam and Eve and it has been separating homes ever since. In modern times, his plan is to divide us at home and the fruit of division will cause us to be divided at church. His deception today is not about forbidden fruit but to cause us to look at one another only as husbands and wives and not as brothers and sisters in Christ, first. Remember what the Apostle John told us in 1 John 4:20, when it says anyone who claims to love God but hates his brother is a liar. If we are liars, then how do we expect to operate the power which comes by faith and works by love. It is impossible and that is the result we all know far too well.

As a Body of Christ, the devil has fixated on a few issues that do nothing to save the institution of marriage. We first need to turn the power back on and then address these issues in the world. We would rather fight these battles using the arm of the flesh than using the power of God because it would mean we would have to address what we have been avoiding all of this time .

It is easy to pretend we love each other when a black congregation visits a white one. That is a form of godliness. The real battle for love is at home. It started when Satan was allowed to get in between Adam and Eve and it has been raging ever since. This goes on throughout the world. Divorces among believers is piling up and very few are speaking against it because we do not understand the implications. We have been deceived into thinking it is a private matter between a man and his wife. We do not realize how the one case between that one man and one wife is impacting us a Body.

Remember the story of Achan in Joshua chapter 7? In this account, the disobedience of one man caused the whole camp to be defeated at Ai and 36 righteous men had to die when the sin went unaddressed. There are scores of believers today who believe it is okay to hate and remain separated from their brother. We are under a period of grace but we are still one body and one bride. We have a huge percentage of the Body of Christ who think it is okay to divorce and separate from one another. We have another large portion living silently in hatred with one another and many are wondering why God's power doesn't work.

It is time to turn on the light. It is time to restore love in the Church by having love restored at home. Christ is waiting for us to be the bride he made us to be and to be the salt and light we have been called to be. It is time to turn the light on and expose the devil for who he really is as a liar and a thief. And it is time to turn the light on and repent for the years of silent hatred we have for another has been allowed to fester in the dark.

It is time to expose the many ways we have been secretly satisfying our thirsts for lust instead of husbands loving their wives and wives respecting their husbands.

It is time to turn the light on and walk in love and forgiveness. Imagine as God shines His light on us and we are prepared to deal with the aftermath of what will happen when our wives find out what we have been doing after work, in private times and in the dark. Are our churches ready when husbands find out what their wives have been doing as the result of the lack of love, affection and respect husbands have refused to share with them? We have been allowed to stay in the dark according to Matthew 13:23-40 because the wheat and tares have been allowed to grow together. According to 1 Peter 4:17, the time has come for judgment to begin with the house of God.

When the light turns on, if God had not restored this redemptive work called marriage restoration, then families would have been devastated and churches decimated as individuals would have played out Satan's pre-programmed response in marriages when issues of infidelity are discovered. Through our culture, he has preprogrammed us to kick out our spouses, call our divorce attorneys and let the hate flow. The devil knows the light is coming and that is why he has been working feverishly to maintain the status quo. But the Lord is once again ahead of him and unmasking his treacherous ways. God's message of marriage restoration and marriage resurrection are His redemptive works that are for those who are really called by his name to return to him, repent of their ways, and once again He will hear from heaven and heal the land. These won't have to fear the light shining because instead of destruction they will find restoration, instead of brokenness they will find peace, instead of hatred they will be offered love and instead unforgiveness them will be restored in forgiveness. This is God's plan and it is now released into the Earth. The light is coming and soon it will shine on all corners of the world.

Turn the light on in your home and then pass the light on in the home to your left and to your right. As we turn the lights on at home, it will cause the light

shine once again and as bright as the noonday in our churches. The power of God and love will flow and the lost will be beckoned to that light. Turn on the light and pass it on.

Scripture:

> "And he opened his mouth and taught them, saying: Blessed (happy, to be envied, and spiritually prosperous-with life-joy and satisfaction in God's favor and salvation, regardless of their outward conditions] are the poor in spirit (the humble, who rate themselves insignificant), for theirs is the kingdom of heaven.
>
> Blessed and enviably happy [with a happiness produced by the experience of God's favor and especially conditioned by the revelation of His matchless grace] are those who mourn, for they shall be comforted!
>
> Blessed (happy, blithesome, joyous, spiritually prosperous- with life-joy and satisfaction in God's favor and salvation, regardless of their outward conditions) are the meek (the mild, patient, long-suffering), for they shall inherit the earth!
>
> Blessed and fortunate and happy and spiritually prosperous (in that state in which the born-again child of God enjoys His favor and salvation) are those who hunger and thirst for righteousness (uprightness and right standing with God), for they shall be completely satisfied!
>
> Blessed (happy, to be envied, and spiritually prosperous – with life-joy and satisfaction in God's favor and salvation, regardless of their outward conditions) are the merciful, for they shall obtain mercy!
>
> Blessed (happy, enviably fortunate, and spiritually prosperous – possessing the happiness produced by the experience of God's favor and especially conditioned by the revelation of His grace, regardless of their outward conditions) are the pure in heart, for they shall see God!
>
> Blessed (enjoying enviable happiness, spiritually prosperous –

255

with life-joy and satisfaction in God's favor and salvation, re-gardless of their outward conditions) are the makers and main-tainers of peace, for they shall be called the sons of God!

Blessed and happy and enviably fortunate and spiritually pros-perous (in the state in which the born-again child of God enjoys and finds satisfaction in God's favor and salvation, regardless of his outward conditions) are those who are persecuted for righteousness' sake, for theirs is the kingdom of heaven!

Blessed (happy, to be envied, and spiritually prosperous-with life-joy and satisfaction in God's favor and salvation, regardless of your outward conditions) are you when people revile you and persecute you and say all kinds of evil things against you falsely on My account.

Be glad and supremely joyful, for your reward in heaven is great (strong and intense), for in this same way people perse-cuted the prophets who were before you.

You are the salt of the earth, but if salt has lost its taste (its strength, its quality), how can its saltiness be restored? It is not good for anything any longer but to be thrown out and trodden underfoot by men.

You are the light of the world. A city set on a hill cannot be hidden. Nor do men light a lamp and put it under a peck mea-sure, but on a lampstand, and it gives light to all in the house.

Let your light so shine before men that they may see your moral excellence and your praiseworthy, noble and good deeds and recognize and honor and praise and glorify your Father who is heaven."

(MATTHEW 5:2 -16 AMP)

WIFE'S COMMENTARY

Section 3

The issues of the last year have been some of the worst experiences of my entire life. Dealing with the shame of being disloyal to my husband and my life's moral compass have shaken me to the core. Many times, we are worst on ourselves when something negative happens and I have beat myself up many times, asking how I found myself in such a compromised position with my husband and how I would be able to repair the many fractured relationships that had been broken.

Over time, I have come to see that despite the excruciating pain and conviction I endured because of my life choices, I have experienced some of the best times of my life. Before the experience I did not have a true understanding of the depth of God's love, mercy, and forgiveness. My husband taught me what unconditional love looked like. For, despite how impossible our situation looked and despite the heartache he endured, he accepted me with open and loving arms in a way that only the Father could do.

Through this experience I learned the difference between conviction and condemnation. I realized that conviction is what saved me but condemnation was trying to grip me and keep me bound. By meditating on God's Word day and night, I have been able to renew my mind to have the mind of Christ. Through this experience, my purpose has become more clear.

In the past I often wondered and asked God why I didn't have a testimony. Growing up in the church, I was accustomed to hearing people talk about how God had saved them from a life of drugs or from an illness that threatened to take their life. I always felt left out because I didn't feel that I had a story, especially not a situation as dramatic as life or death. After going through all that I've gone through now I can see that God has looked ahead and made provision. I definitely have a story. I can testify and tell others how God saved my marriage and how He healed me from a host of maladies that threatened to steal my joy and my very life.

In less than two years I've endured and overcome PTSD, severe depression, an eating disorder, two surgeries, life threatening hypertension and a near divorce. As a result of God's love, I have gained peace that I can't explain and am looking forward to the day when I can tell my story to help others deal with situations that are keeping them from experiencing God's best in their lives and in the lives of their loved ones.

If you or someone you know is contemplating or attempting a separation or divorce, tell them that it is never too late for a miracle. Let them know that with man something may seem impossible but with God, all things really are possible. My husband and I were separated six months and had already gone to one divorce hearing before I had an encounter with God that snatched me out of the grip of the enemy, enabling me to repent. Though I spent many days in a psychiatric hospital because I had many issues to overcome, your experience does not need to be dramatic. All it takes is a change of heart to line up your will with God's Word. Once I changed my mind and began to seek God's help through His Word, everything began to line up.

Don't give up on yourself or your spouse. And don't lose faith. God's Word says in Hebrews 11:6 that without faith it is impossible to please God. Once you begin to please God, your life will begin to change. It's a promise.

SPECIAL COMMENTARY BY JASON JONES

RESTORATION AFTER INFIDELITY

Scripture Context: 2 Samuel 11 and 12

By the world's standards, this commentary could be called "Confessions of an Adulterer," or a similar title of some such. But as the Word says, "If the Son therefore shall make you free, ye shall be free indeed," (John 8:36) making such a title inappropriate in a Kingdom context.

The purpose of this commentary is to show you how God can not only re-store a relationship broken by infidelity but also can forge a relationship based on forgiveness and restoration between an injured spouse and the adulterer. More importantly, if you have been involved in an extramarital affair as the adulterer, this commentary is aimed to show you that the sin does not make you a bad person, instead someone who fell for the enemy's deception. God can and will forgive you of what was done just as He did for King David. After all, David was an adulterer, yet his sin did not prevent him from becoming a man after God's own heart (Acts 13:22).

My story parallels the story of David and Bathsheba found in 2 Samuel 11 and 12 in that there are four parts to the story: The Sin, The Cover-Up, The Conviction, and The Restoration.

> *"Marriage is honorable, and the bed undefiled, but whore-mongers and adulterers God shall judge."*
>
> (HEBREWS 13:4)

During a Sunday service, my pastor gave a sermon entitled, "Did God Really Say?" which addressed sexual immorality in today's spiritually and morally lax society. The central theme of the sermon was based on if God spoke against and cast judgment on those who involved themselves in sexual immorality. As he spoke, I hung on to the pastor's every word. Little did I know that his ser-mon would serve as a foreshadowing of my story.

The Sin

My story doesn't begin with me looking for a woman to start a relationship. Instead, it starts with a decision. I had determined that I didn't need to think too much about my pastor's sermon. While I was believing God for a mate, finding one wasn't my top priority.

As a matter of fact, I was going about my daily life when I met her. Nearly a month after my Pastor's sermon, I had just gotten paid for completing work at a client's office and I wanted to celebrate the completion of the deal by having a pizza and a ginger ale at a local pub.

I remember seeing her having a conversation with another woman, whom I later learned was her aunt, and an older gentleman as they sat in the corner of the bar. Soon, I decided to strike up a conversation with her. We began by discussing fraternities and sororities. Not long into the conversation, she explained that she was married but had recently filed for divorce. It was obvious that she was Christian and we both felt a spiritual connection that evening. We exchanged telephone numbers. The following day, I called her and we met for brunch with her aunt and son after church the upcoming Sunday.

Several days later, it was her birthday. I purchased an inexpensive birthday present for her and a card about friendship. When I presented it to her, she expressed so much elation and gratitude for such a touching gift that I made a critical mistake. Pulling her close, I kissed her on the lips. It was a brief encounter because she had plans to spend time with her family. I reached out to her again and we spent more time together. Within several weeks, we were fully engaged in a sexual relationship. It started as an innocent friendship but quickly escalated into a full-blown extra-marital affair.

Now, what would prompt a Christian man to commit adultery with a married woman? There are several factors that all relate to that decision I mentioned earlier. First, there is the impact of the many relationship rejections I experienced as a teen and young adult. Then it was my firm belief that because of all of the rejection I experienced in the past, I saw myself as unattractive and therefore, I thought God's laws of sexual immorality did not apply to me. In my heart, I believed that no woman would be interested in me in sexually, so I didn't think I needed to be concerned about adultery or sexual immorality. I was married once before but that relationship lacked intimacy and here I found myself sitting across from an attractive, independent, and brilliant woman interested in me. With every touch, my commitment to God and His Word disappeared.

It wasn't long before our relationship extended beyond a physical engagement. We had become emotionally entangled. We discussed everything – our fears, insecurities, goals, ambitions, you name it, we talked about it. We exchanged support and encouragement with each other and we felt like we were in love. We spent all the time we could together and we communicated frequently throughout the day. It was with her encouragement that I decided to take the Certified Public Accountant Exam and upon successfully completing it, I was offered a job across the country. I had some concern about relocating when our relationship was just blooming but felt that our love was strong enough to last beyond the distance.

Justification

Yes, I knew she was still married but I comforted my understanding of her situation with the knowledge that she had filed for divorce and soon she would be free. She had characterized her husband as emotionally abusive and a control freak whom she felt was overly protective of her. Based on her description, I developed my own unfavorable opinion of him by comparing him to a former boss who was micromanager. He was the kind of person who justified his own faults by virtue of his title. He was excessively demanding and overly critical to others.

It was easy with her description of him and my own perceptions to not give him any consideration at all. During some of our conversations when she would bring up her husband, I would see him as my former supervisor and I would transfer my feelings of disdain towards my old boss to her husband. Though I didn't know him, I felt anger towards her husband because it sounded as if he was trying to sabotage her life. I saw her as someone trying to gain her freedom and in my opinion she had every right to depart from him. She seemed to be the victim in all of this, I thought. As for why she was leaving after so many years of his oppression, I figured it was better late than never.

As her divorce hearing got closer, the conversations involving her husband increased to the point I was getting tired of hearing about him and his underhanded antics and adventures. I just knew that it would be only a matter of time she would gain her divorce and she would be free to be married to me.

Our Relationship

In just over two months from the time we met, our relationship went from sexual to her fully being my partner. She helped me financially as I readied for my relocation. One day she explained if I was going to be with her I had to dress better and she followed that up by discarding half my wardrobe. She then took me shopping and purchased a few trendy items so I could begin replacing my wardrobe. She lent her credit card to me along with a small down payment so I could have a car. Though she told me she expected me to reimburse her fully, I saw her gestures as very generous as we became what I had hoped were lifelong partners.

Prior to my relocation, I moved into her home for a few weeks. We were deluded into believing we were in love by becoming increasingly dependent on one another. By this time, we weren't sexually intimate as we once were. We had talked about getting married after the divorce was final so, in an attempt to honor God, we ended the sexual intimacy. However, we were extremely emotionally connected to one another and continued in this blissful state until the day our relationship was discovered by her husband.

The Cover-Up

During our time together, we made what was in hindsight flimsy efforts to conceal our affair. Although we were seen together in public occasionally, we never posted any pictures or discussed our relationship on social media. She held an executive position at work and occasionally, she had galas or events to attend. She never invited me to attend these events. Even when she went to church, she would go alone for fear of being discovered.

One day, however, our hidden romance came to the light. While I was staying at her house, I heard a knock at the front door. I opened it quickly, thinking she may have lost her keys but as it turned out, it was her husband at the door. He was there to deliver her mail that had stacked up at their marital home. He introduced himself as her husband and asked me how I knew her. I lied to him by telling him I was a friend of hers from her hometown. I was so nervous; I gave him my real name. After hearing my name, he promptly left.

There began to be visible signs our relationship was negatively impacting her relationships with her children, but I continued to justify our actions by believing one day I would be able to attend church with her, attend her galas and even gain acceptance from her children when the divorce finalized. I further justified our relationship by believing that because I didn't meet her until after her relationship with her husband was over, I was not involved in destroying a marriage. After all, I figured, the marriage was destroyed long before I ever met her. Did my presence compound the problem? Sure, but I told myself that I was no home wrecker.

Though there were only occasional verbal squabbles with her grown children, there seemed to be a sigh of relief that our relationship was no longer hidden. It seemed everything was on track for us to be together forever. Little did we realize this feeling would be short-lived. The enemy's trap had begun to take the life out of its captives.

Conviction and Repentance

One of the things I learned about her soon after we met was she was dealing with a number of health issues and had been given a leave of absence from work to get restored to health. What I learned later is not long after she started her leave of absence she decided to file for divorce.

It seemed that soon after her husband discovered our relationship everything between us started to fall apart. First, her health significantly deteriorated. In fact, most weekends she spent in a hospital emergency room. Her mental health suffered as well. It seemed to me overnight, she went from being a strong, independent woman to being ill, fragile, and extremely needy.

The affair began to fall apart under its own sinful foundation. My relocation became a greater physical barrier than was anticipated. With my relocation and her alone to face her life, we witnessed her life come apart right before our very eyes. Not being able to work brought about great financial strain as her health continued to deteriorate. All these things were indirectly beginning to take a toll on our relationship; I still was totally in love with her in the midst of all the ungodly chaos going on in her life.

At the time, I didn't recognize God's involvement through all the chaos. She and I would just swing from one crisis to the next, trying to hold on to each other as tight as possible. It was becoming clear, however, that with each crisis, the grip became weaker and weaker.

In the final days of our relationship, she became incredibly afraid she was being followed. One day she called me on the telephone stating she felt her husband had been following her. I later learned, however, he was out of the country on vacation during that time and there was never anyone following her. Now I know the whole story, I believe her feeling was conviction coming to her heart.

That same week she had planned to come visit me for a brief visit but that trip would never happen. She never made it on the airplane. Instead, she spent the night in a hotel room nearly 100 miles from the airport and while I don't know all the details of what happened to her that night, I know the results.

I received a "Dear John" text telling me that our relationship was over. The following day, I received a call from my pastor who shared with me the details of a conversation he had with her husband. It became clear to me through that exchange her husband knew about the relationship and kept abreast of our actions, yet, he didn't interfere. It was only after the events of the night before did he finally decide to step forward.

As I spoke to my pastor, those lessons of his sermon months ago started to come back to me as I finally stepped back to take a look at my life. He got me to finally realize for the first time I was in the midst of an affair, I had laid aside my Christian values, and I was very much walking in sin. He reminded me sin has its consequences (Romans 6:23) and the very first consequence for me was to face the husband whom I wronged.

Before I called her husband, I got on my knees and prayed a humble heartfelt "Psalms 51" type of prayer repenting for what I had done and the hurt I had caused in the process. I asked God to withhold His judgment against me, although I knew I fully deserved it. In His mercy, God did forgive me.

Now I had to face her husband. I realize most people would have asked God for forgiveness but would have somehow justified not calling the husband. Trust me, that thought crossed my mind a hundred times. Our initial phone conversation was not pleasant as one would expect but on the whole it wasn't as bad as I thought it would be. After the first phone call, her husband called me back moments later much calmer than before. This time he was concerned about me and helping me be restored as a brother in Christ. We spent over two hours talking that night and he was gracious by giving me insight about her, her life, and family I hadn't known. He was concerned about my well-being. He wasn't judgmental but I could tell he was hurt by the whole thing. Over the next couple of days, we spent hours talking over the telephone. He was kind enough to take my call no matter the hour. He even prayed with me multiple times; he became my brother and my friend.

Healing and Restoration

As part of my reconciliation to them, her husband and I have come to financial arrangements to allow me to repay all of the financial benefits I received from her during our time together. It is important to me I make things right with them and with me. Though the first few months after our relationship ended were awfully lonesome and my heart yearned for her badly, I took comfort my relationship with God was restored. With Christ, I have moved on with my life.

Over the last few months, I have come to know her husband and I have learned he is not at all like the man she told he was or I imagined him to be. I have learned whatever happened to her that night in the hotel, she is a changed person also. Not only has she reconciled with her husband but she no longer suffers from all those various physical and mental health issues. Her life has been restored even greater than it was.

Some interesting things have taken place in the midst of all of this and I've learned a few things about myself and the relationship. For one, I learned I was living a lie. While we had feelings for one another, our feelings we not based on anything real. There were many life challenges she was struggling to address and instead of facing them head on she ran from them. Her time with me gave her the distraction she needed before she could face her issues and deal with them appropriately.

Only by God's grace and mercy, a marriage was not only saved and restored, but a friendship between a husband and his wife's infidel was formed, a very unlikely outcome even in the best of circumstances.

One Final "Word"

If you are or have ever been involved as the "third wheel" in an extramarital affair, know just as God forgave David and myself, He can forgive you, too. Know even if you repent and ask for forgiveness there may be consequences for your sin, but you will also find grace and mercy as reconciliation and healing takes place.

The first thing you will need to do is to pray a Psalms 51 prayer, admit what you have done and own up to your faults and misgivings that led to the sin. Repent and ask God for forgiveness. Most importantly, don't be afraid to seek the forgiveness of others. They may or may not be as forgiving as her husband was in my case but once you receive the forgiveness of God, you really don't need their forgiveness. Your repentance does help to start the healing process for all involved.

God will bless you for taking these steps. Once you receive God's forgiveness, leave your sins at the altar and don't walk in condemnation. This is not God's desire for you and don't let others shame you into feeling condemnation, either. This is just as wrong as the sin. Embrace God's love every day. Spend time listening to God in His Word and it won't be long that you will have a healed heart and you will find the person He has for you.

"Blessed is he whose transgression is forgiven, whose sin is covered. Blessed is the man unto whom the Lord imputeth not iniquity and in whose spirit there is no guile."

(PSALMS 32:1-2)

REFERENCES

About.com. (2016, February 10). *Eros.htm*. Retrieved from AboutReligion.com: christanity.about.com/od/glossary/a/Eros.htm

American Civil Liberties Union. (2016, February 15). *Should You Get A Civil Union in Illinois*. Retrieved from ACLU.org: http://civilunions.aclu-il.org/?page_id=2

Barna Group. (2014, April 8). *The State of the Bible: 6 Trends for 2014*. Retrieved from Barna.org: https://www.barna.org/barna-update/culture/664-the-state-of-the-bible-6-trends-for-2014#.VsJRfPIrLW

Barna Group. (2015, February). *State of the Bible 2015*. Retrieved from AmericanBible.org: http://www.americanbible.org/uploads/content/State_of_the_Bible_2015_report.pdf

Beam, J. (2007, October 5). *Why Should a Married Couple Separate?* Retrieved from Crosswalk: http://www.crosswalk.com/family/marriage/when-should-a-married-couple-separate-11556106.html

Bible Hub, Inc. (2016, April 26). *Chen*. Retrieved from Biblehub.com: Becoming one flesh doesn't just automatically happen because you get married. It happens because of conscience decisions made by Adam to love his wife and give to her the role in his life that God created for her. It happens when Eve finds that openness,

Commentary, P. (2016, February 10). *Matthew19-8.htm*. Retrieved from Biblehub.com: www.bible-hub.com/matthew/19-8.htm

Dictionary.com. (2016, February 15). *Civil Unions*. Retrieved from Dictionary.com: http://dictionary.reference.com/browse/civil-u

Greta, C. (2016, February 15). *Why Civil Unions Aren't Enough*. Retrieved from Alternet.org: http://www.alternet.org/story/57722/why_civil_unions_aren't_enough

Hold, B. H. (2016, January 21). *Statistics*. Retrieved from Brokenheartonhold.com: http://www.bro-kenheartonhold.com/statistics/

Internet Brands, Inc. (2016, February 26). *How Much Will My Divorce Cost and How Long Will It Take?* Retrieved from Nolo.com: www.nolo.com/legal-encyclodepia/ctp/cost-of-divorce

Just Answer, LLC. (2016, February 16). *Questions About Marriage Reconcilation Law*. Retrieved from JustAnswer.com: http://www.justanswer.com/topics-reconciliation/

Know-Jesus.com. (2016, February 23). *Being Deceived*. Retrieved from Bible.Knowing-Jesus.com: http://bible.knowing-jesus.com/topics/Being-Deceived

Magloff, L. D. (2010, March 26). *The Average Cost of Divorce*. Retrieved from LegalZoom.com: http://info.legalzoom.com/average-cost-divorce-20103.html

Marriage Helper, Inc. (2016, February 24). *About Us*. Retrieved from MarriageHelper.com: http://www.marriagehelper.com/about-us

Marriage in America, N. S. (2016, January 20). *Statistics*. Retrieved from Brokenheartonhold.com: http://www.brokenheartonhold.com/statistics

Medical Arts Studio, Inc. (2016, April 6). *Rib Cage*. Retrieved from MedicalArtsLibrary.com: http://www.medicalartlibrary.com/ribcage/

Merriam-Webster, Inc. (2016, April 6). *Completeness*. Retrieved from Merriam-Webster.com: http://www.merriam-webster.com/dictionary/completeness

Merriam-Webster, Inc. (2016, April 6). *Counterpart*. Retrieved from Merriam-Webster.com: http://www.merriam-webster.com/dictionary/counterpart

Merriam-Webster, Inc. (2016, February 20). *Flash Flood*. Retrieved from Merriam-Webster: http://www.merriam-webster.com/dictionary/flash%20flood

Merriam-Webster, Inc. (2016, February 20). *Lifeboat*. Retrieved from Merriam-Webster.com: http://www.merriam-webster.com/dictionary/lifeboat

Merriam-Webster, Inc. (2016, April 6). *Provision*. Retrieved from Merriam-Webster.com: http://www.merriam-webster.com/dictionary/provision

Merriam-Webster, Inc. (2016, April 6). *Purpose*. Retrieved from Merriam-Webster.com: http://www.merriam-webster.com/dictionary/purpose

Merriam-Webster, Inc. (2016, April 1). *Restitution*. Retrieved from Merriam-webster.com: http://www.merriam-webster.com/dictionary/restitution

Pulpit Commentary. (2016, February 10). *Matthew19-8.htm*. Retrieved from Biblehub.com: www.biblehub.com/matthew/19-8.htm

Reich, L. (2008, June 1). *Growing Fruit Trees from Seeds*. Retrieved from Motherearthnews.com: http://www.motherearthnews.com/organic-gardening/growing-fruit-trees-zmaz08jjzmcc.aspx?PageId=1

Religion Division of Lily Endowment, Inc. (2016, February 26). *Church Giving*. Retrieved from ReligionInsights.org: http://www.religioninsights.org/articles/church-giving-tied-gratitude-and-sense-mission

Strong's, C. D. (1994). Lexical Aids To The Old Testament. In D. S. Zodhiates, *The Complete Word Study Old Testament - KJV* (p. 2364). Chattanooga: AMG Publishers.

The American Heritage Dictionary. (2001). In D. Publishing, *The American Heritage Dictionary, 21st Century Reference* (p. 754). New York City: Random House, Inc.

UK Daily, M. (2014, August 20). *Do You Regret Getting Divorce? Astonishing 50% of People Wish They Had Never Ended Their Marriage*. Retrieved from UKDailyMail.com: http://www.dailymail.co.uk/femail/article-2727716/Is-going-separate-ways-really-good-idea-Astonishing-50-divorcees-regret-breaking-partner.html

REFERENCES

Vines and Hogg, V. E. (2016, February 10). *Love (Noun and Verb) Vine's Expository Dictionary of New Testament Words.* Retrieved from Studybible.info: http://studybible.info/vines/Love%20(Noun%20and%20Verb)

Whetstone, B. P. (2016, March 1). *Marriage, Crisis, Discernment Counseling, Separation, Infidelity.* Retrieved from Doctorbecky.com: http://doctorbecky.com/relationships/marriage-crisis-separation-infidelity/

William J Doherty, P. F. (2016, January 21). *Statistics.* Retrieved from Brokenheartonhold.com: http://www.brokenheartonhold.com/statistics

Womack, A. (2016, February 10). *Hardness of Heart: A Condition You May Have and Not Even Know It.* Retrieved from Awmi.net: www.awmi.net/reading/teaching-articles,hardness__heart

Zodhiates, S. T. (1994). Dictionary. In D. S. Zodhiates, *The Complete Word Study Dictionary New Testament* (pp. 385-386). Chattanooga: AMG Publishers.

PRAYER OF SALVATION

"For God so loved the world that he gave his one and only Son, that whoever believes in him shall not perish but have eternal life."

(JOHN 3:16 NIV)

If you don't know Jesus Christ as your Savior and Lord, then the biblical truths and lessons learned in this content packed book will not work for you.

But the good news is that today, in fact, right we can change that. God sent Jesus to redeem us from an eternal separation from Himself and through the work Jesus did, you can now receive God's free gift of salvation.

To receive salvation today, pray this prayer:

Lord Jesus,

Come into my heart today

and save me from all of my sins.

I believe that you came to redeem the whole world

and that includes me.

I declare that I believe in my heart

that God raised you from the dead and because I believe

I receive you as Savior and confess you as Lord of my life.

I know that your love for me is eternal.

Thank you for saving me.

In Jesus name, Amen.

Welcome to the Family!

Dr. Reginald and Renea Morris

ABOUT THE AUTHORS

Reginald and Renea Morris are the founding pastors of Restoration Church International a fellowship of believers which encourage people to embrace God's love to become all they were created to be located in Athens, OH. The couple also have a discreet personal ministry focus of helping high profile Christian ministers, politicians, business leaders, professional athletes and entertainers walk out the love of Christ to bring restoration to their troubled marriages and family life.

For more information, for other messages and teaching from Reginald or Renea, or to contact their ministry, email, call or write:

Reginald Morris Ministries

P.O. Box 943

Athens, OH 45701

Telephone: (614) 448-1825

Reginald@reginaldmorris.com

You can also visit their ministry website, get in touch, and get more online at:

www.ResurrectMyMarriage.com

or

www.ReginaldMorris.com

FREE! DOWNLOAD
THE "BOOK OF PRAYERS" TODAY!

Take all that you have learned in Resurrect Your Dead Marriage to a whole new level with this download of the "Book of Prayers".

This eBook is meant to add to enhance your ability to draw upon everything you learned about saving your marriage by giving you the same prayers that the author(s) used during their own successful marriage resurrection.

This book is free to you as a reader of "Resurrect Your Dead Marriage" and a gift from the authors. *Download a copy for yourself and then feel free to tell a friend.

Get your free eBook today, by visiting

www.ReginaldMorris.com/freeoffer.

Order code needed to obtain your free downloaded copy: restoration

*Registration required to access free eBook for download. One copy per registered email will download.

Printed copies of the "Book of Prayers" available for purchase on

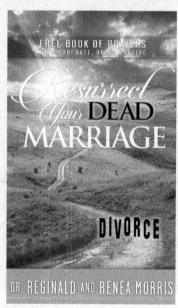

Printed in the USA
CPSIA information can be obtained
at www.ICGtesting.com
JSHW012049140824
68134JS00035B/3333